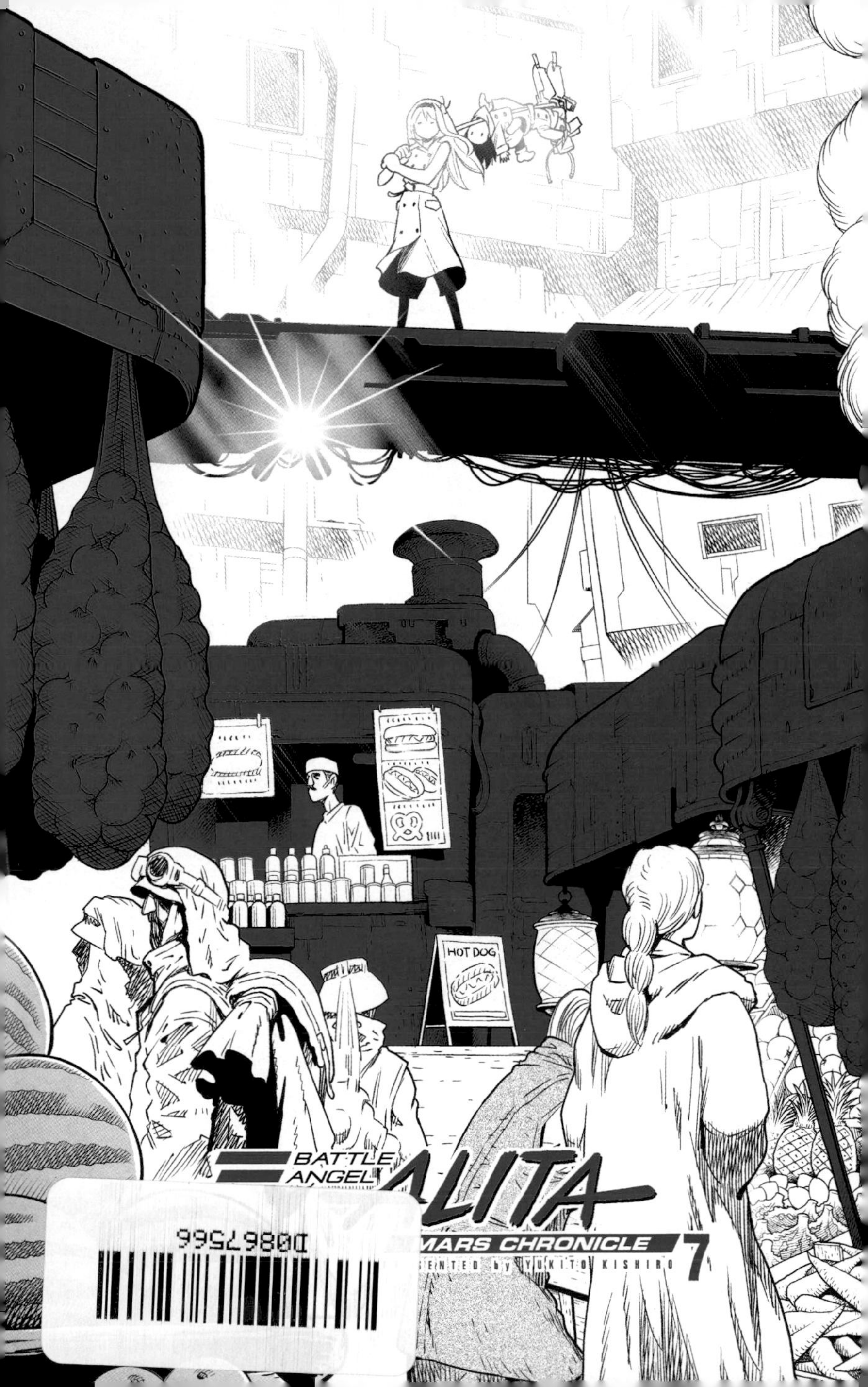
HOT DOG
BATTLE
ANGEL
ALITA
MARS CHRONICLE
7
YUKITO KISHIRO

BATTLE ANGEL ALITA MARS CHRONICLE

PRESENTED by YUKITO KISHIRO

CONTENTS

ADDITIONAL STAFF:
TSUTOMU KISHIRO / EMIYA KINARI

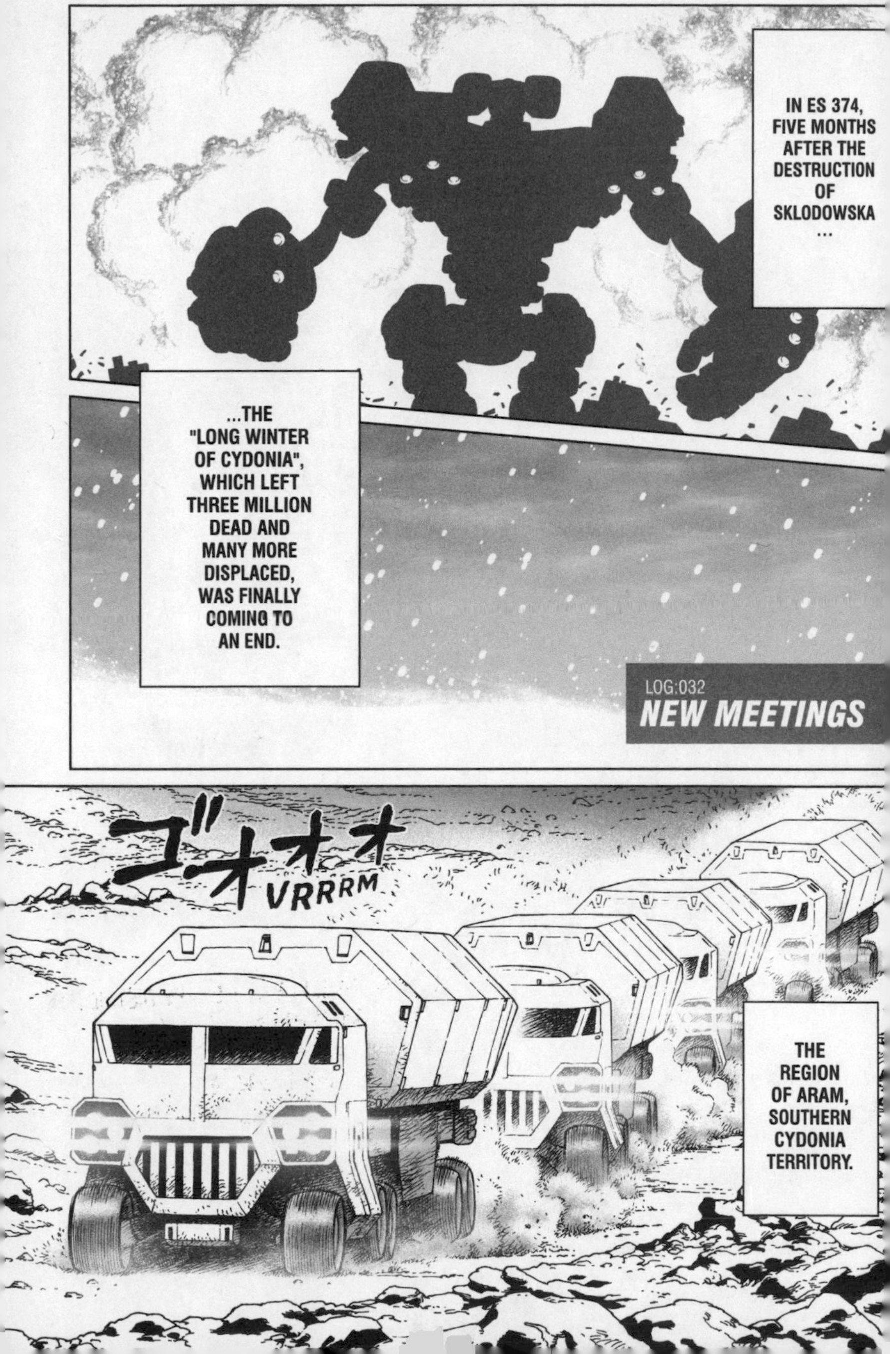
IN ES 374, FIVE MONTHS AFTER THE DESTRUCTION OF SKLODOWSKA ...
...THE "LONG WINTER OF CYDONIA", WHICH LEFT THREE MILLION DEAD AND MANY MORE DISPLACED, WAS FINALLY COMING TO AN END.
LOG:032
NEW MEETINGS
ゴオオオ
VRRRM
THE REGION OF ARAM, SOUTHERN CYDONIA TERRITORY.

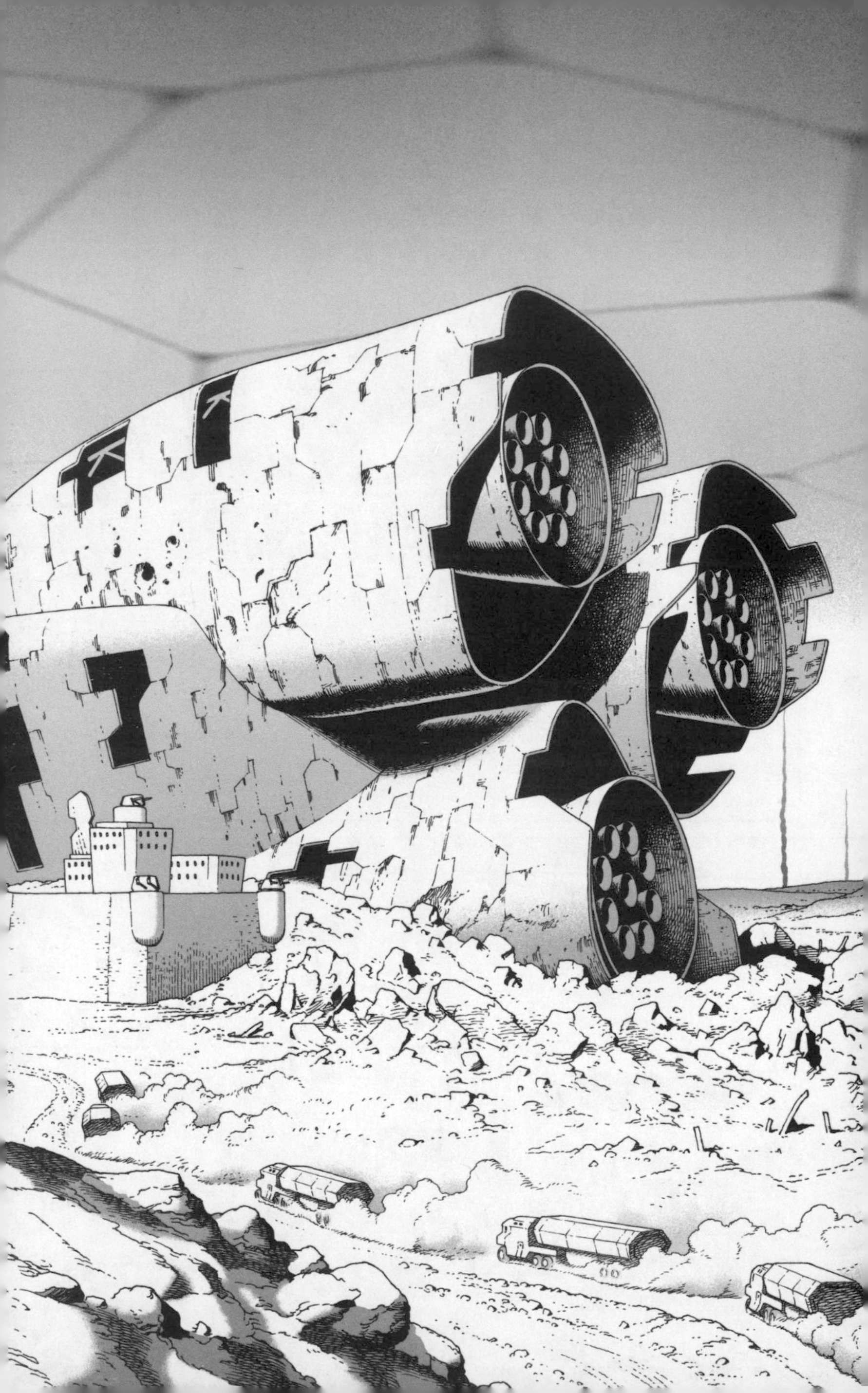

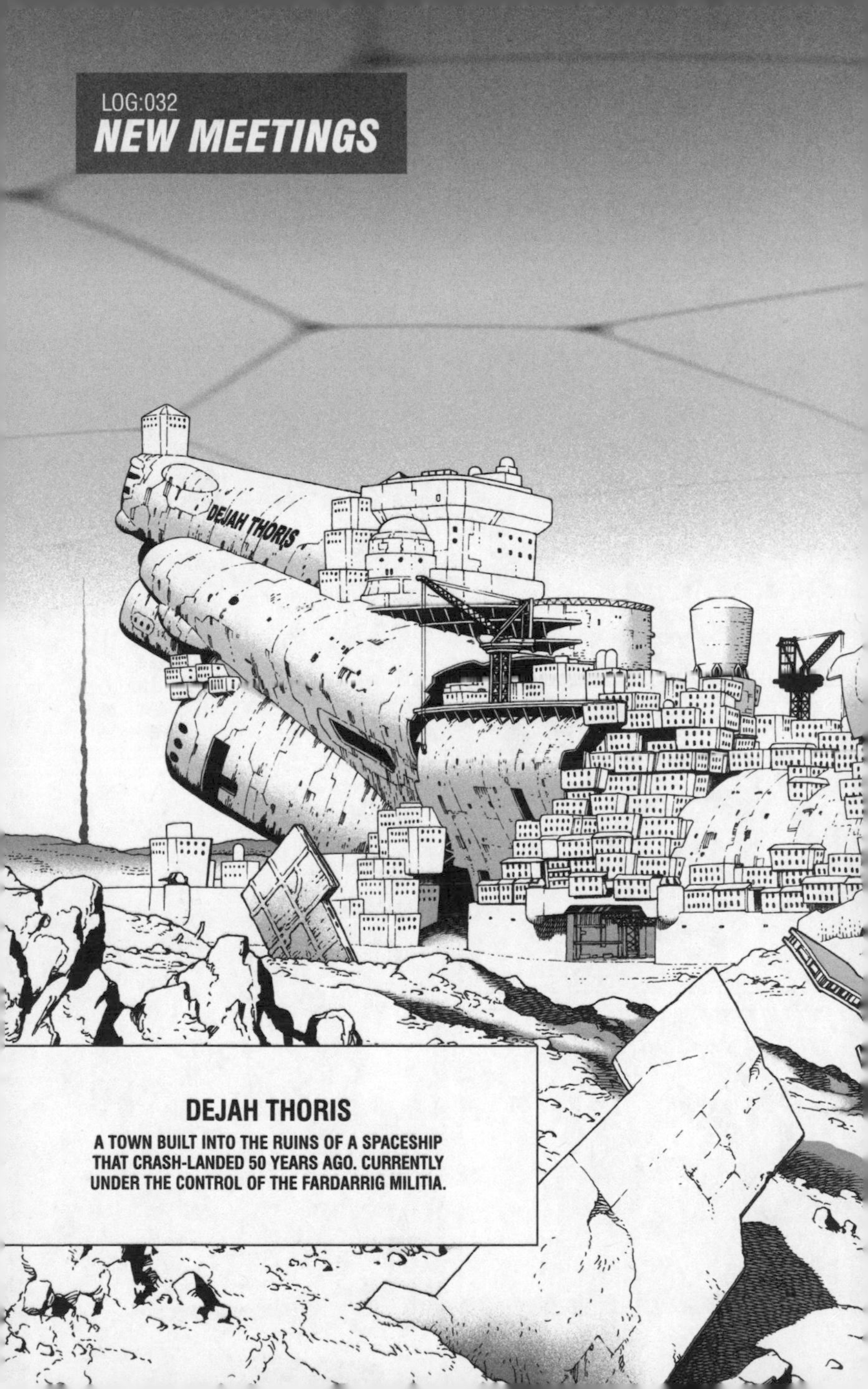
LOG:032
NEW MEETINGS
DEJAH THORIS
DEJAH THORIS
A TOWN BUILT INTO THE RUINS OF A SPACESHIP THAT CRASH-LANDED 50 YEARS AGO. CURRENTLY UNDER THE CONTROL OF THE FARDARRIG MILITIA.

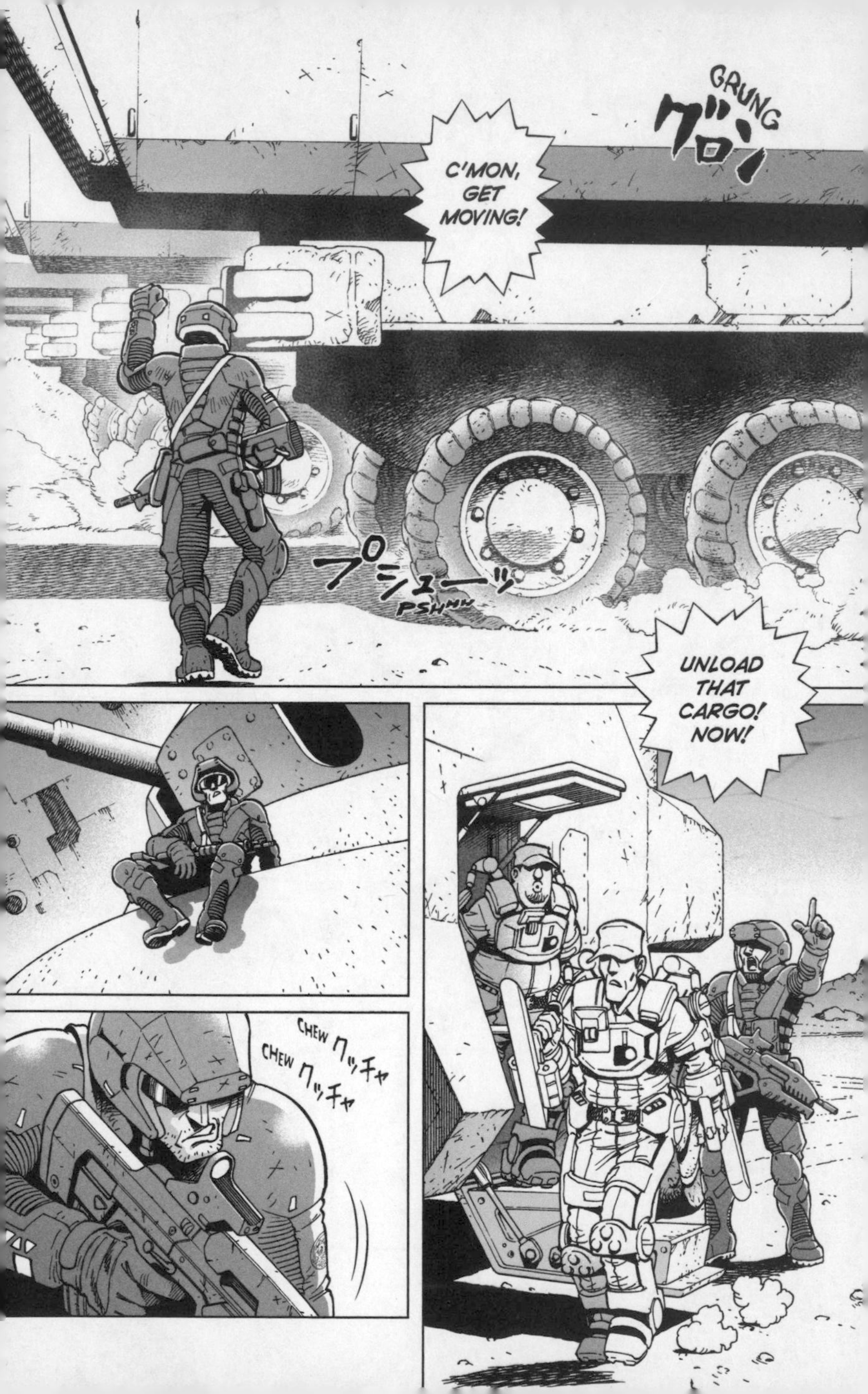

GRUNG
グロン
C'MON, GET MOVING!
プシューッ
PSHMW
UNLOAD THAT CARGO! NOW!
CHEW クッチャ
CHEW クッチャ

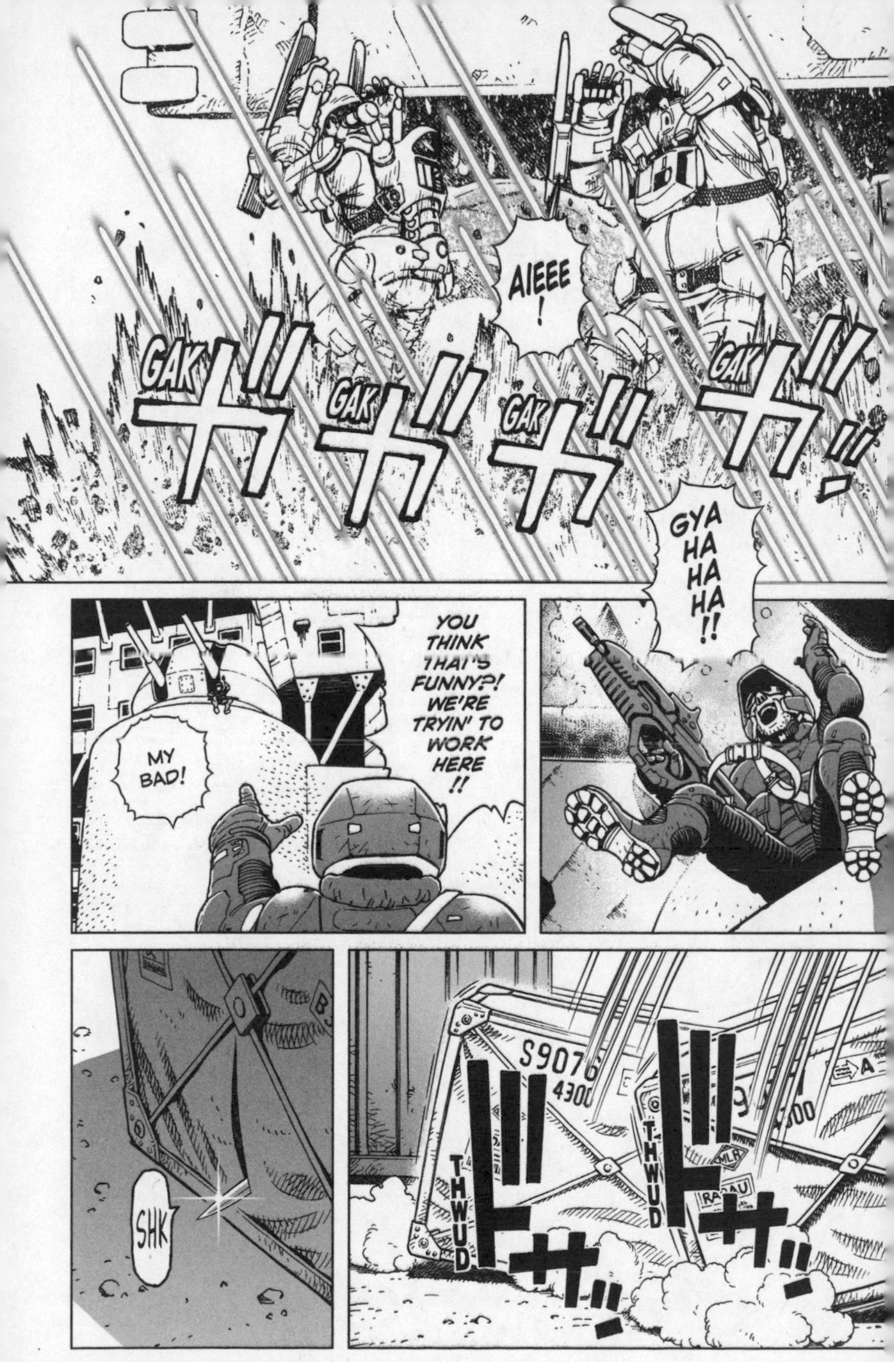
AIEEE!
GAK
GAK
GAK
GAK
GYA HA HA HA!!
YOU THINK THAT'S FUNNY?! WE'RE TRYIN' TO WORK HERE!!
MY BAD!
THWUD
THWUD
SHK

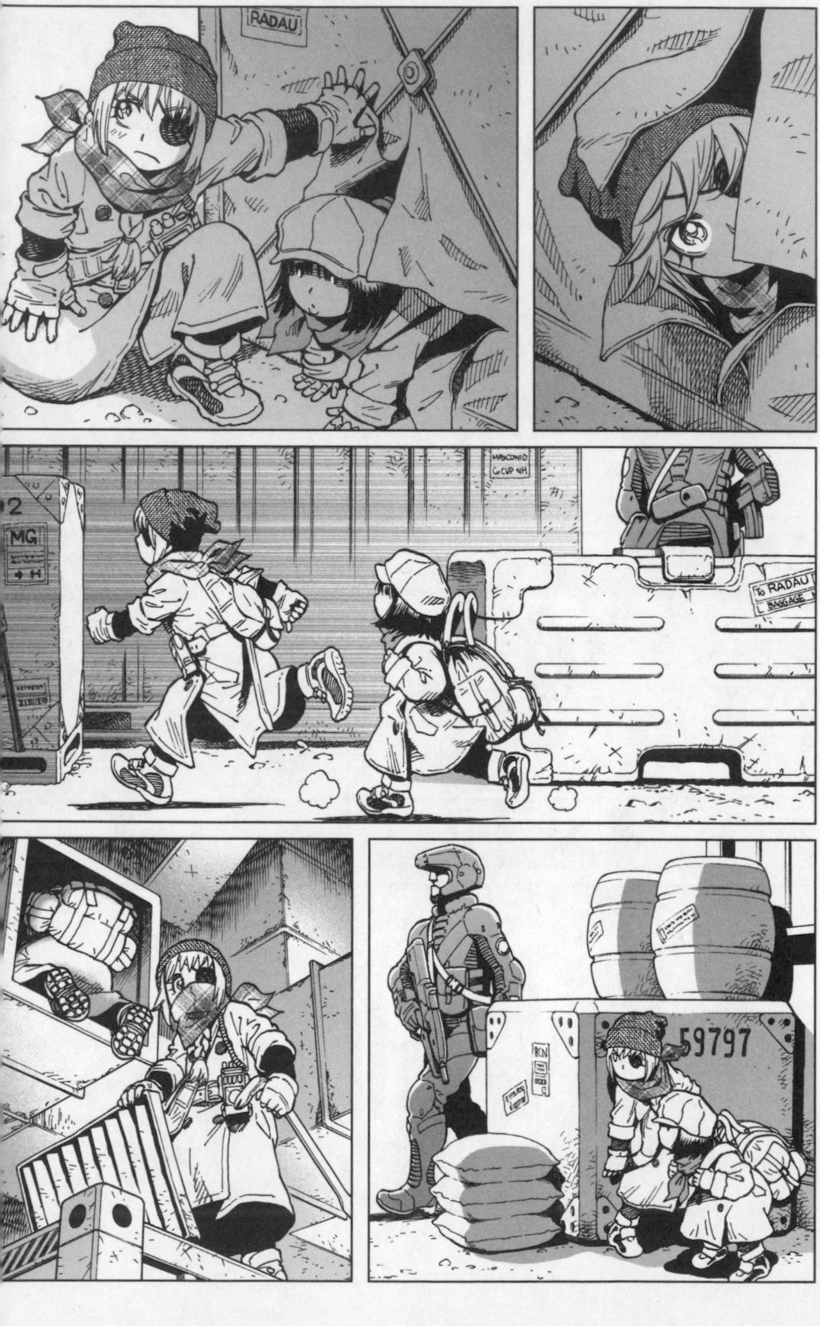
RADAU
To RADAU
BAGGAGE
2
MG
59797

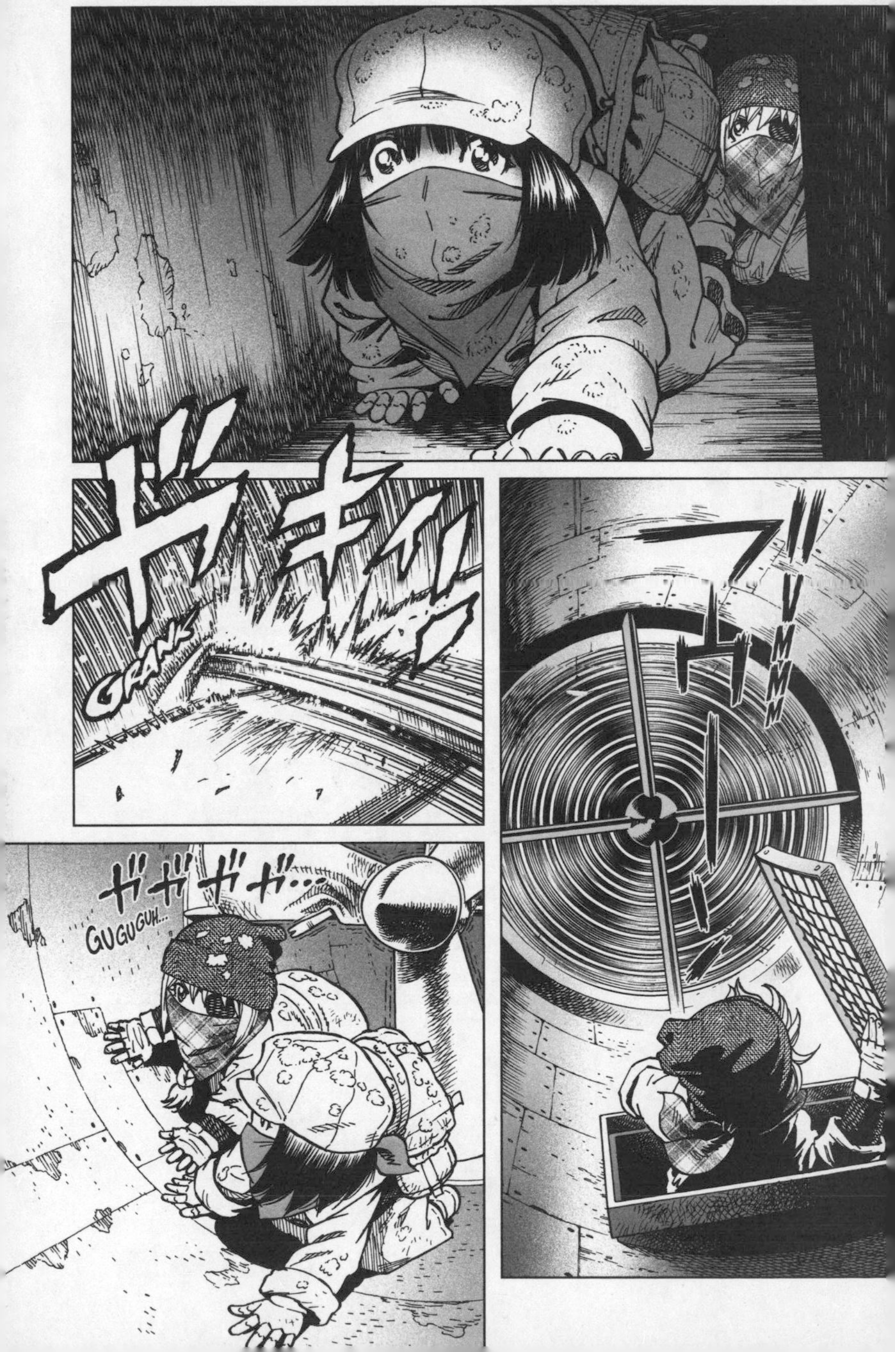
ブウー
VMMMM!!
ギャキィ!!
GRANK
ガガガガ…
GUGUGUH...

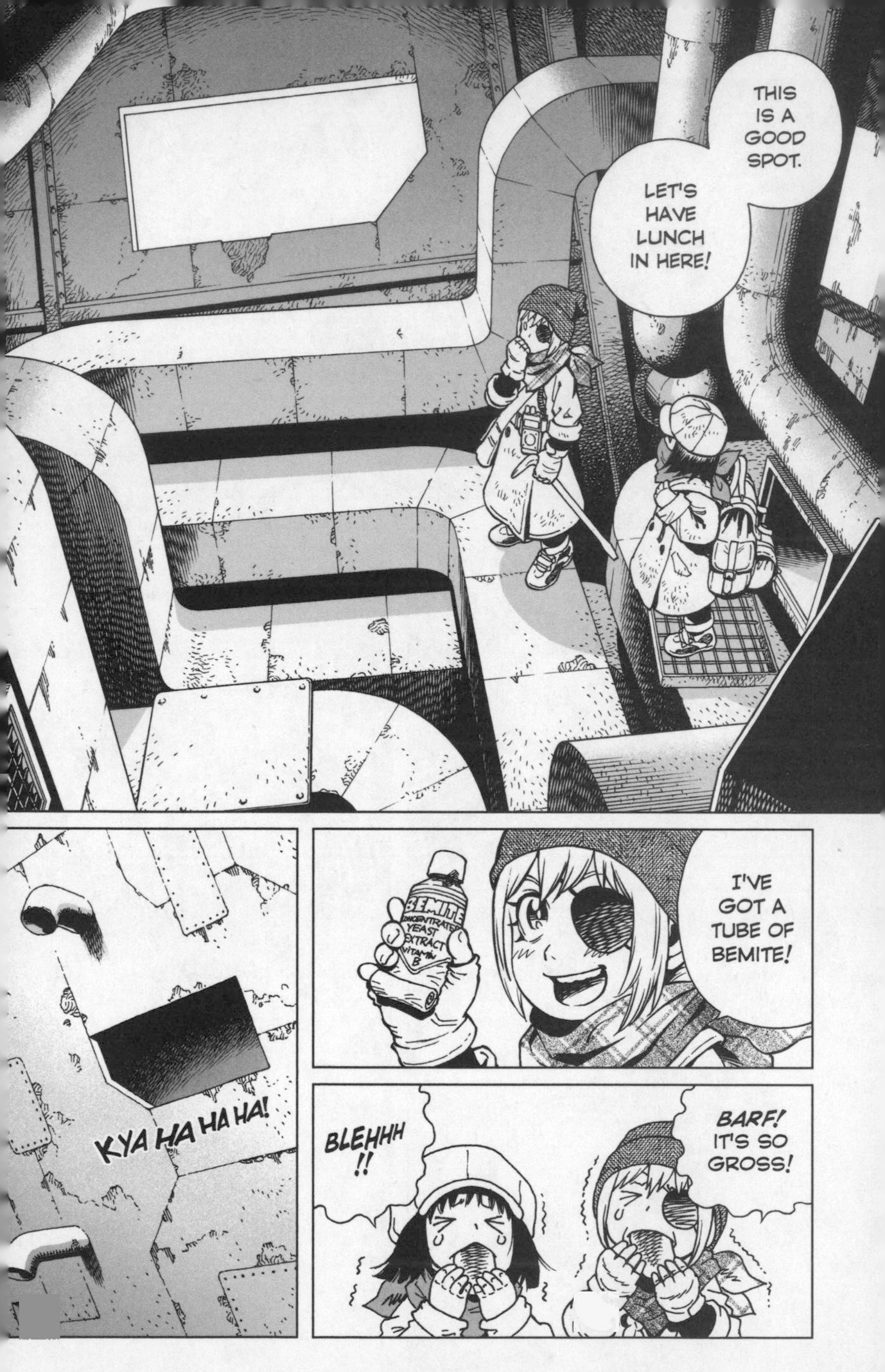
THIS IS A GOOD SPOT.
LET'S HAVE LUNCH IN HERE!
I'VE GOT A TUBE OF BEMITE!
BEMITE CONCENTRATED YEAST EXTRACT VITAMIN B
BARF! IT'S SO GROSS!
BLEHHH !!
KYA HA HA HA!

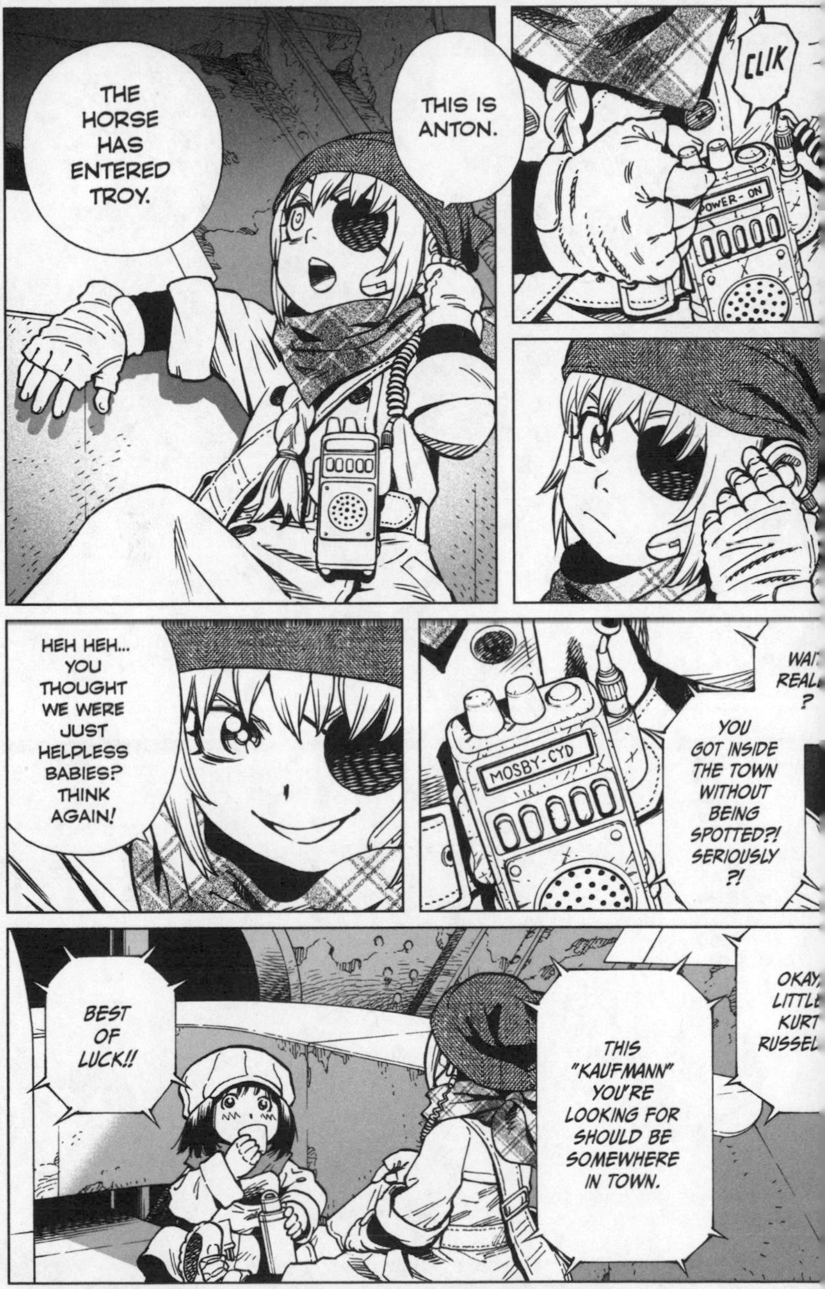
CLIK
POWER-ON
THIS IS ANTON.
THE HORSE HAS ENTERED TROY.
WAI REAL ?
YOU GOT INSIDE THE TOWN WITHOUT BEING SPOTTED?! SERIOUSLY?!
MOSBY-CYD
HEH HEH... YOU THOUGHT WE WERE JUST HELPLESS BABIES? THINK AGAIN!
OKAY, LITTLE KURT RUSSEL
THIS "KAUFMANN" YOU'RE LOOKING FOR SHOULD BE SOMEWHERE IN TOWN.
BEST OF LUCK!!

***KURT RUSSELL:** American actor (1951-). Played Snake Plissken, the eye-patch-wearing hero of John Carpenter's *Escape from New York* (

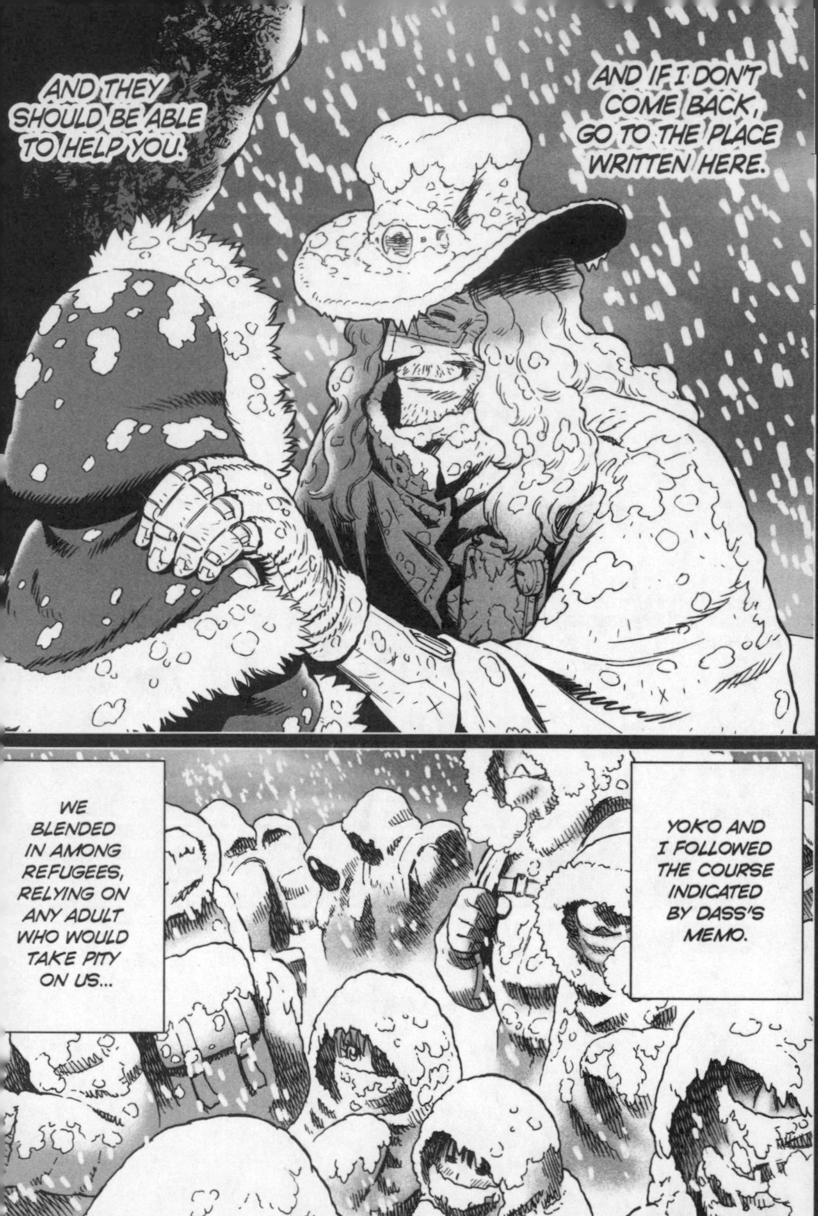
AND IF I DON'T COME BACK, GO TO THE PLACE WRITTEN HERE.
AND THEY SHOULD BE ABLE TO HELP YOU.
YOKO AND I FOLLOWED THE COURSE INDICATED BY DASS'S MEMO.
WE BLENDED IN AMONG REFUGEES, RELYING ON ANY ADULT WHO WOULD TAKE PITY ON US...

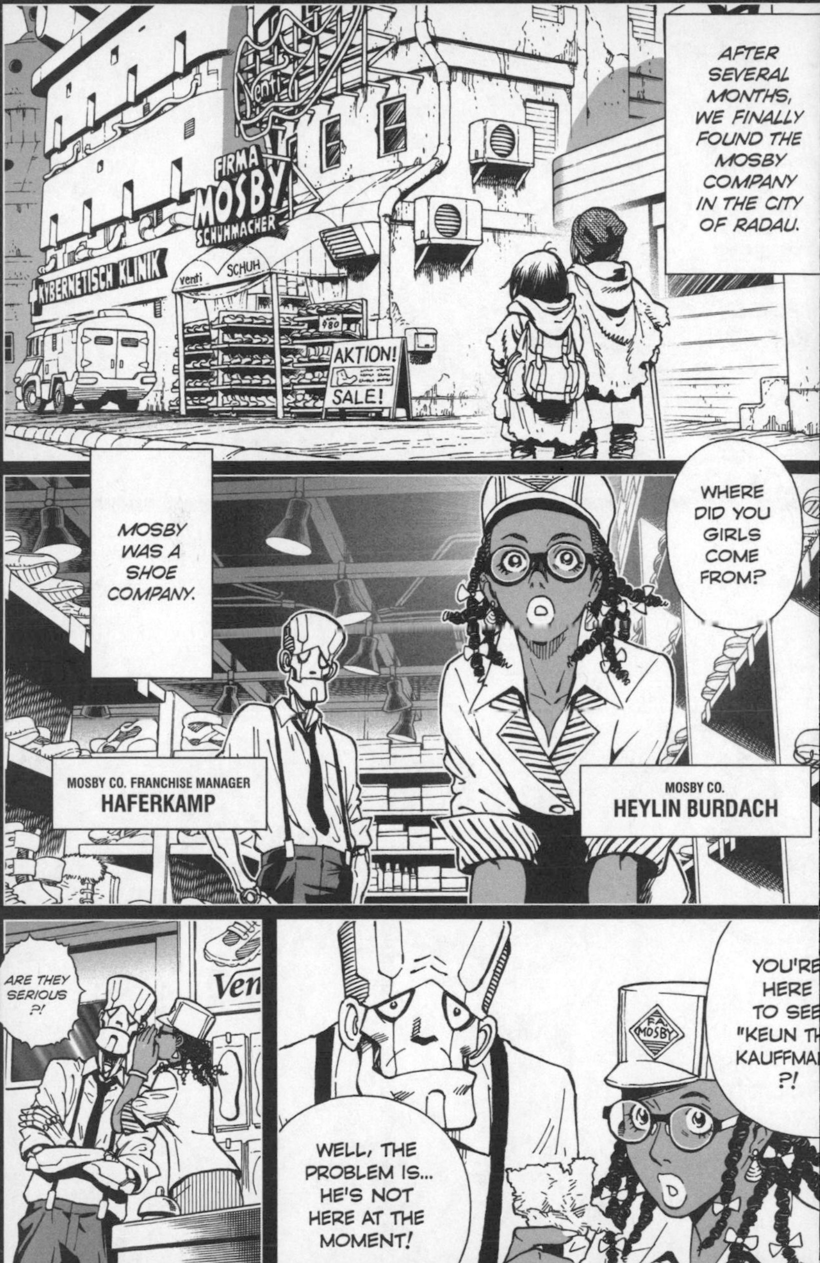

AFTER SEVERAL MONTHS, WE FINALLY FOUND THE MOSBY COMPANY IN THE CITY OF RADAU.
Venti
FIRMA MOSBY SCHUHMACHER
KYBERNETISCH KLINIK
Venti SCHUH
AKTION!
SALE!
WHERE DID YOU GIRLS COME FROM?
MOSBY WAS A SHOE COMPANY.
MOSBY CO. HEYLIN BURDACH
MOSBY CO. FRANCHISE MANAGER HAFERKAMP
YOU'RE HERE TO SEE "KEUN TH KAUFFMA ?!
FA MOSBY
WELL, THE PROBLEM IS... HE'S NOT HERE AT THE MOMENT!
ARE THEY SERIOUS ?!
Ven

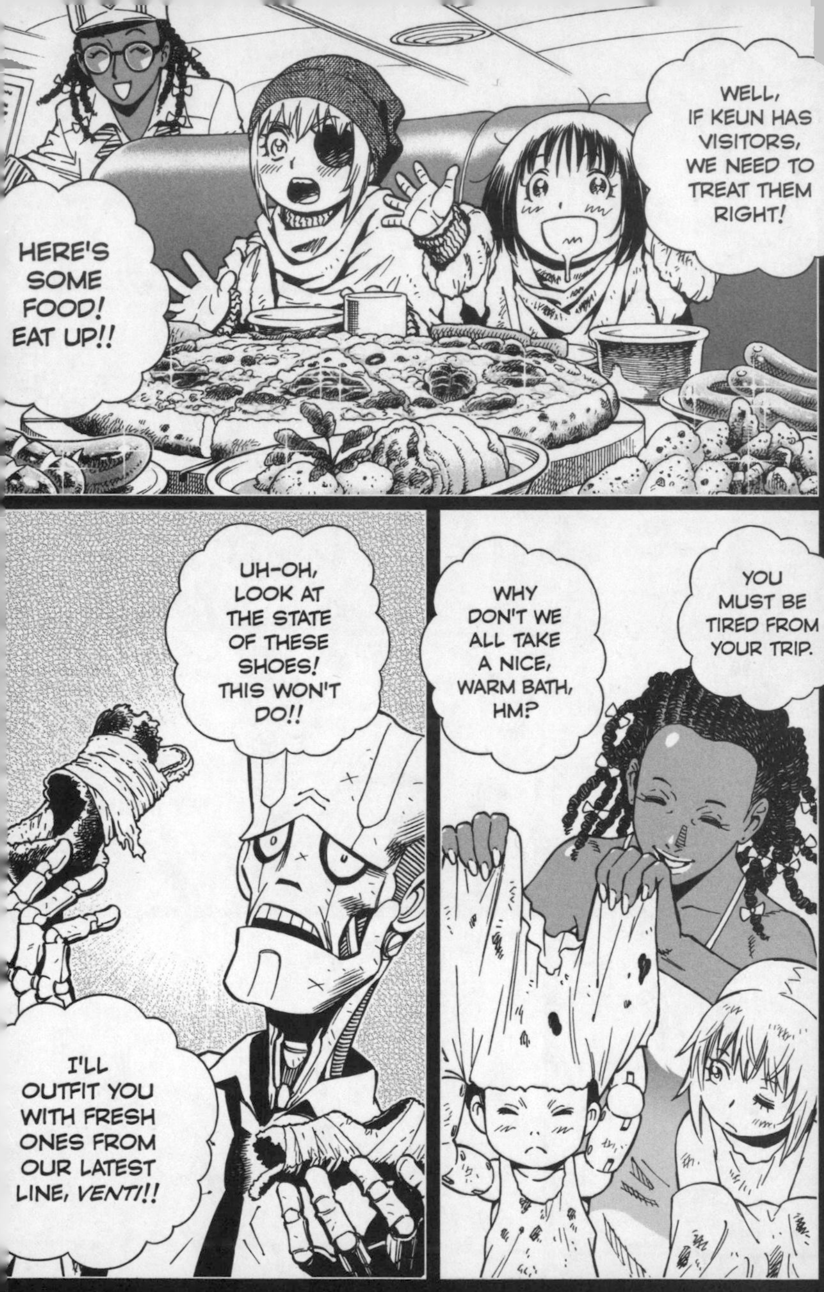
WELL, IF KEUN HAS VISITORS, WE NEED TO TREAT THEM RIGHT!
HERE'S SOME FOOD! EAT UP!!
YOU MUST BE TIRED FROM YOUR TRIP.
WHY DON'T WE ALL TAKE A NICE, WARM BATH, HM?
UH-OH, LOOK AT THE STATE OF THESE SHOES! THIS WON'T DO!!
I'LL OUTFIT YOU WITH FRESH ONES FROM OUR LATEST LINE, *VENTI*!!

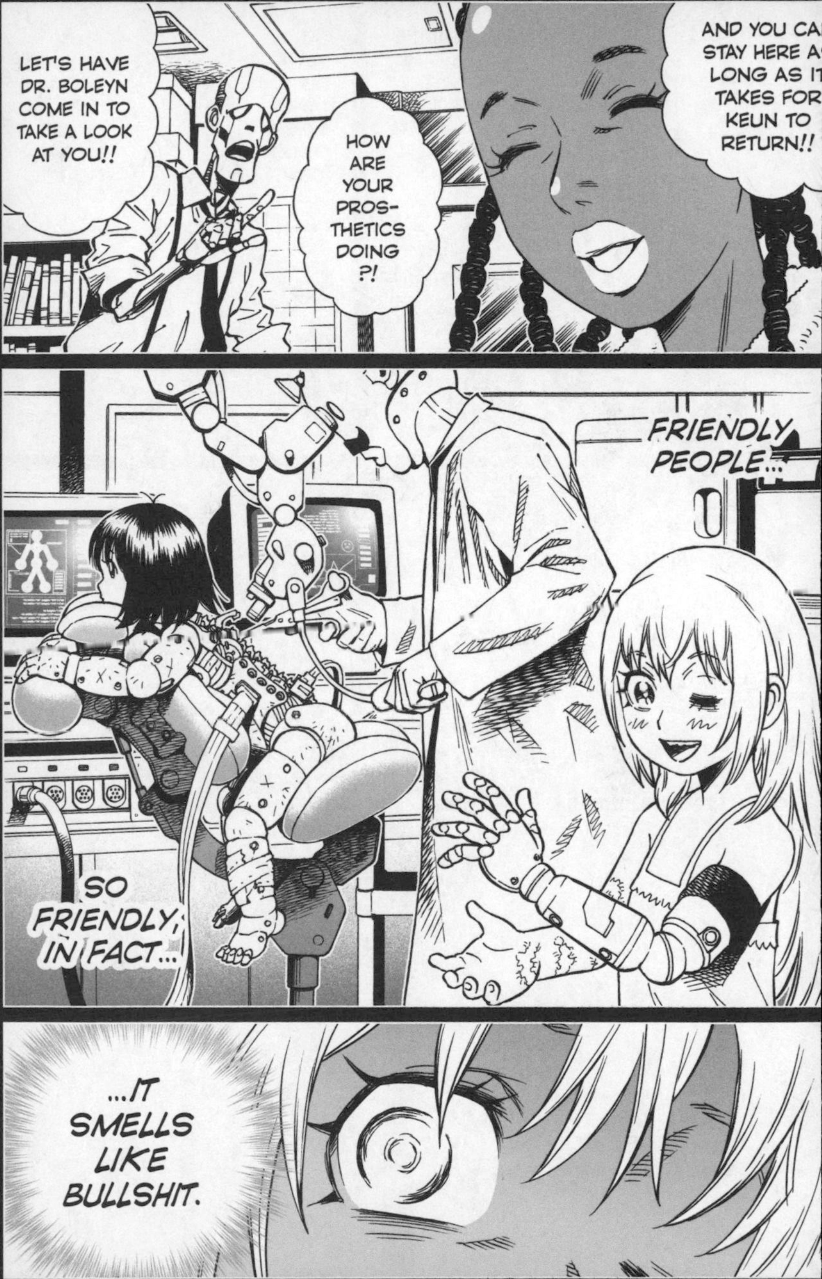
AND YOU CA STAY HERE AS LONG AS IT TAKES FOR KEUN TO RETURN!!
HOW ARE YOUR PROS-THETICS DOING ?!
LET'S HAVE DR. BOLEYN COME IN TO TAKE A LOOK AT YOU!!
FRIENDLY PEOPLE...
SO FRIENDLY, IN FACT...
...IT SMELLS LIKE BULLSHIT.

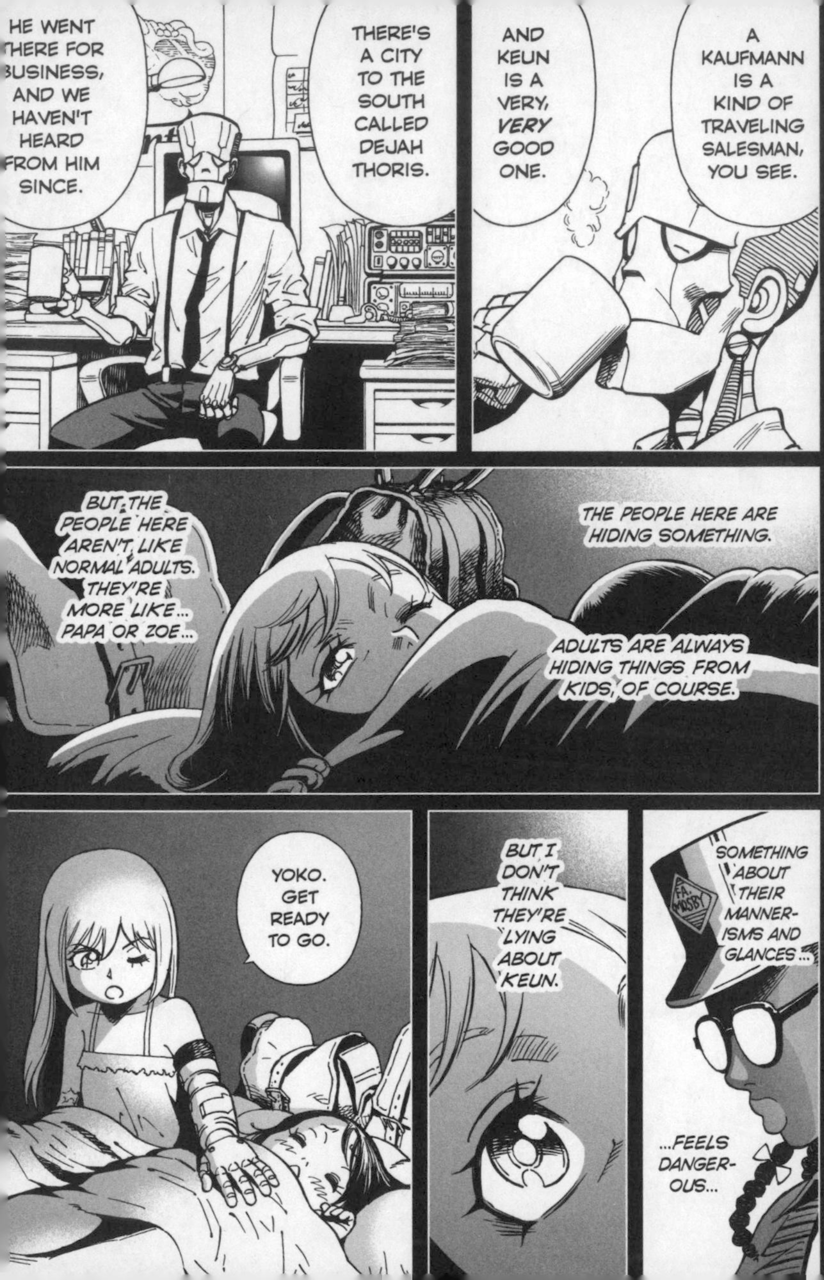
A KAUFMANN IS A KIND OF TRAVELING SALESMAN, YOU SEE.
AND KEUN IS A VERY, *VERY* GOOD ONE.
THERE'S A CITY TO THE SOUTH CALLED DEJAH THORIS.
HE WENT THERE FOR BUSINESS, AND WE HAVEN'T HEARD FROM HIM SINCE.
THE PEOPLE HERE ARE HIDING SOMETHING.
ADULTS ARE ALWAYS HIDING THINGS FROM KIDS, OF COURSE.
BUT THE PEOPLE HERE AREN'T LIKE NORMAL ADULTS. THEY'RE MORE LIKE... PAPA OR ZOE...
SOMETHING ABOUT THEIR MANNERISMS AND GLANCES...
...FEELS DANGEROUS...
F.A. MOSBY
BUT I DON'T THINK THEY'RE LYING ABOUT KEUN.
YOKO. GET READY TO GO.

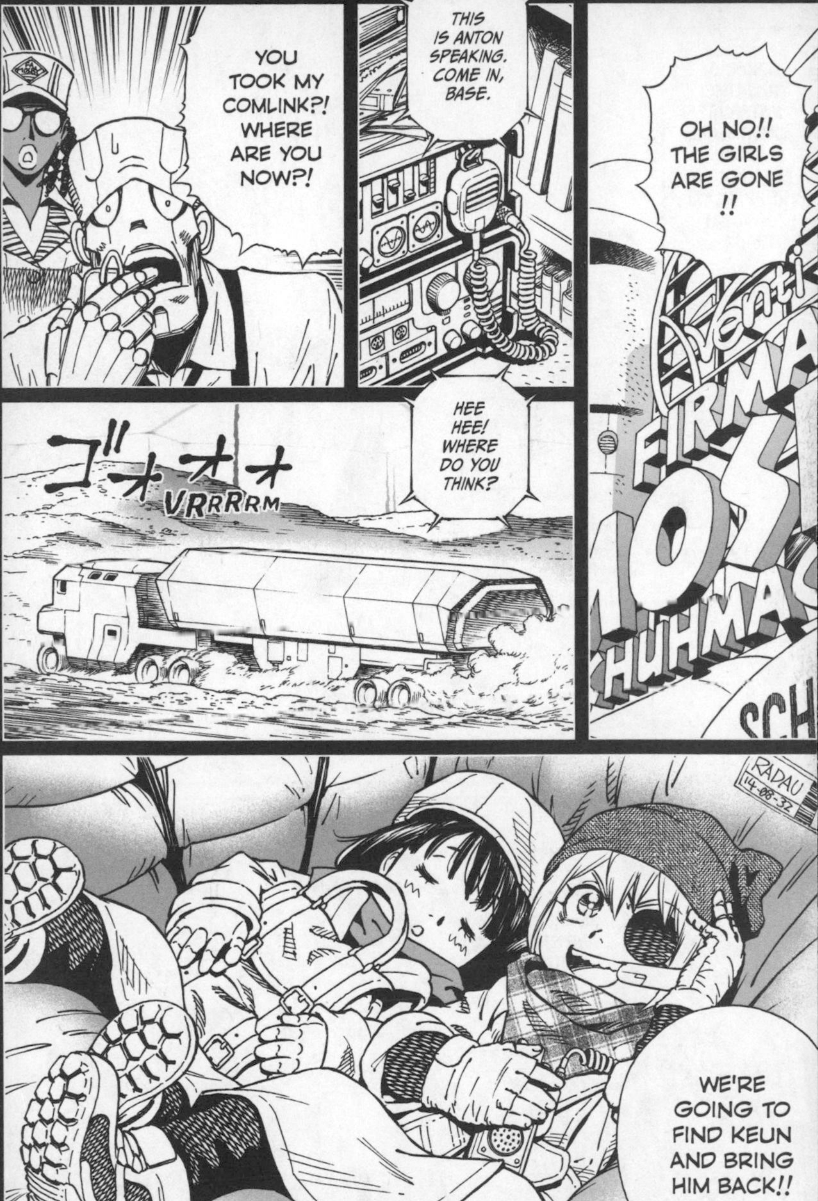
OH NO!! THE GIRLS ARE GONE!!
THIS IS ANTON SPEAKING. COME IN, BASE.
YOU TOOK MY COMLINK?! WHERE ARE YOU NOW?!
ゴオオオ
VRRRRM
HEE HEE! WHERE DO YOU THINK?
RADAU
14-08-32
WE'RE GOING TO FIND KEUN AND BRING HIM BACK!!

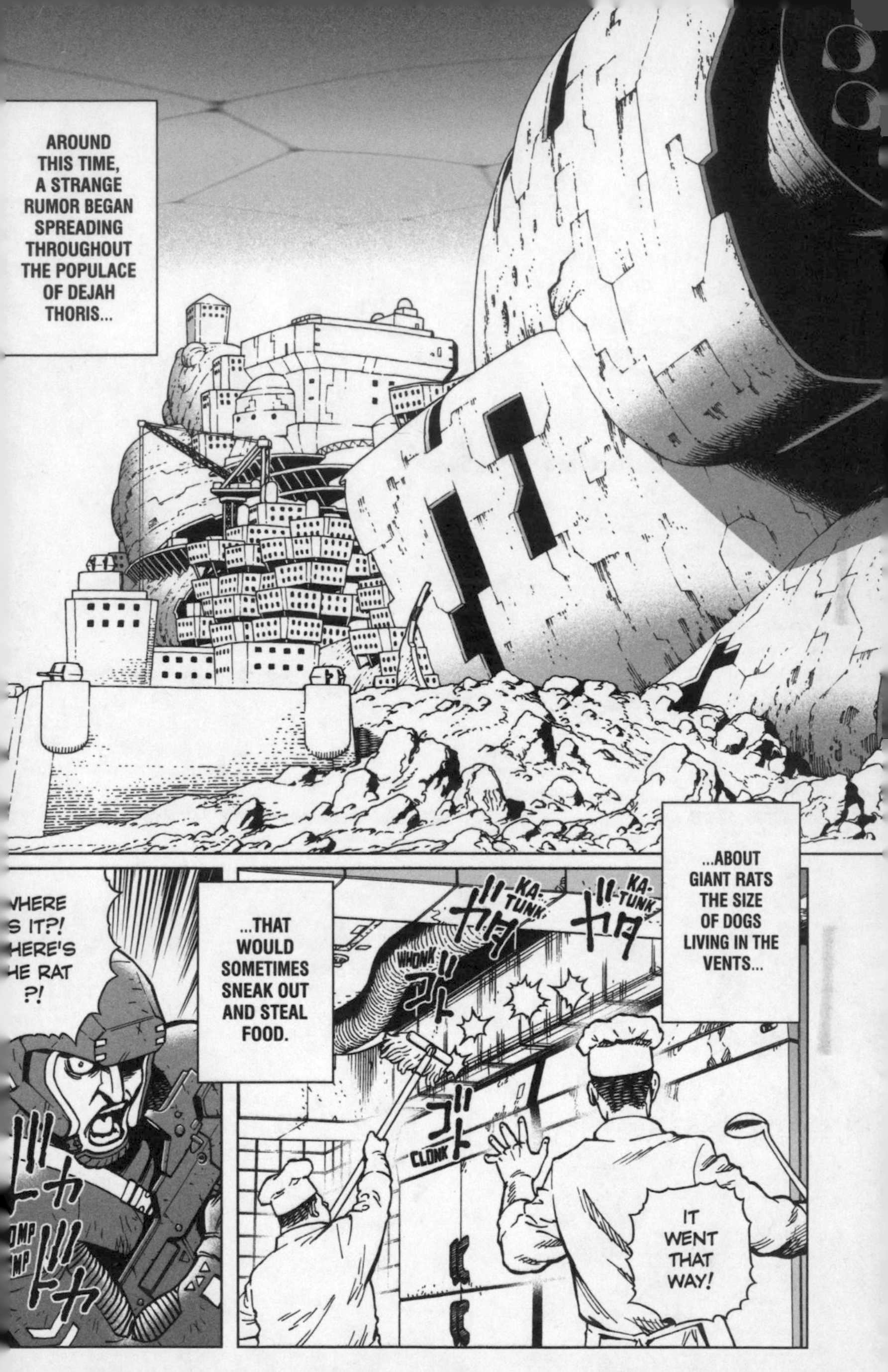

AROUND THIS TIME, A STRANGE RUMOR BEGAN SPREADING THROUGHOUT THE POPULACE OF DEJAH THORIS...
...ABOUT GIANT RATS THE SIZE OF DOGS LIVING IN THE VENTS...
KA-TUNK
KA-TUNK
...THAT WOULD SOMETIMES SNEAK OUT AND STEAL FOOD.
WHONK
CLONK
IT WENT THAT WAY!
WHERE S IT?! HERE'S HE RAT ?!

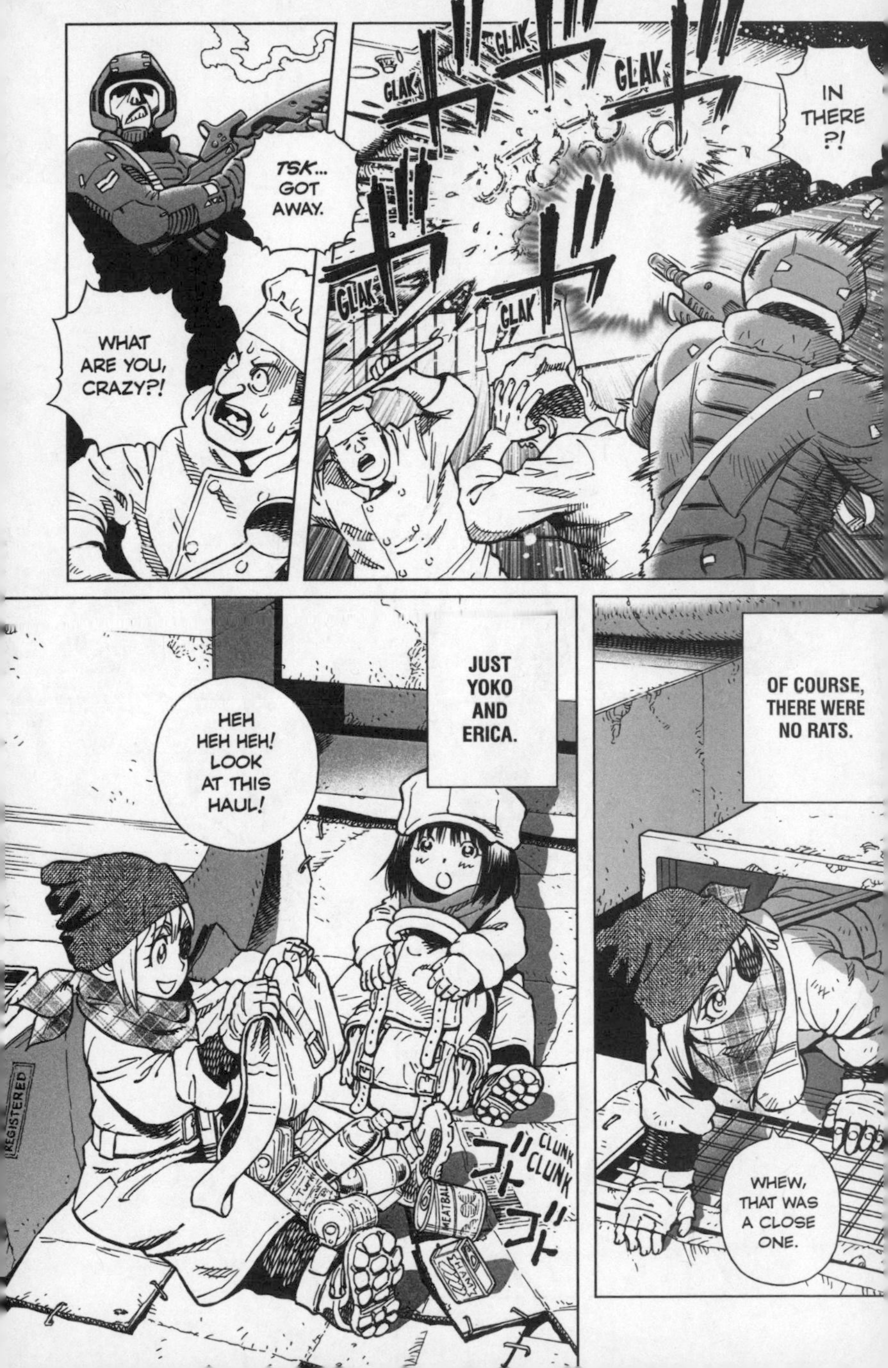
IN THERE ?!
GLAK
GLAK
GLAK
GLAK
GLAK
TSK... GOT AWAY.
WHAT ARE YOU, CRAZY?!
OF COURSE, THERE WERE NO RATS.
WHEW, THAT WAS A CLOSE ONE.
JUST YOKO AND ERICA.
HEH HEH HEH! LOOK AT THIS HAUL!
CLUNK CLUNK
MEATBALL
REGISTERED

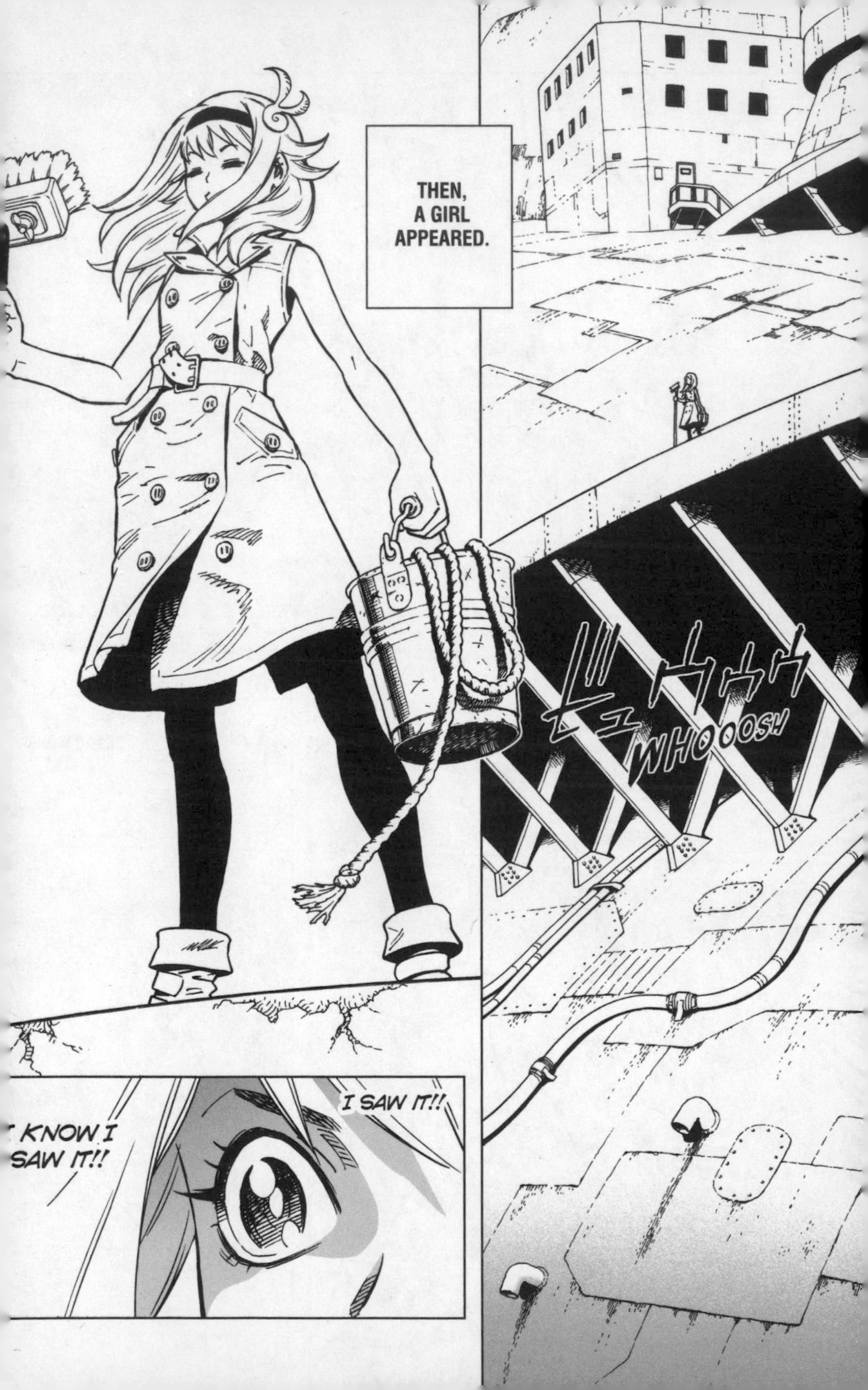
ビュウウウ
WHOOOSH
THEN, A GIRL APPEARED.
I SAW IT!!
KNOW I SAW IT!!

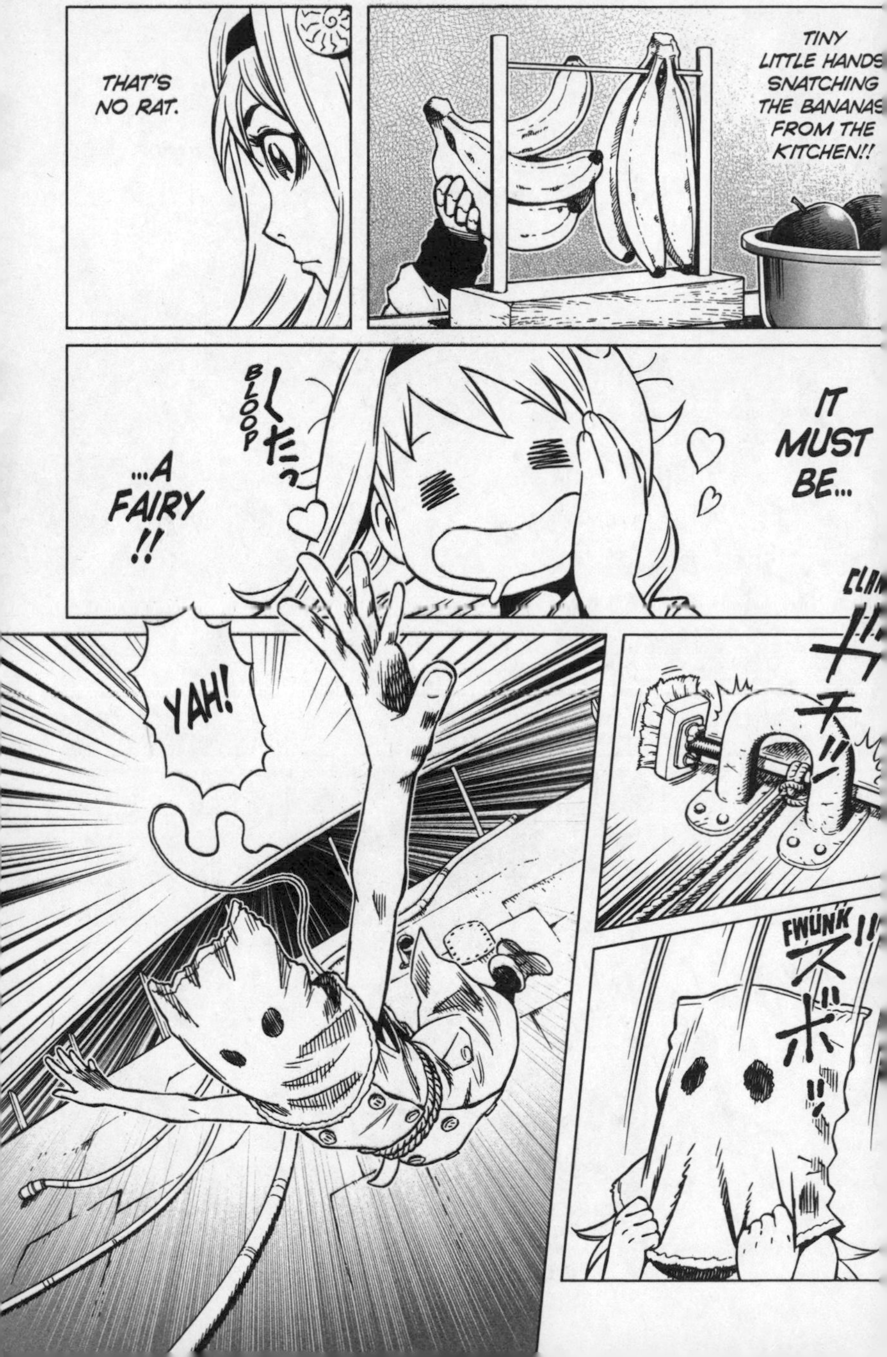
TINY LITTLE HANDS SNATCHING THE BANANAS FROM THE KITCHEN!!
THAT'S NO RAT.
IT MUST BE...
BLOOP
...A FAIRY!!
CLAN
FWUNK!!
YAH!

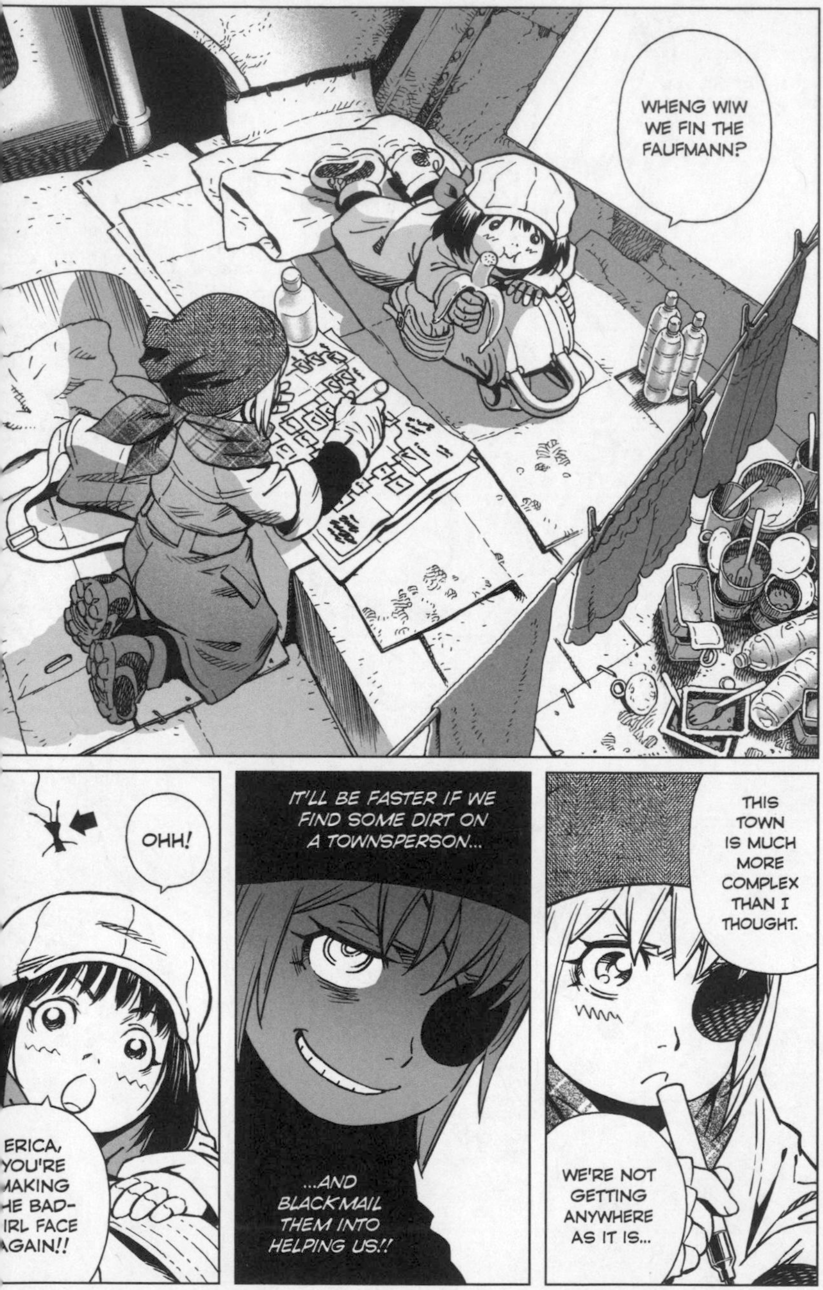
WHENG WIW WE FIN THE FAUFMANN?
THIS TOWN IS MUCH MORE COMPLEX THAN I THOUGHT.
WE'RE NOT GETTING ANYWHERE AS IT IS...
IT'LL BE FASTER IF WE FIND SOME DIRT ON A TOWNSPERSON...
...AND BLACKMAIL THEM INTO HELPING US!!
OHH!
ERICA, YOU'RE MAKING HE BAD-IRL FACE AGAIN!!

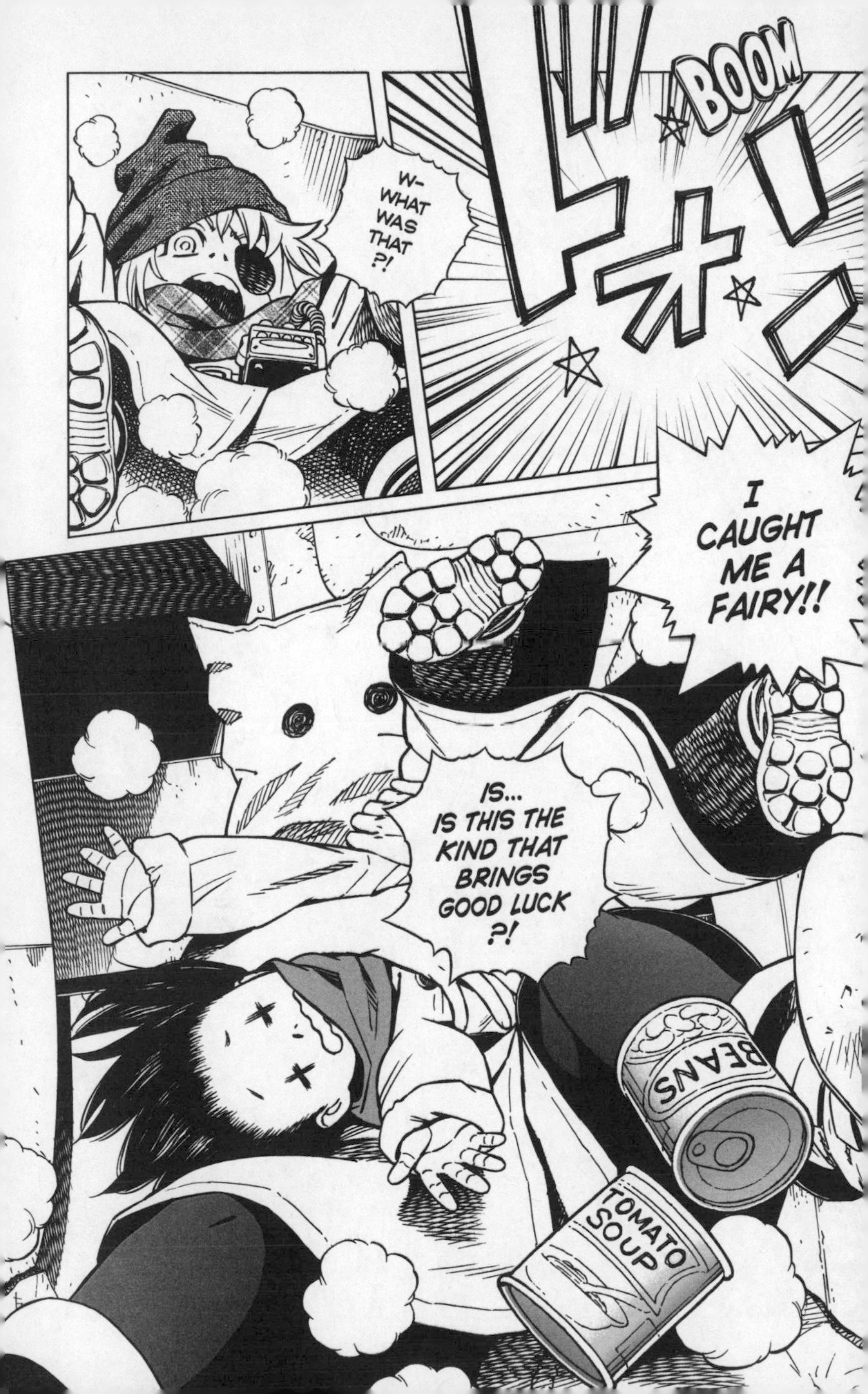
BOOM
W-WHAT WAS THAT ?!
I CAUGHT ME A FAIRY!!
IS... IS THIS THE KIND THAT BRINGS GOOD LUCK ?!
BEANS
TOMATO SOUP

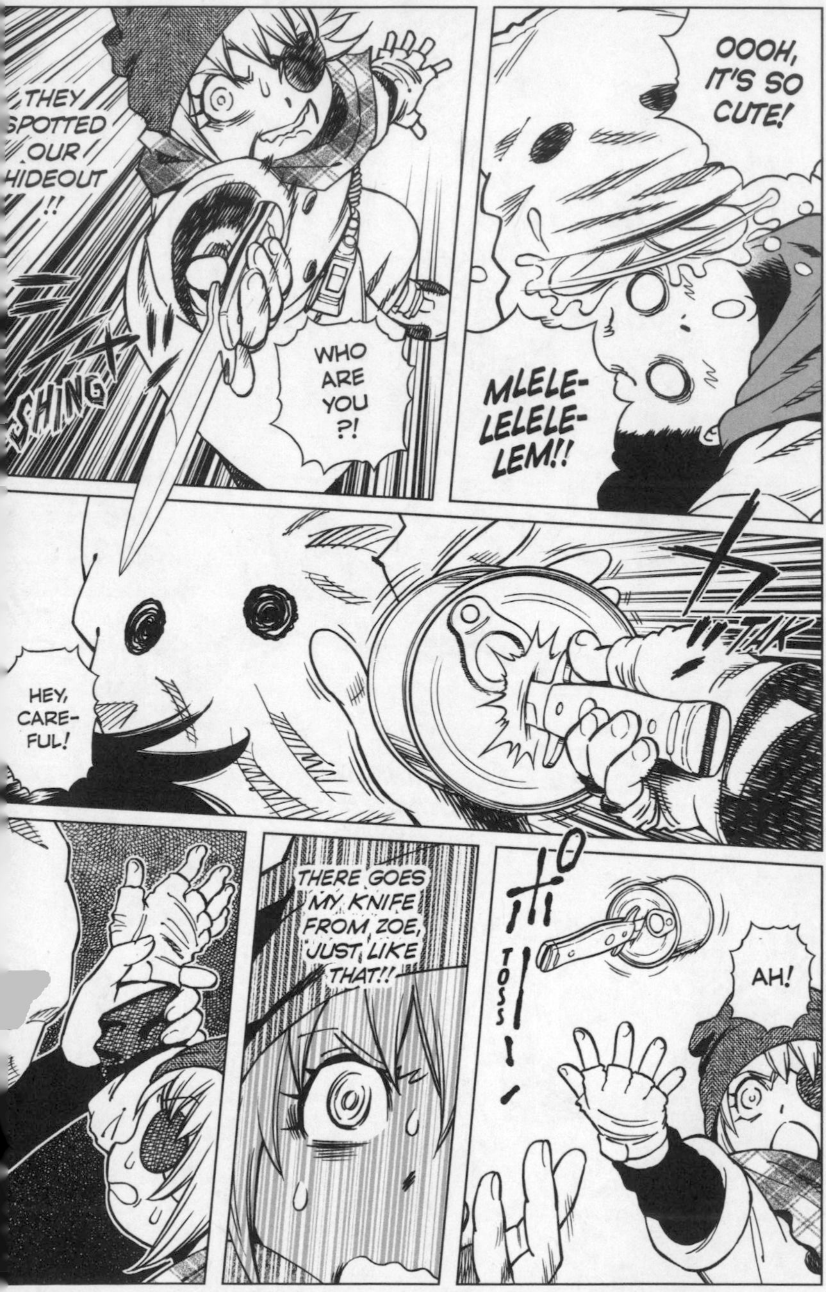
OOOH, IT'S SO CUTE!
MLELE-LELELE-LEM!!
THEY SPOTTED OUR HIDEOUT!!
WHO ARE YOU?!
SHING
TAK
HEY, CAREFUL!
AH!
TOSS
THERE GOES MY KNIFE FROM ZOE, JUST LIKE THAT!!

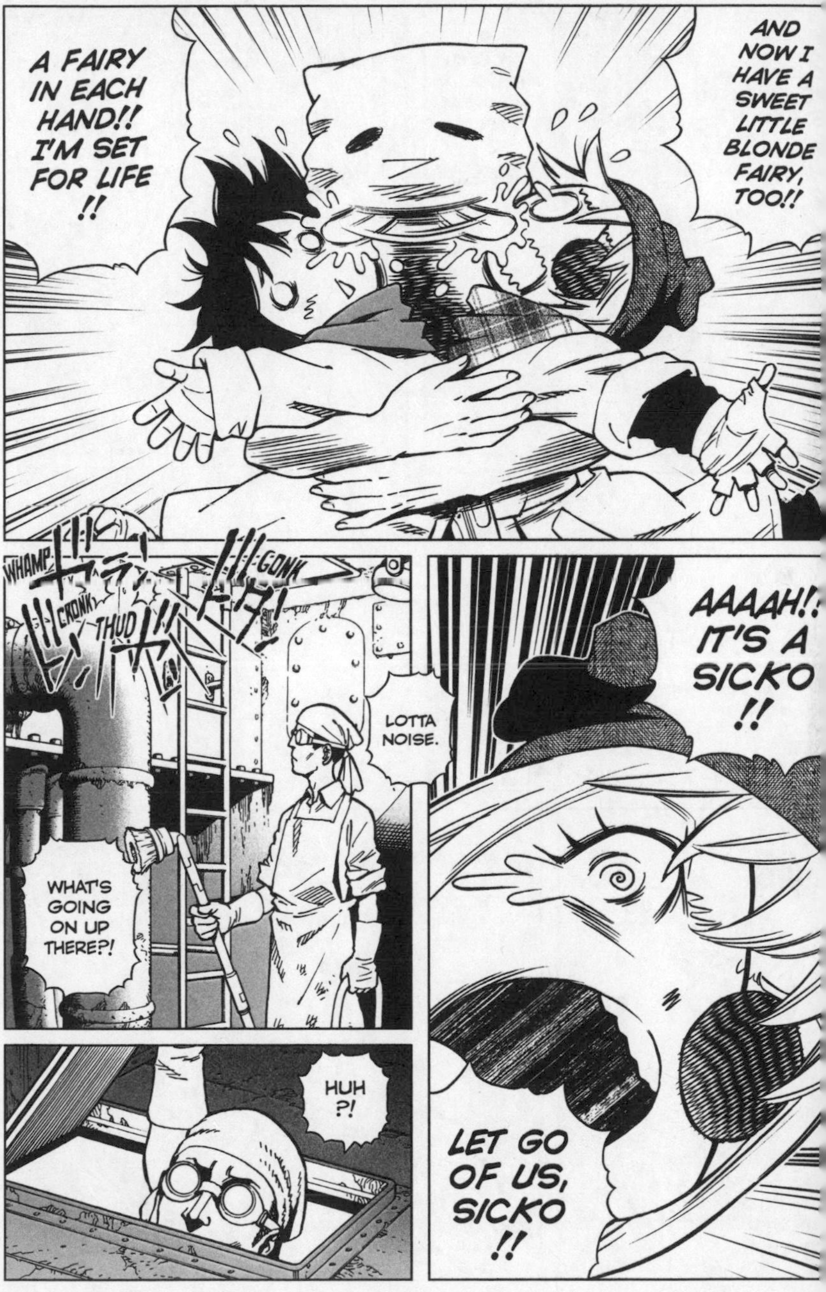
AND NOW I HAVE A SWEET LITTLE BLONDE FAIRY, TOO!!
A FAIRY IN EACH HAND!! I'M SET FOR LIFE!!
AAAAH!! IT'S A SICKO!!
LET GO OF US, SICKO!!
GONK
WHAMP
CRONK
THUD
LOTTA NOISE.
WHAT'S GOING ON UP THERE?!
HUH?!

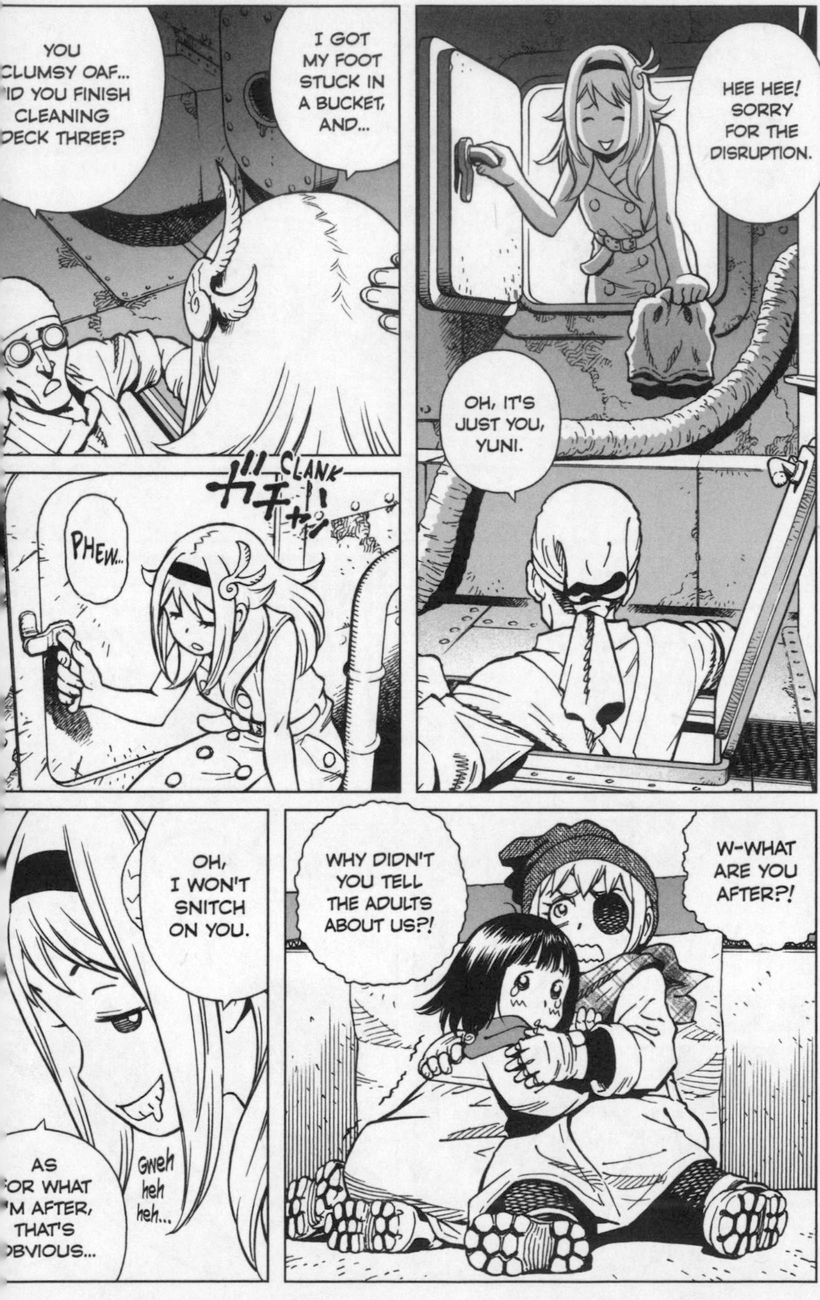
HEE HEE! SORRY FOR THE DISRUPTION.
I GOT MY FOOT STUCK IN A BUCKET, AND...
YOU CLUMSY OAF... DID YOU FINISH CLEANING DECK THREE?
OH, IT'S JUST YOU, YUNI.
CLANK
PHEW...
W-WHAT ARE YOU AFTER?!
WHY DIDN'T YOU TELL THE ADULTS ABOUT US?!
OH, I WON'T SNITCH ON YOU.
Gweh heh heh...
AS FOR WHAT I'M AFTER, THAT'S OBVIOUS...

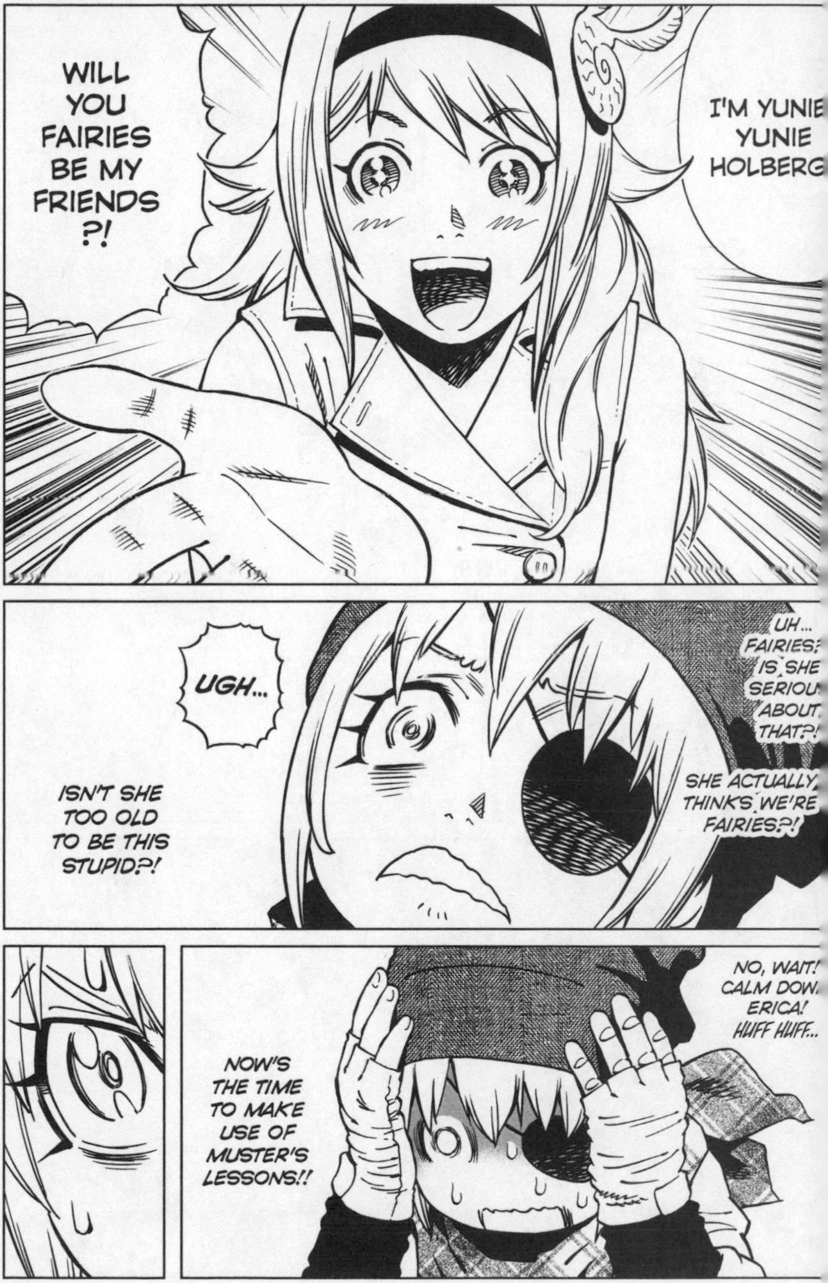
I'M YUNIE YUNIE HOLBERG
WILL YOU FAIRIES BE MY FRIENDS ?!
UH... FAIRIES? IS SHE SERIOU ABOUT THAT?!
SHE ACTUALLY THINKS WE'RE FAIRIES?!
UGH...
ISN'T SHE TOO OLD TO BE THIS STUPID?!
NO, WAIT! CALM DOW ERICA! HUFF HUFF...
NOW'S THE TIME TO MAKE USE OF MUSTER'S LESSONS!!

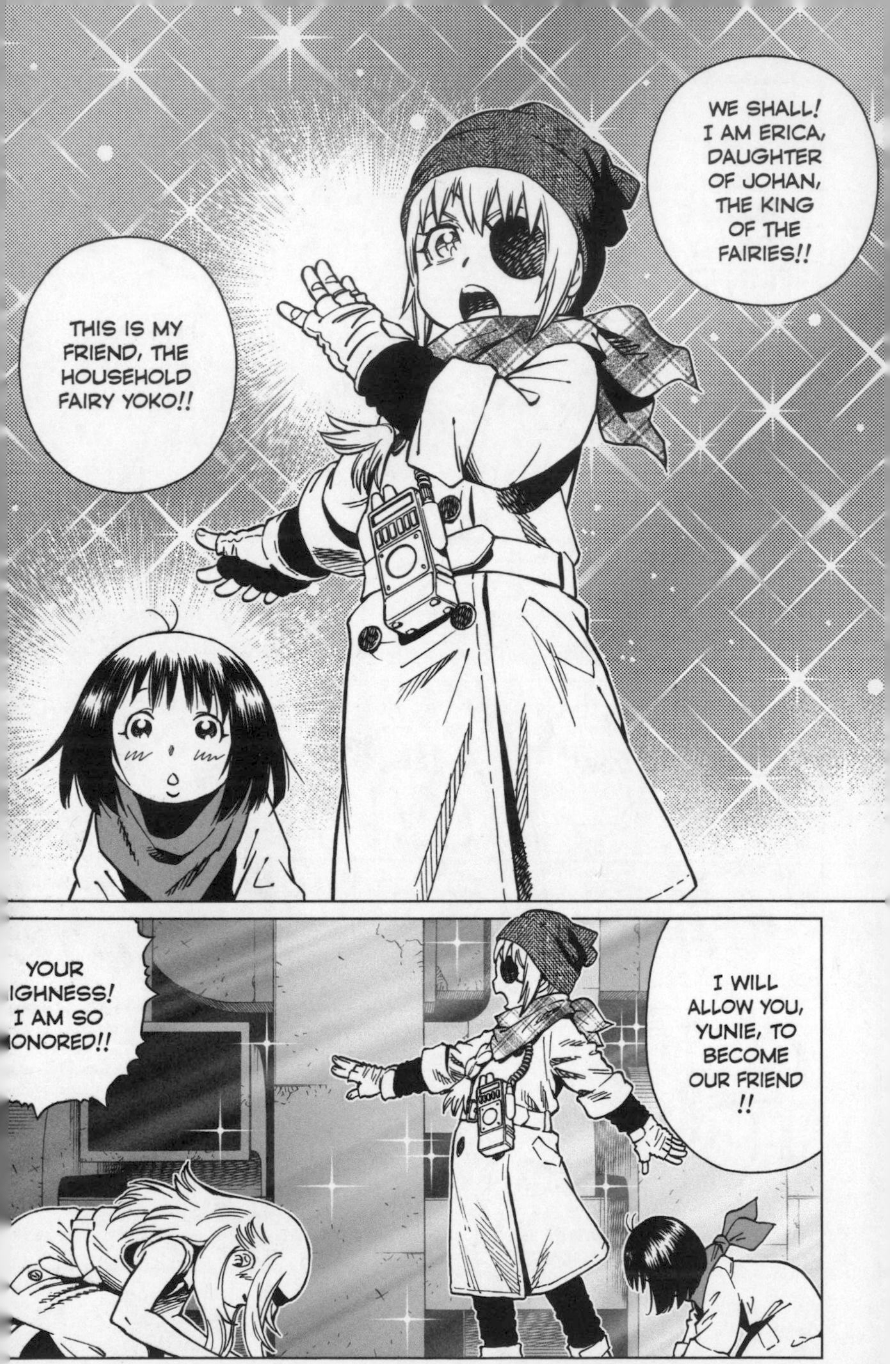
WE SHALL! I AM ERICA, DAUGHTER OF JOHAN, THE KING OF THE FAIRIES!!
THIS IS MY FRIEND, THE HOUSEHOLD FAIRY YOKO!!
I WILL ALLOW YOU, YUNIE, TO BECOME OUR FRIEND !!
YOUR IGHNESS! I AM SO ONORED!!

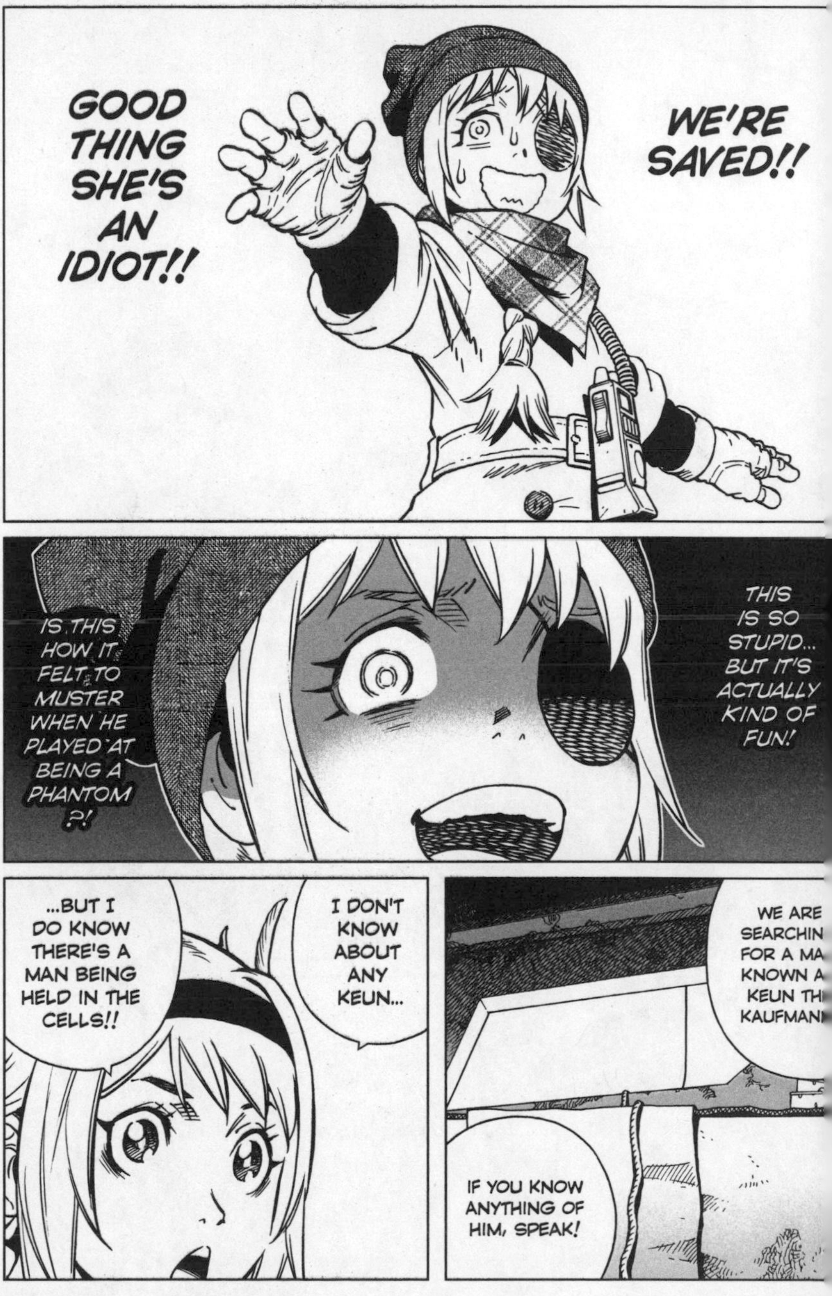
WE'RE SAVED!!
GOOD THING SHE'S AN IDIOT!!
THIS IS SO STUPID... BUT IT'S ACTUALLY KIND OF FUN!
IS THIS HOW IT FELT TO MUSTER WHEN HE PLAYED AT BEING A PHANTOM ?!
WE ARE SEARCHIN FOR A MA KNOWN A KEUN TH KAUFMAN
IF YOU KNOW ANYTHING OF HIM, SPEAK!
I DON'T KNOW ABOUT ANY KEUN...
...BUT I DO KNOW THERE'S A MAN BEING HELD IN THE CELLS!!

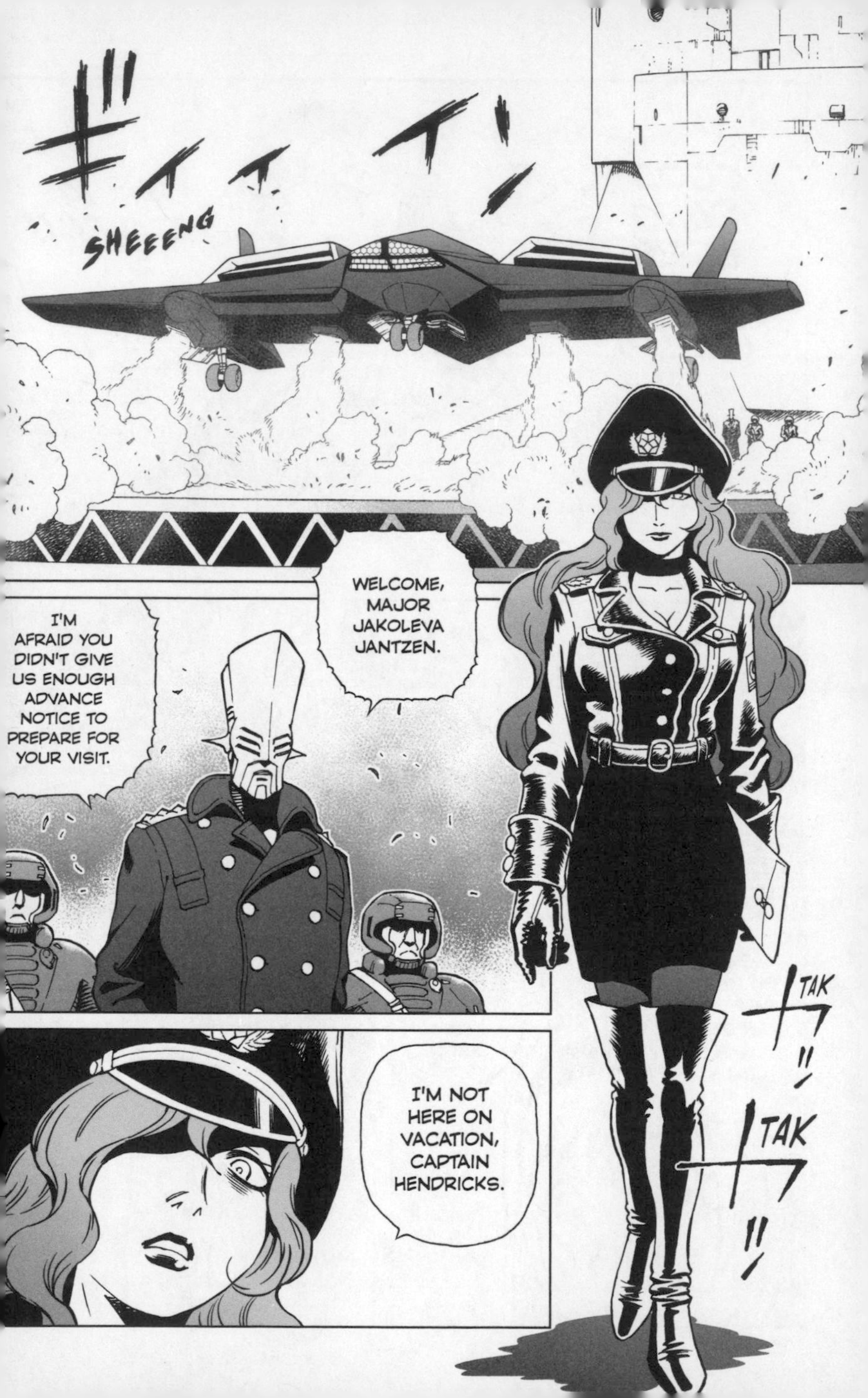
SHEEENG
TAK
TAK
WELCOME, MAJOR JAKOLEVA JANTZEN.
I'M AFRAID YOU DIDN'T GIVE US ENOUGH ADVANCE NOTICE TO PREPARE FOR YOUR VISIT.
I'M NOT HERE ON VACATION, CAPTAIN HENDRICKS.

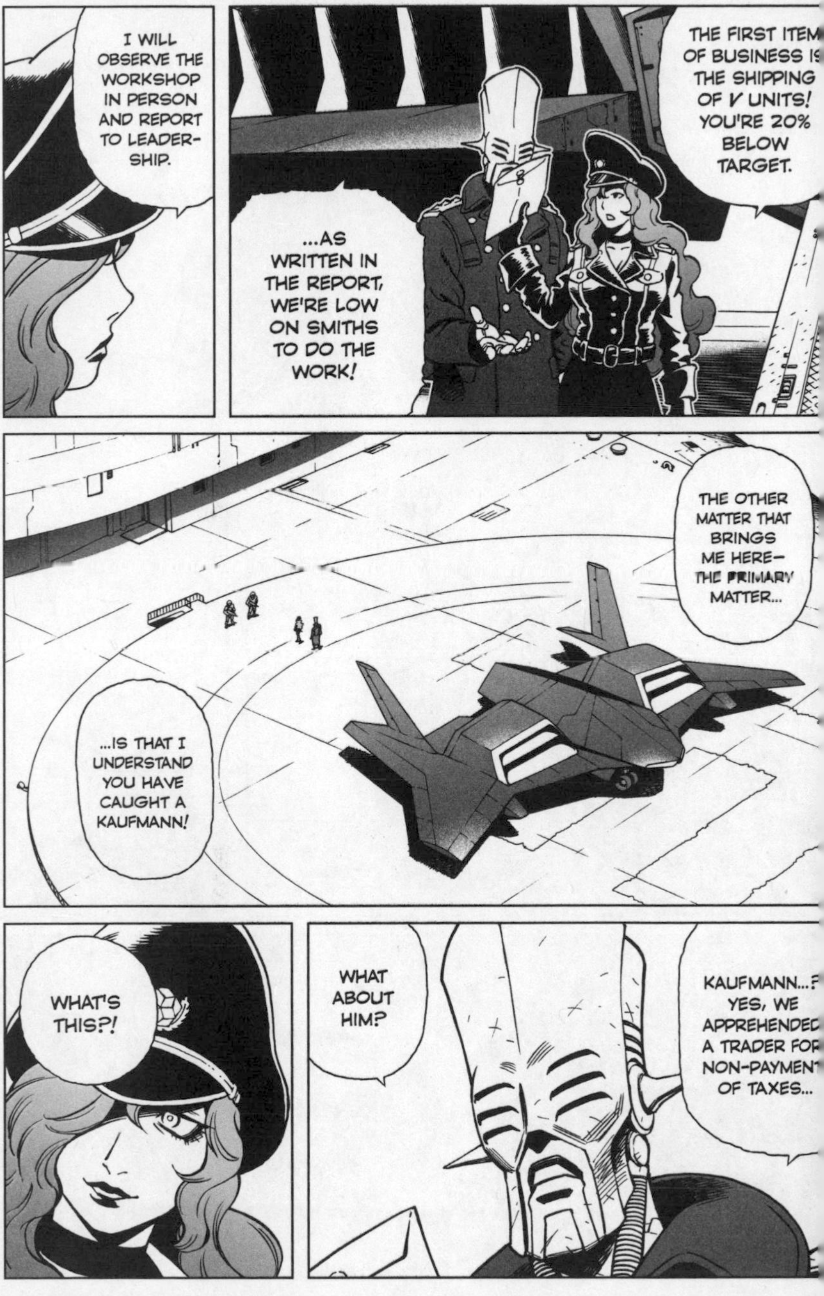

THE FIRST ITEM OF BUSINESS IS THE SHIPPING OF V UNITS! YOU'RE 20% BELOW TARGET.
...AS WRITTEN IN THE REPORT, WE'RE LOW ON SMITHS TO DO THE WORK!
I WILL OBSERVE THE WORKSHOP IN PERSON AND REPORT TO LEADER-SHIP.
THE OTHER MATTER THAT BRINGS ME HERE— THE PRIMARY MATTER...
...IS THAT I UNDERSTAND YOU HAVE CAUGHT A KAUFMANN!
KAUFMANN...? YES, WE APPREHENDED A TRADER FOR NON-PAYMENT OF TAXES...
WHAT ABOUT HIM?
WHAT'S THIS?!

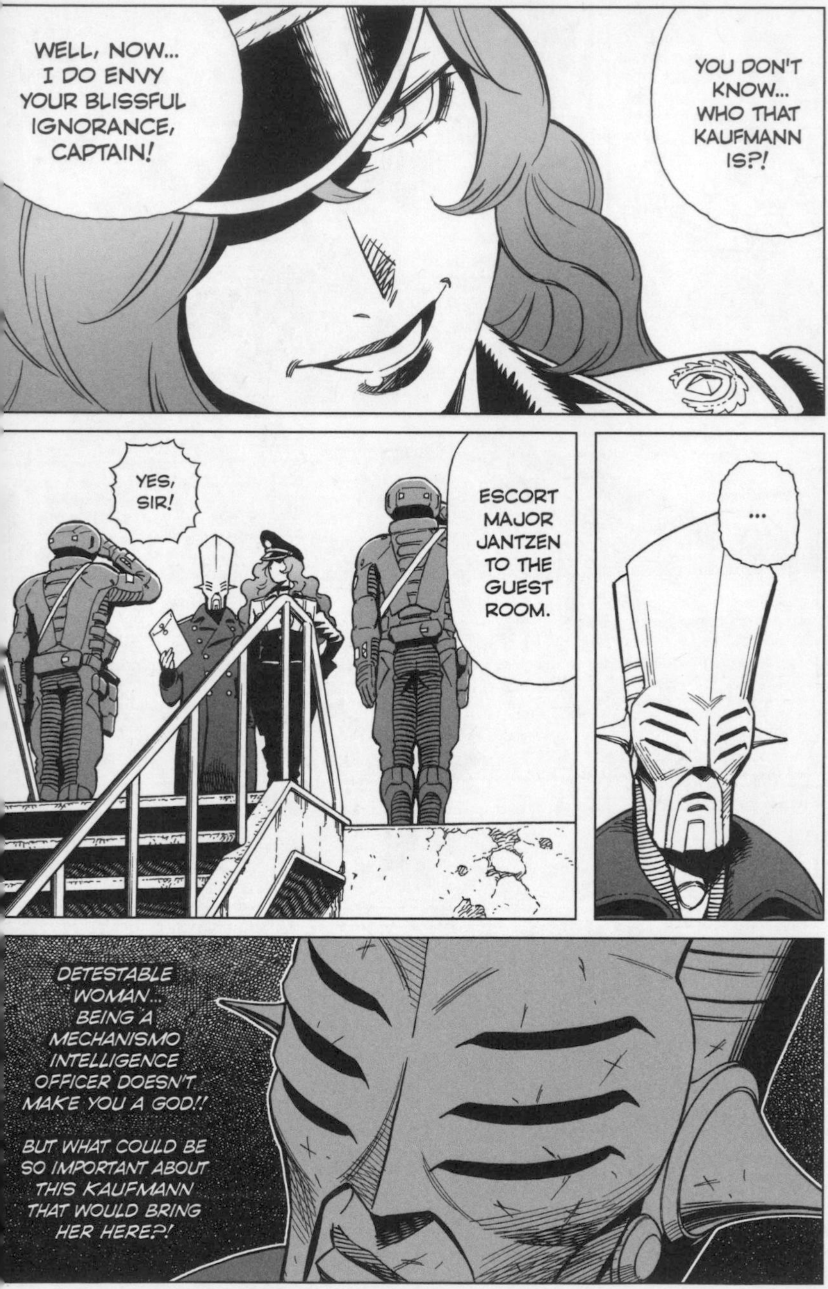
YOU DON'T KNOW... WHO THAT KAUFMANN IS?!
WELL, NOW... I DO ENVY YOUR BLISSFUL IGNORANCE, CAPTAIN!
...
ESCORT MAJOR JANTZEN TO THE GUEST ROOM.
YES, SIR!
DETESTABLE WOMAN... BEING A MECHANISMO INTELLIGENCE OFFICER DOESN'T MAKE YOU A GOD!!
BUT WHAT COULD BE SO IMPORTANT ABOUT THIS KAUFMANN THAT WOULD BRING HER HERE?!

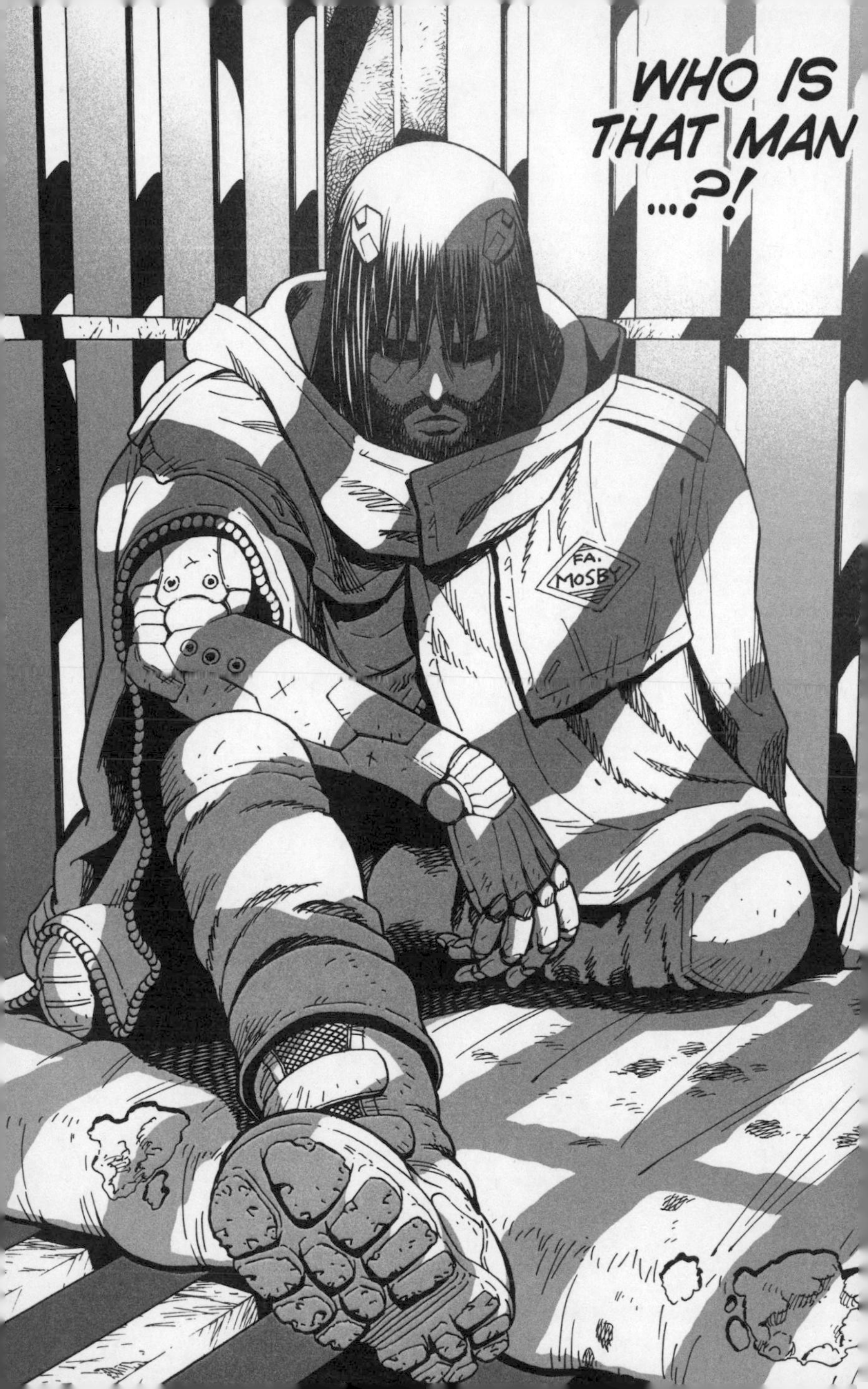
WHO IS THAT MAN ...?!
FA. MOSBY

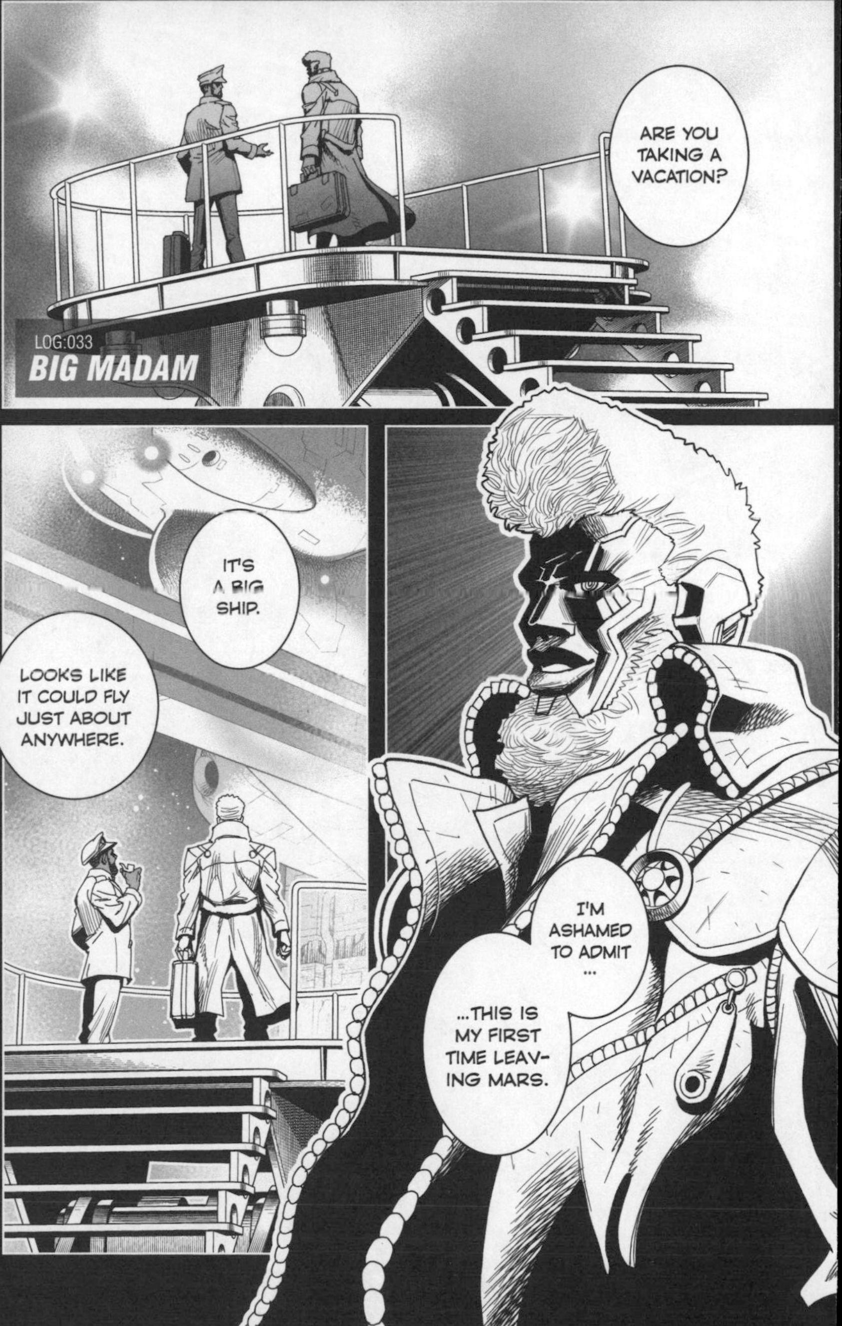
LOG:033
BIG MADAM
ARE YOU TAKING A VACATION?
I'M ASHAMED TO ADMIT ...
...THIS IS MY FIRST TIME LEAV-ING MARS.
IT'S A BIG SHIP.
LOOKS LIKE IT COULD FLY JUST ABOUT ANYWHERE.

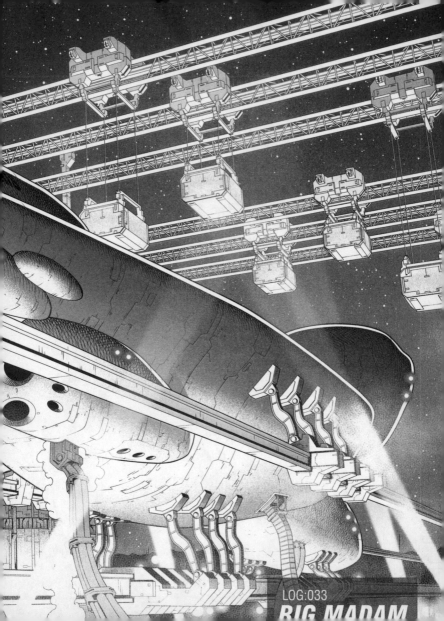

LOG:033
BIG MADAM

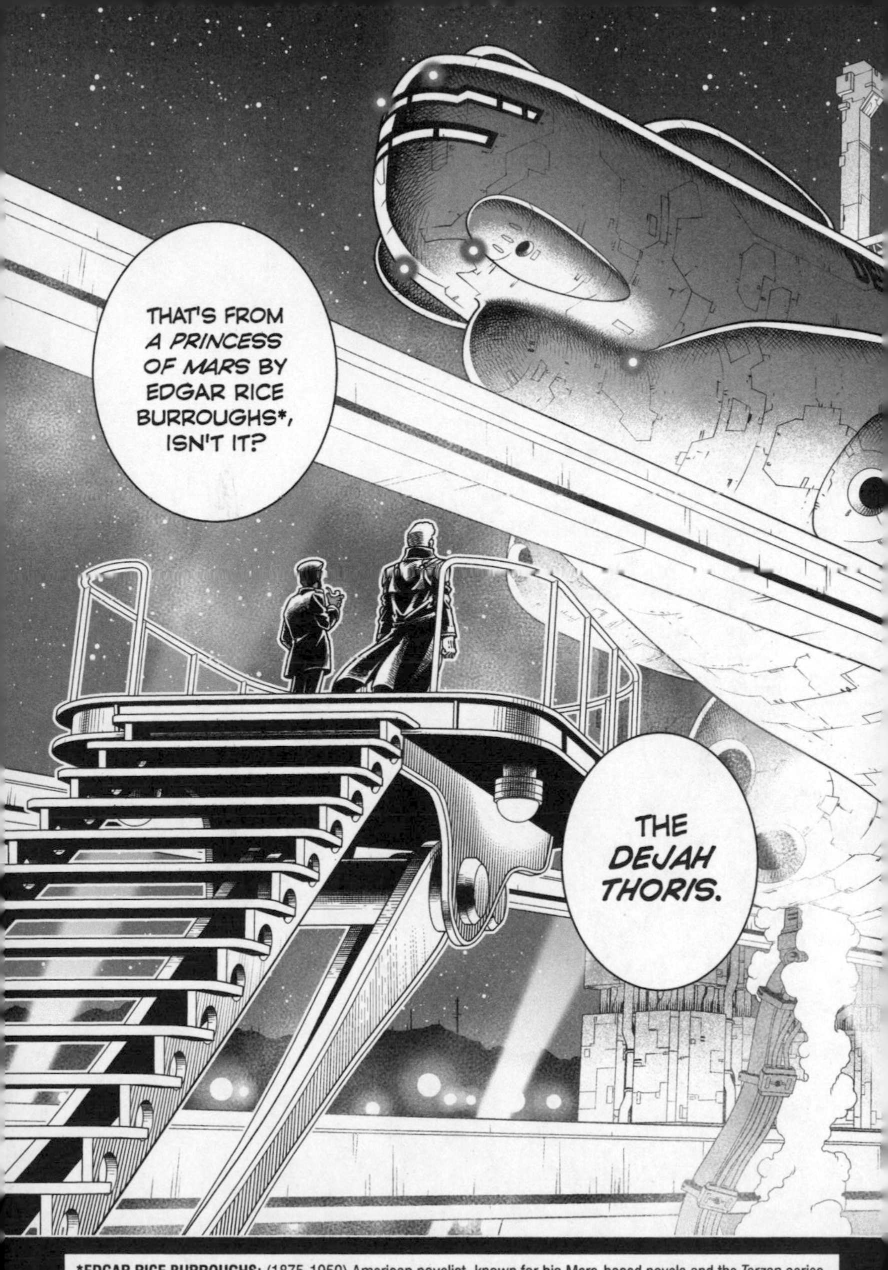
THAT'S FROM *A PRINCESS OF MARS* BY EDGAR RICE BURROUGHS*, ISN'T IT?
THE *DEJAH THORIS.*

***EDGAR RICE BURROUGHS:** (1875-1950) American novelist, known for his Mars-based novels and the *Tarzan* series. Dejah Thoris is the titular character in *A Princess of Mars.*

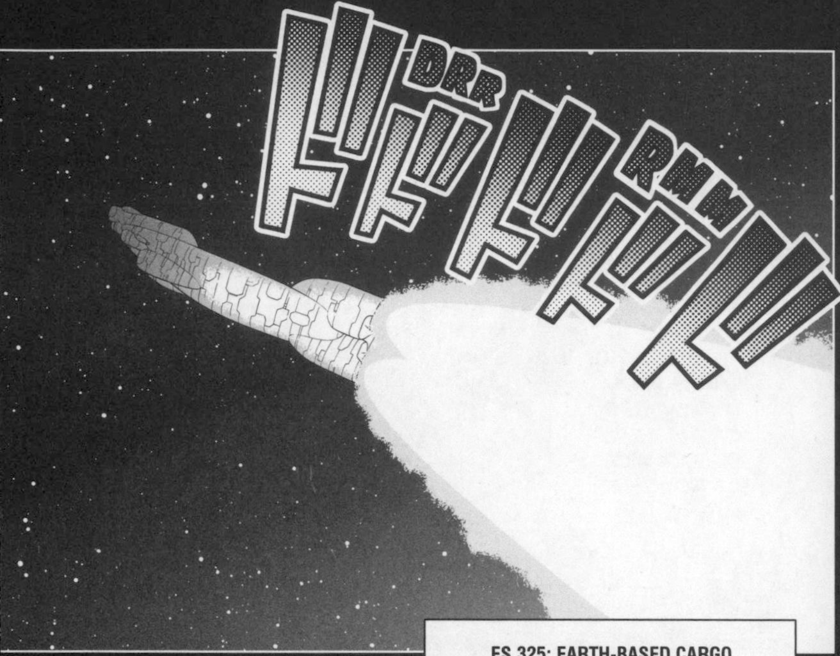
DRR
RMMM

ES 325: EARTH-BASED CARGO SHIP *DEJAH THORIS* DEPARTS NICHOLSON SPACEPORT OF MARS

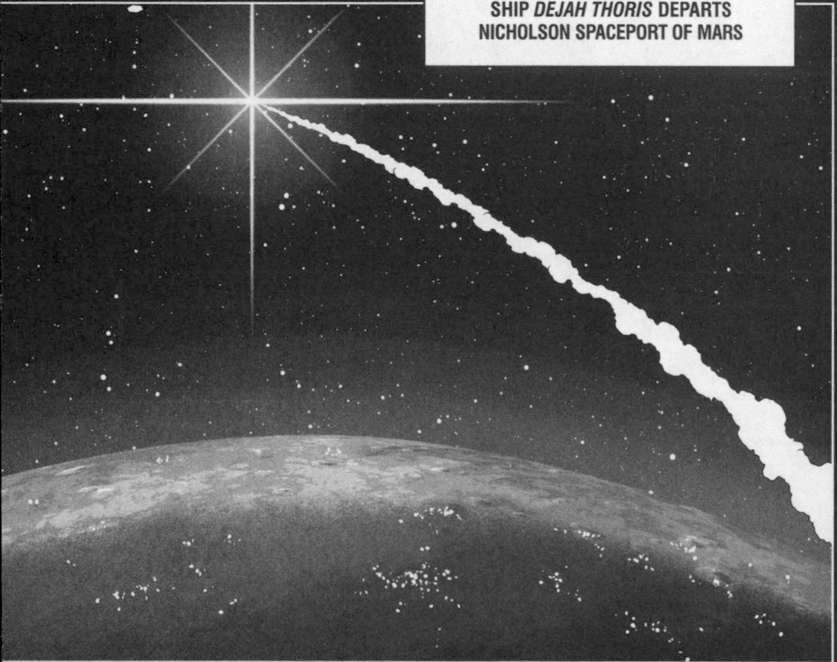

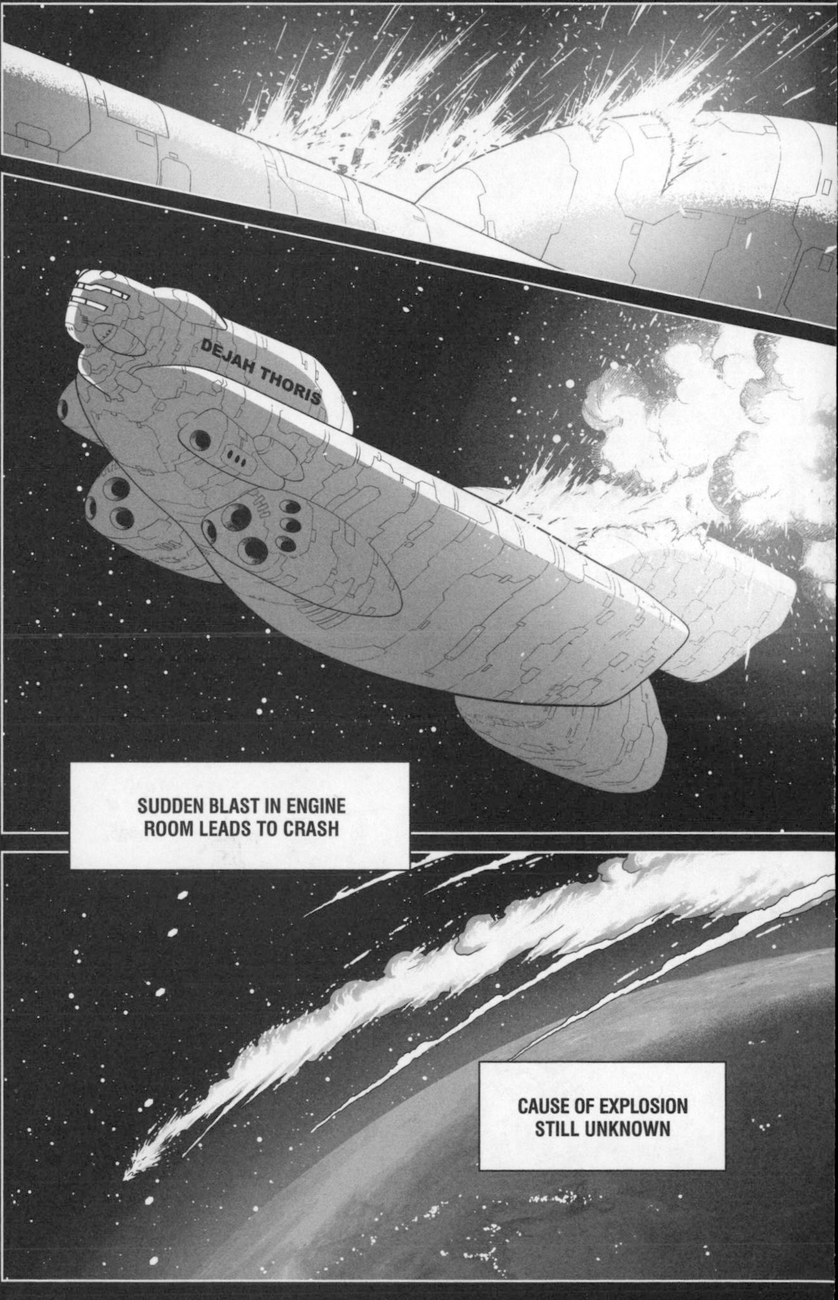
DEJAH THORIS
SUDDEN BLAST IN ENGINE ROOM LEADS TO CRASH
CAUSE OF EXPLOSION STILL UNKNOWN

ES 374

DEJAH THORIS

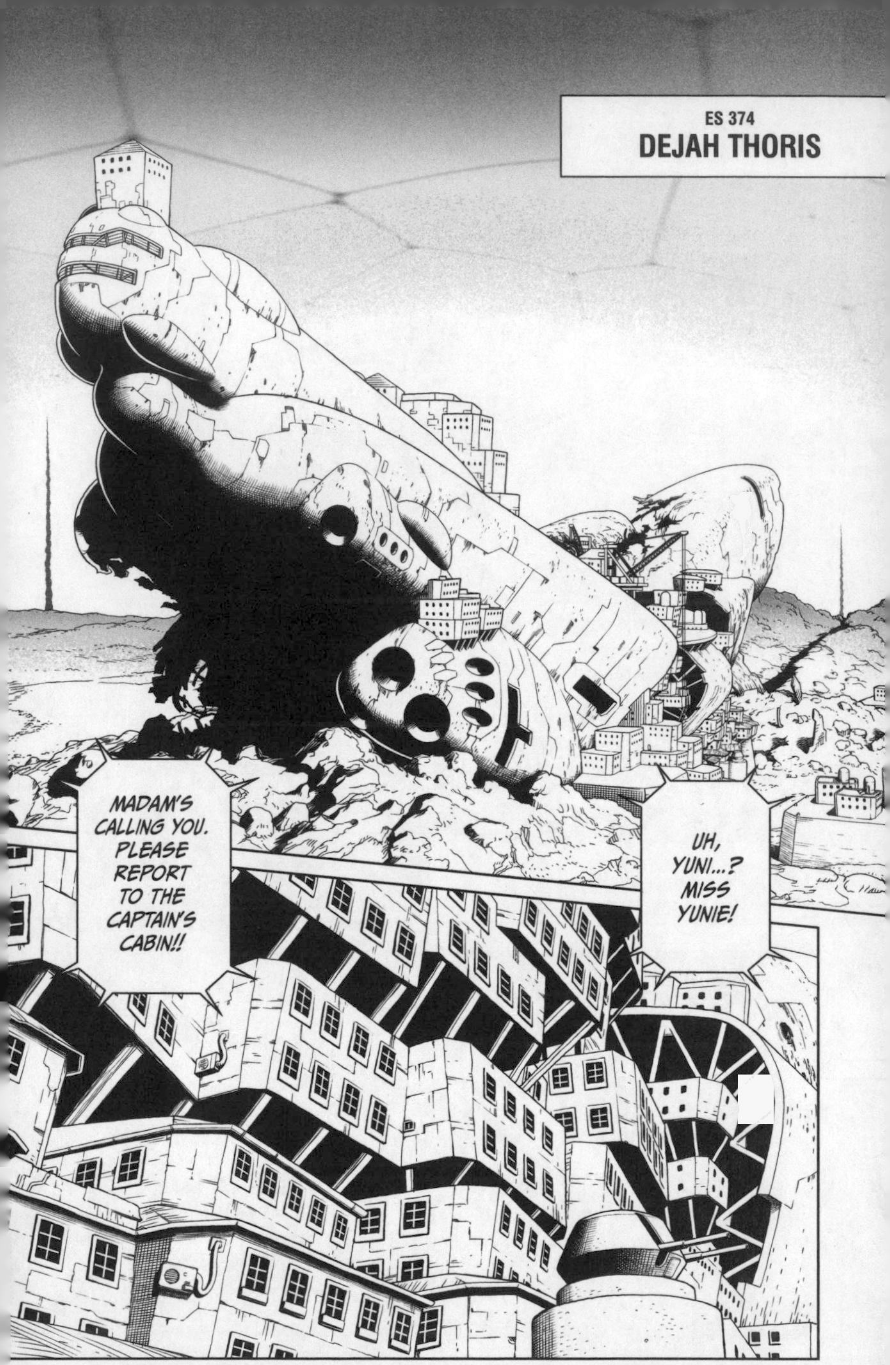
UH, YUNI...? MISS YUNIE!
MADAM'S CALLING YOU. PLEASE REPORT TO THE CAPTAIN'S CABIN!!

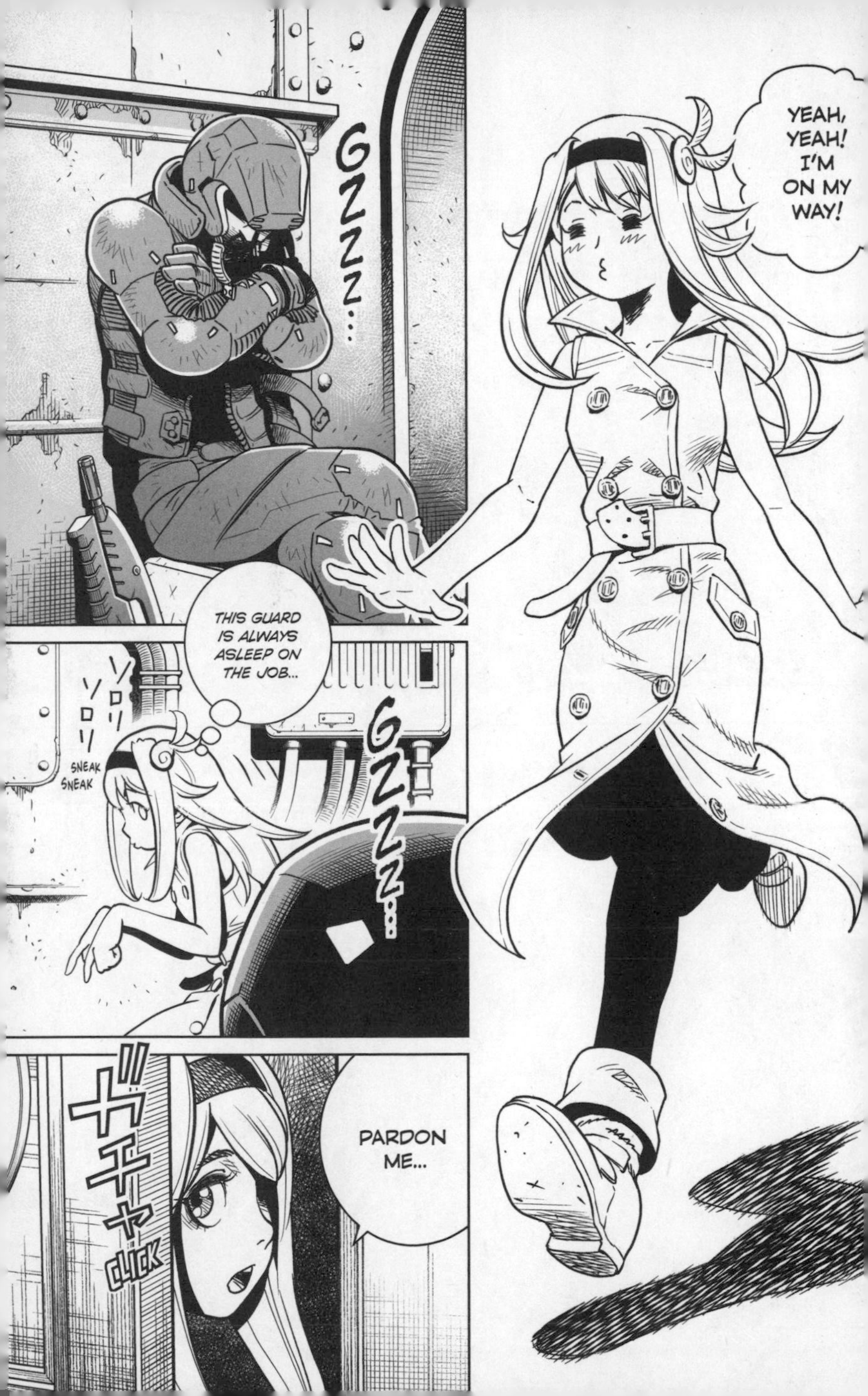
YEAH, YEAH! I'M ON MY WAY!
GZZZ...
THIS GUARD IS ALWAYS ASLEEP ON THE JOB...
ソロリ ソロリ
SNEAK SNEAK
GZZZ...
ガチャ
CLICK
PARDON ME...

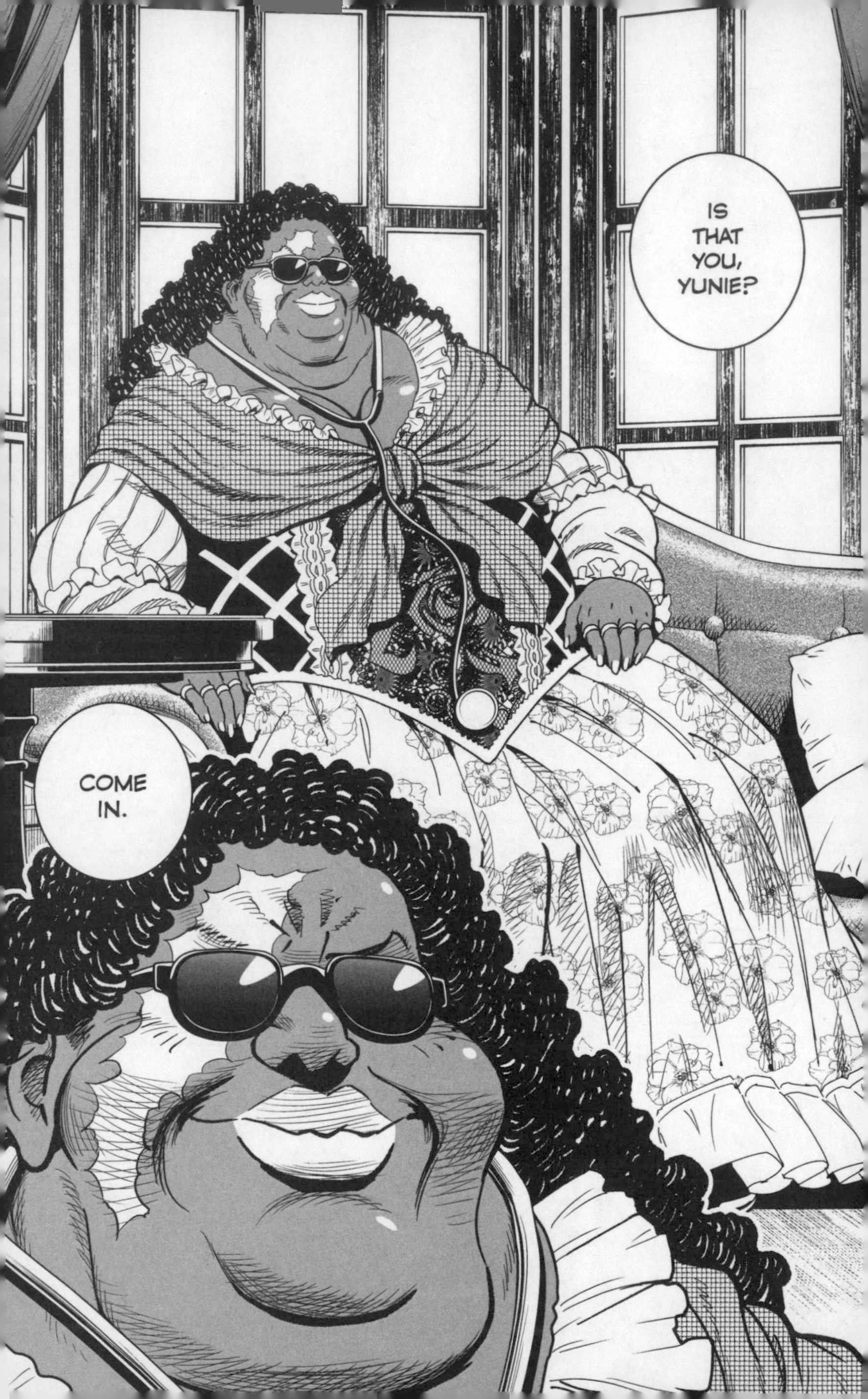
IS THAT YOU, YUNIE?
COME IN.

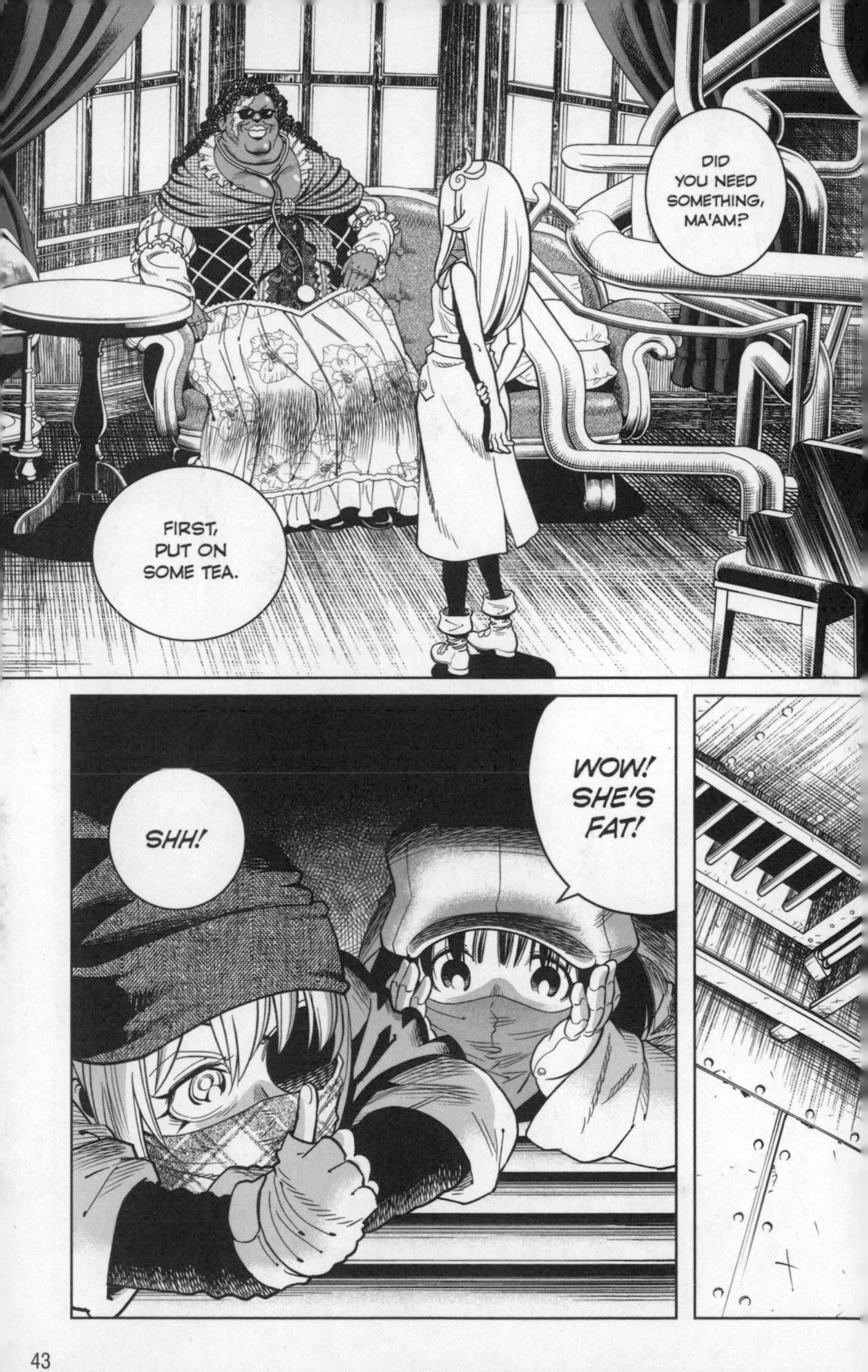
DID YOU NEED SOMETHING, MA'AM?
FIRST, PUT ON SOME TEA.
WOW! SHE'S FAT!
SHH!

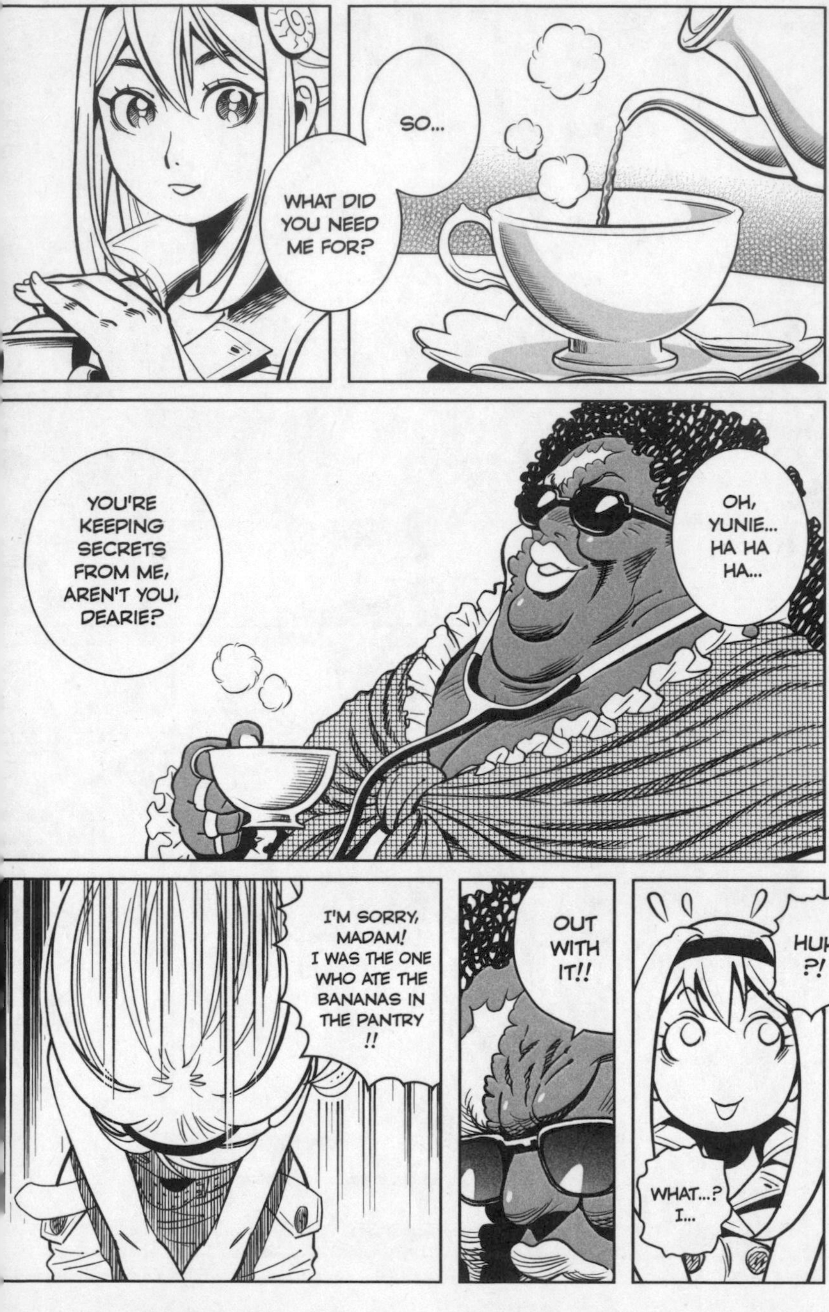
SO...
WHAT DID YOU NEED ME FOR?
OH, YUNIE... HA HA HA...
YOU'RE KEEPING SECRETS FROM ME, AREN'T YOU, DEARIE?
HUH ?!
WHAT...? I...
OUT WITH IT!!
I'M SORRY, MADAM! I WAS THE ONE WHO ATE THE BANANAS IN THE PANTRY !!

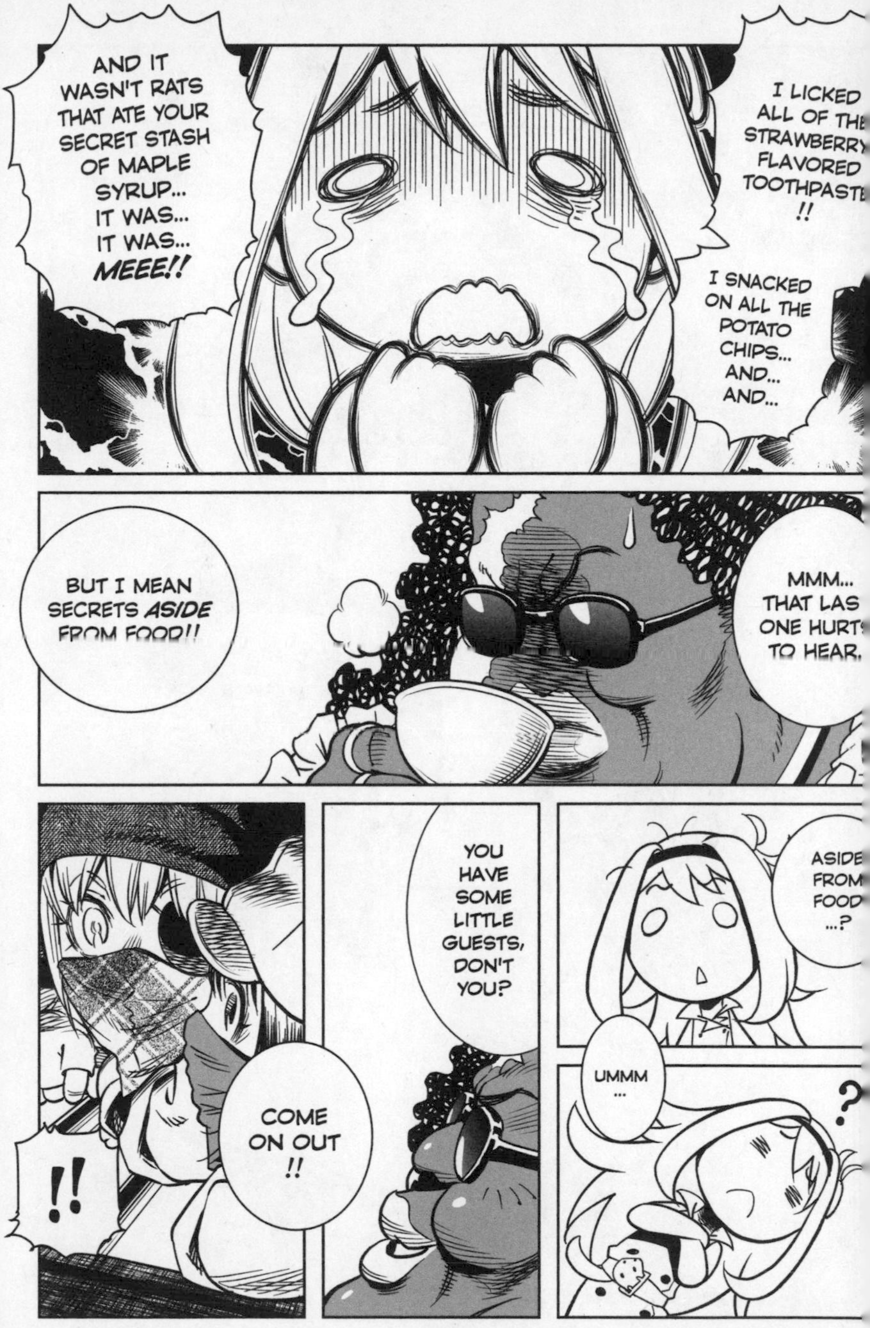
I LICKED ALL OF THE STRAWBERRY FLAVORED TOOTHPASTE !!
I SNACKED ON ALL THE POTATO CHIPS... AND... AND...
AND IT WASN'T RATS THAT ATE YOUR SECRET STASH OF MAPLE SYRUP... IT WAS... IT WAS... *MEEE!!*
MMM... THAT LAS ONE HURT TO HEAR.
BUT I MEAN SECRETS *ASIDE* FROM FOOD!!
ASIDE FROM FOOD ...?
UMMM ...
?
YOU HAVE SOME LITTLE GUESTS, DON'T YOU?
COME ON OUT !!
!!

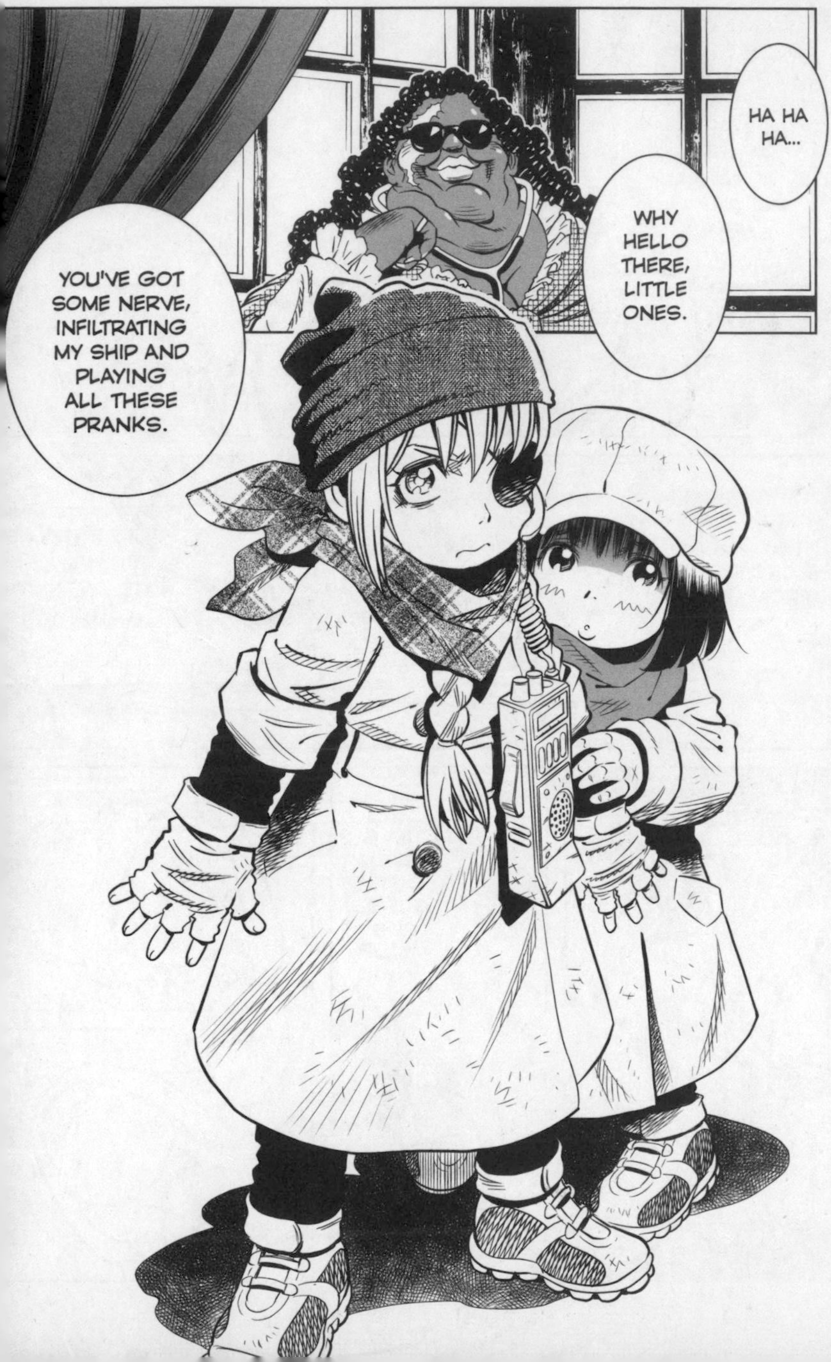
HA HA HA...
WHY HELLO THERE, LITTLE ONES.
YOU'VE GOT SOME NERVE, INFILTRATING MY SHIP AND PLAYING ALL THESE PRANKS.

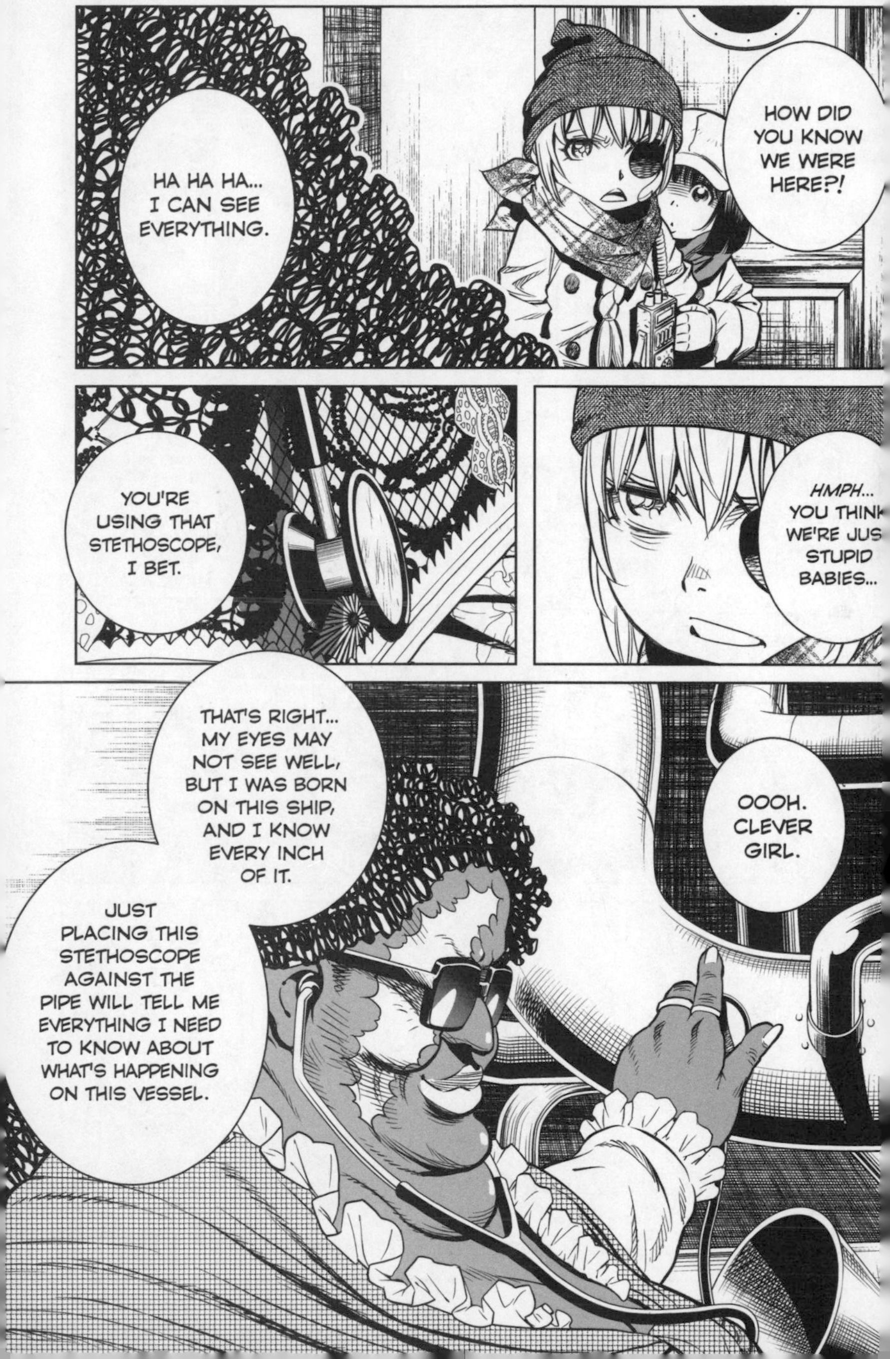
HOW DID YOU KNOW WE WERE HERE?!
HA HA HA... I CAN SEE EVERYTHING.
HMPH... YOU THINK WE'RE JUS STUPID BABIES...
YOU'RE USING THAT STETHOSCOPE, I BET.
OOOH. CLEVER GIRL.
THAT'S RIGHT... MY EYES MAY NOT SEE WELL, BUT I WAS BORN ON THIS SHIP, AND I KNOW EVERY INCH OF IT.
JUST PLACING THIS STETHOSCOPE AGAINST THE PIPE WILL TELL ME EVERYTHING I NEED TO KNOW ABOUT WHAT'S HAPPENING ON THIS VESSEL.

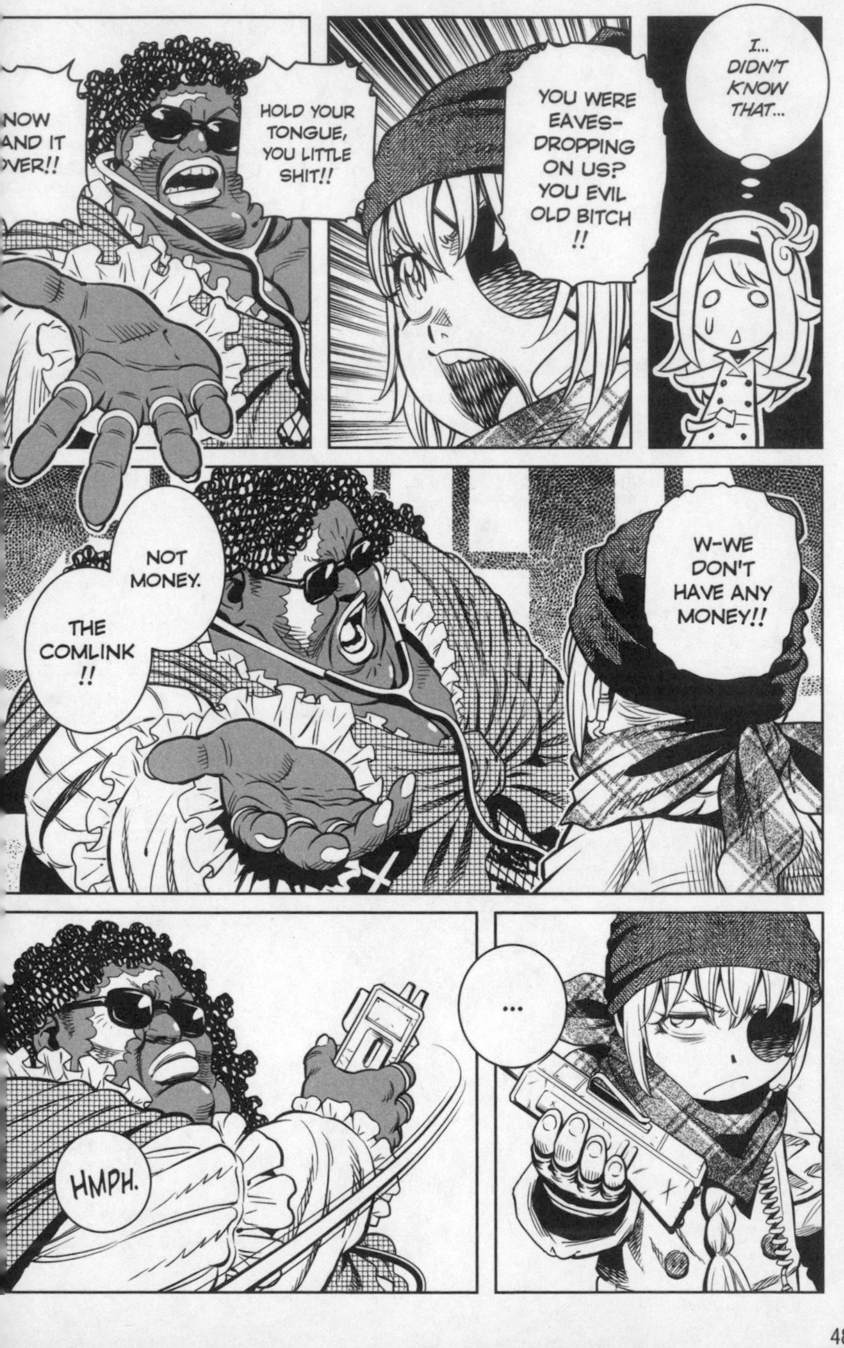
I... DIDN'T KNOW THAT...
YOU WERE EAVES-DROPPING ON US? YOU EVIL OLD BITCH !!
HOLD YOUR TONGUE, YOU LITTLE SHIT!!
NOW AND IT VER!!
W-WE DON'T HAVE ANY MONEY!!
NOT MONEY.
THE COMLINK !!
...
HMPH.

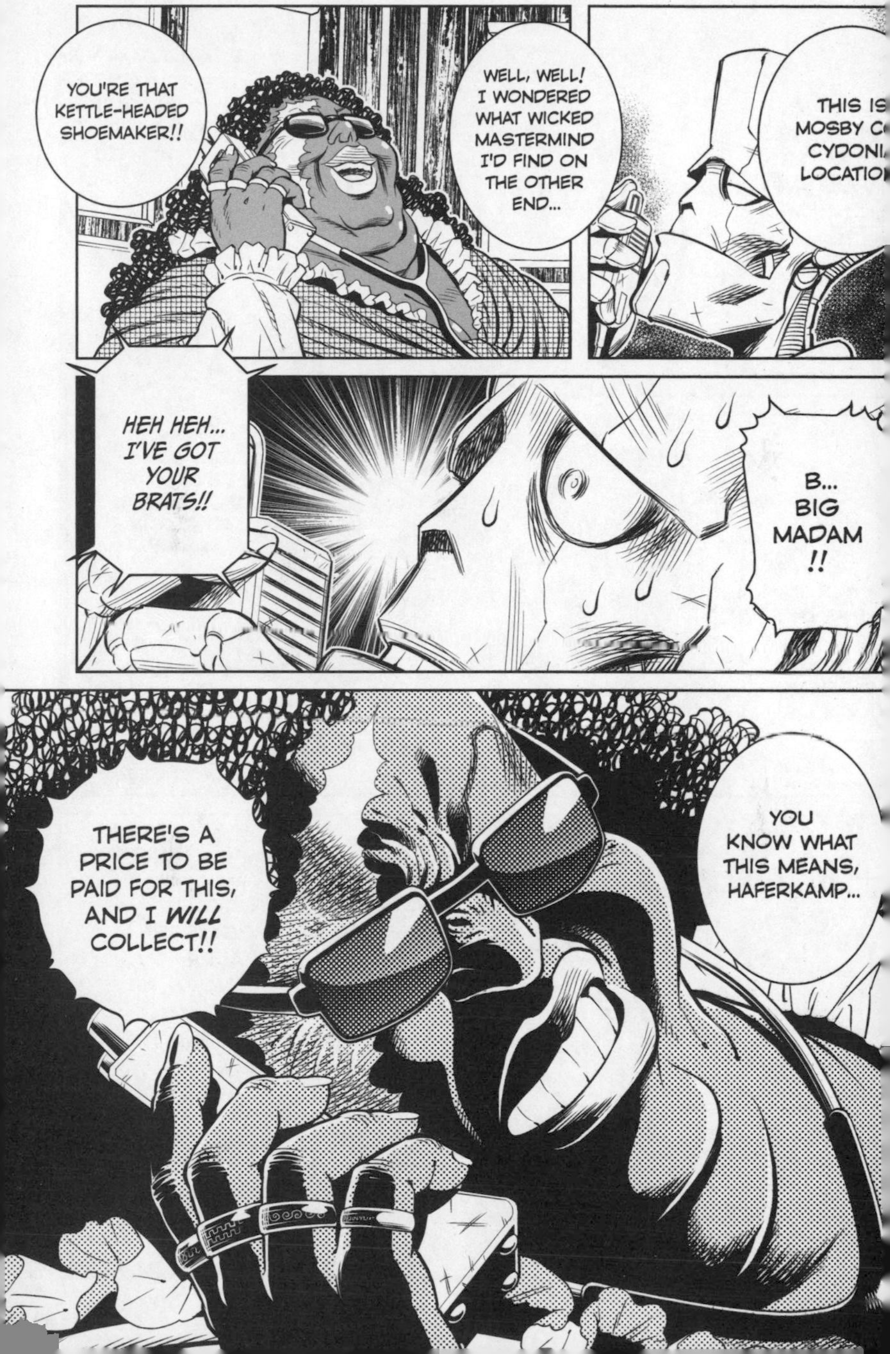
THIS IS MOSBY C CYDONI LOCATIO
WELL, WELL! I WONDERED WHAT WICKED MASTERMIND I'D FIND ON THE OTHER END...
YOU'RE THAT KETTLE-HEADED SHOEMAKER!!
B... BIG MADAM !!
HEH HEH... I'VE GOT YOUR BRATS!!
YOU KNOW WHAT THIS MEANS, HAFERKAMP...
THERE'S A PRICE TO BE PAID FOR THIS, AND I *WILL* COLLECT!!

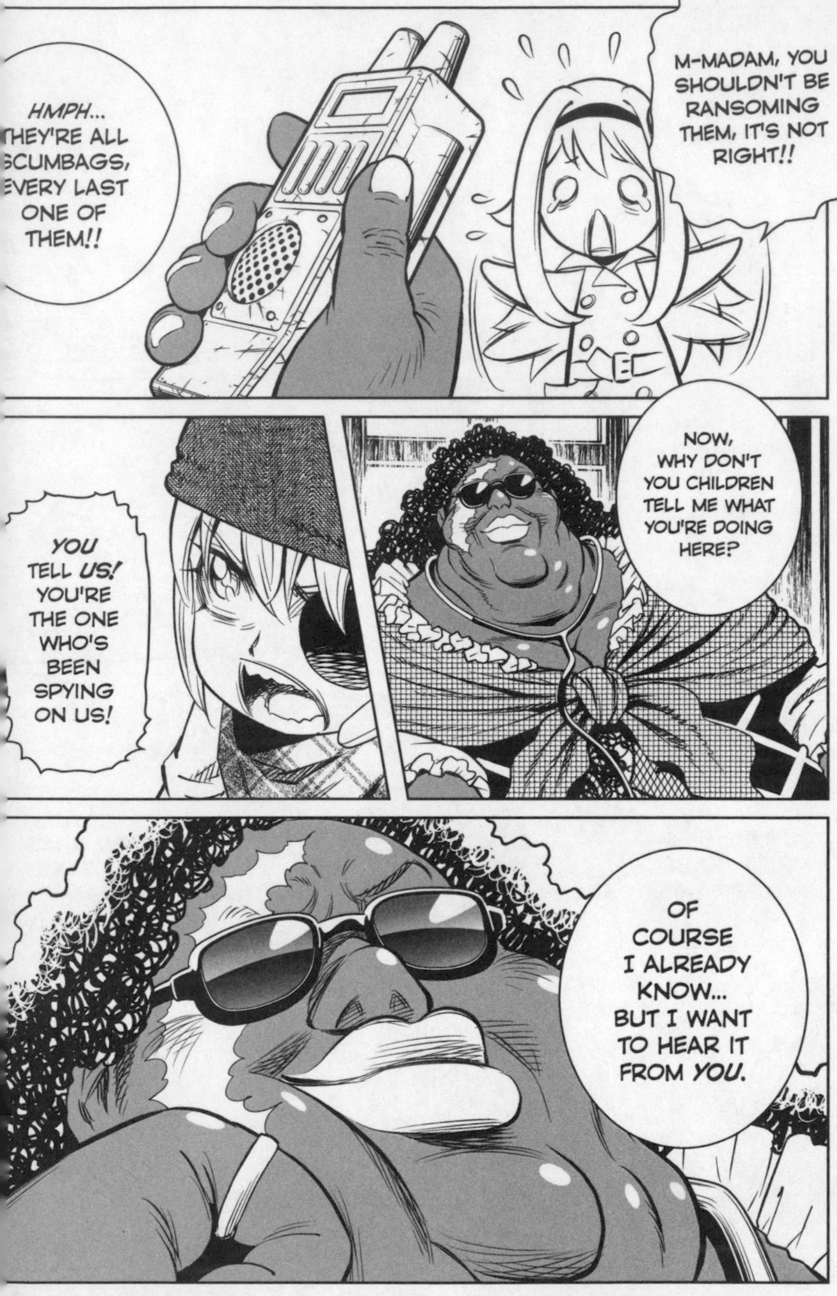
M-MADAM, YOU SHOULDN'T BE RANSOMING THEM, IT'S NOT RIGHT!!
HMPH... THEY'RE ALL SCUMBAGS, EVERY LAST ONE OF THEM!!
NOW, WHY DON'T YOU CHILDREN TELL ME WHAT YOU'RE DOING HERE?
YOU TELL *US!* YOU'RE THE ONE WHO'S BEEN SPYING ON US!
OF COURSE I ALREADY KNOW... BUT I WANT TO HEAR IT FROM *YOU*.

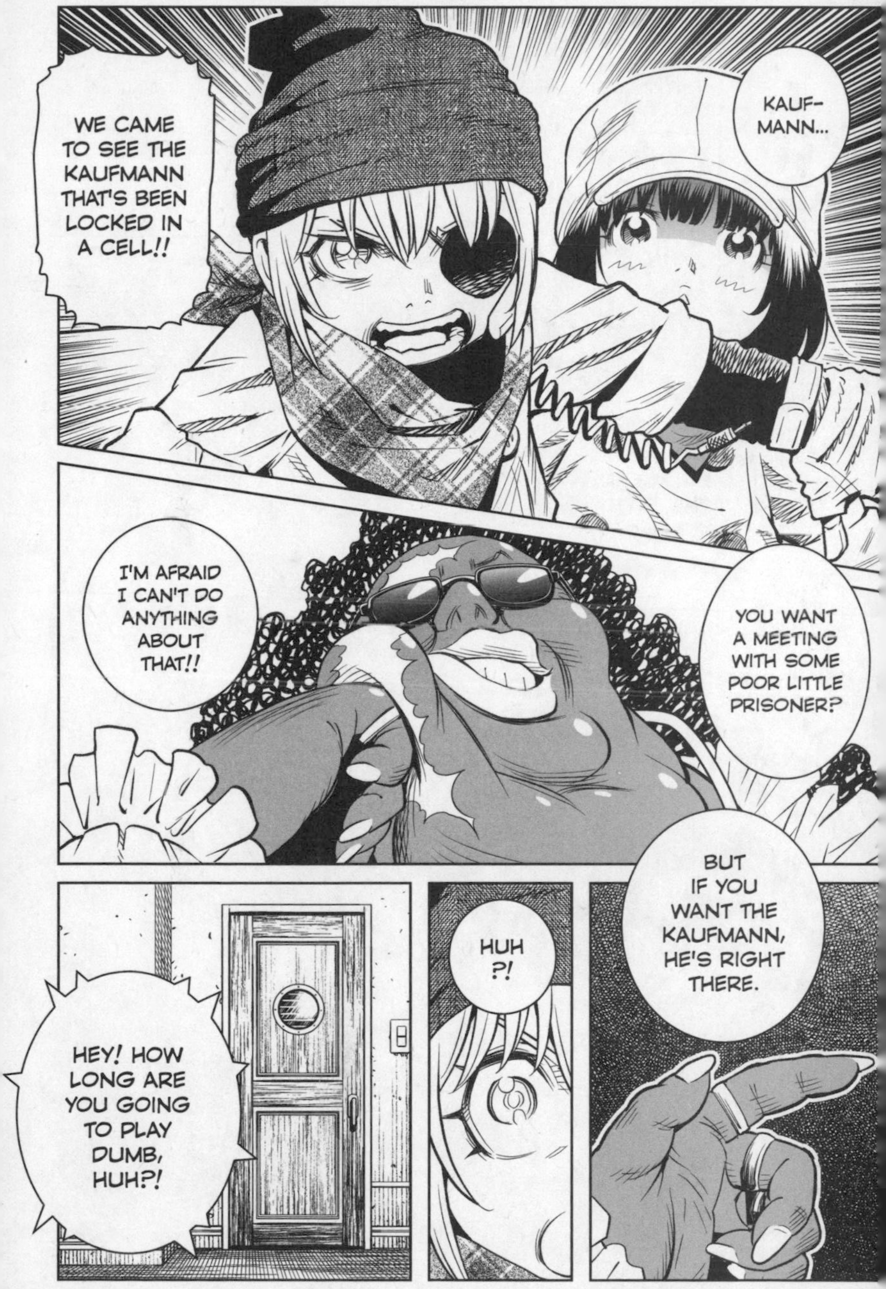
KAUF-MANN...
WE CAME TO SEE THE KAUFMANN THAT'S BEEN LOCKED IN A CELL!!
YOU WANT A MEETING WITH SOME POOR LITTLE PRISONER?
I'M AFRAID I CAN'T DO ANYTHING ABOUT THAT!!
BUT IF YOU WANT THE KAUFMANN, HE'S RIGHT THERE.
HUH?!
HEY! HOW LONG ARE YOU GOING TO PLAY DUMB, HUH?!

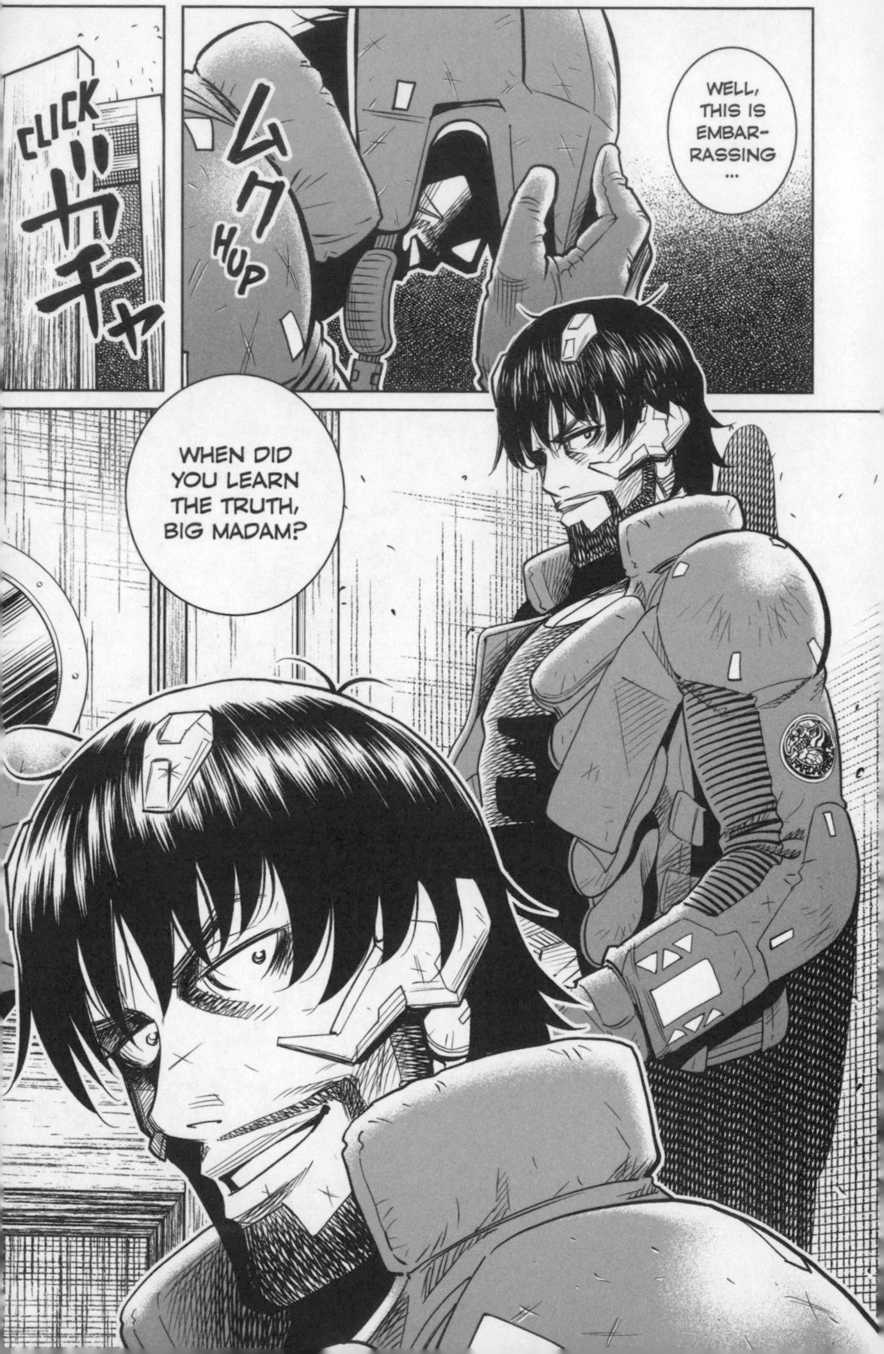
WELL, THIS IS EMBAR-RASSING ...
ムク
HUP
CLICK
ガチャ
WHEN DID YOU LEARN THE TRUTH, BIG MADAM?

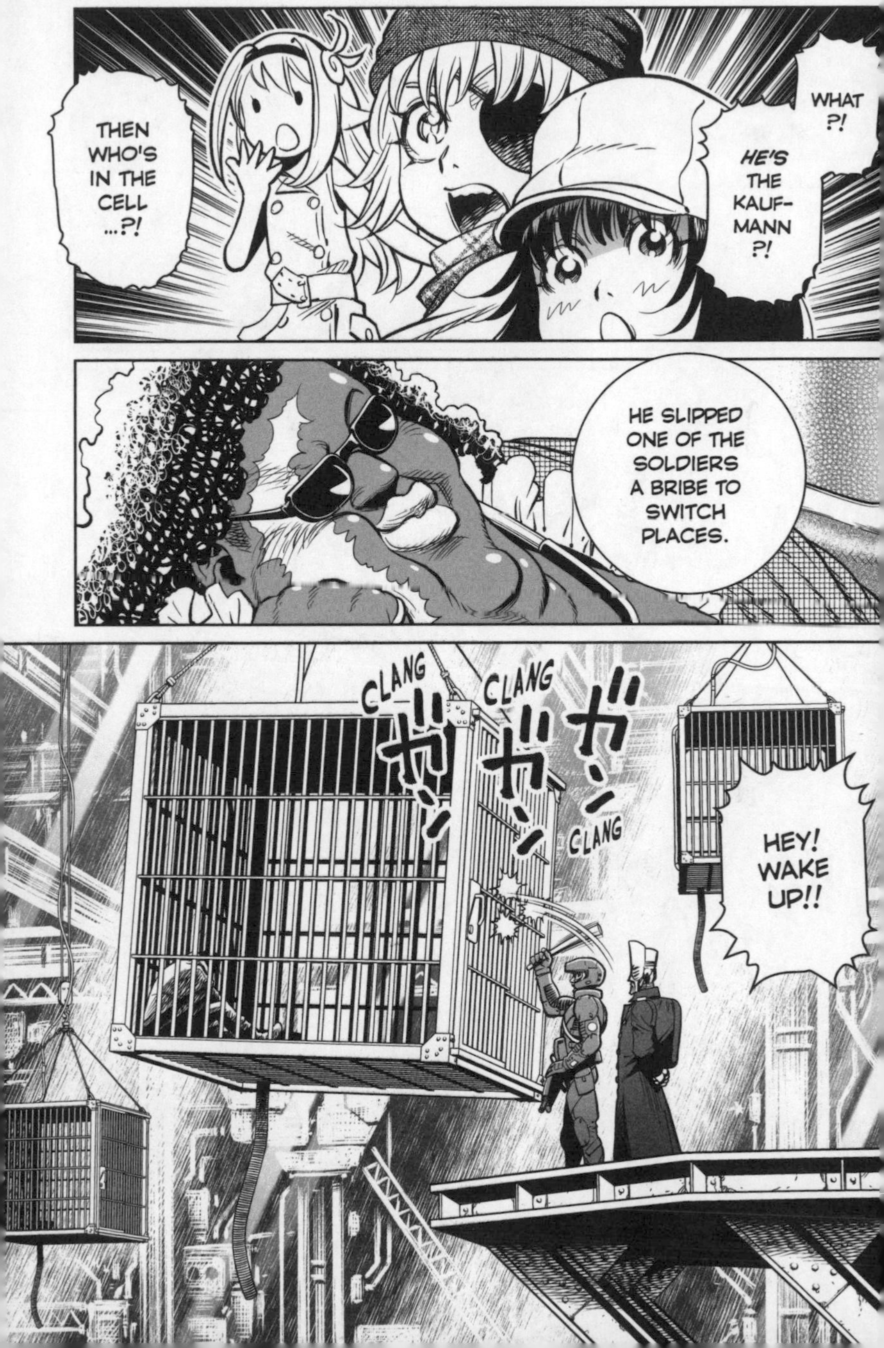
WHAT?!
HE'S THE KAUF-MANN?!
THEN WHO'S IN THE CELL ...?!
HE SLIPPED ONE OF THE SOLDIERS A BRIBE TO SWITCH PLACES.
CLANG
CLANG
CLANG
HEY! WAKE UP!!

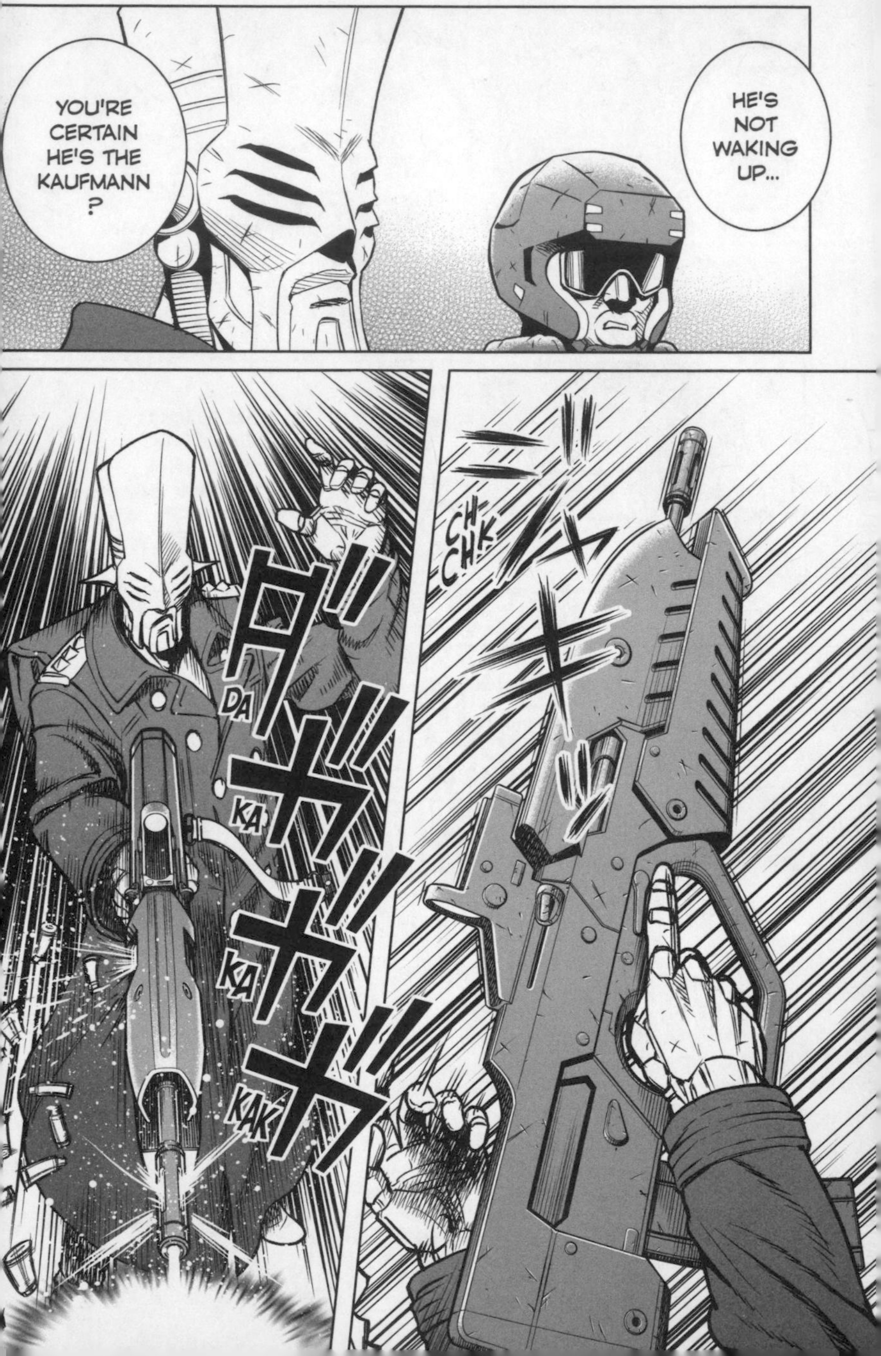
HE'S NOT WAKING UP...
YOU'RE CERTAIN HE'S THE KAUFMANN?
CH CHK
DA KA KA KAK

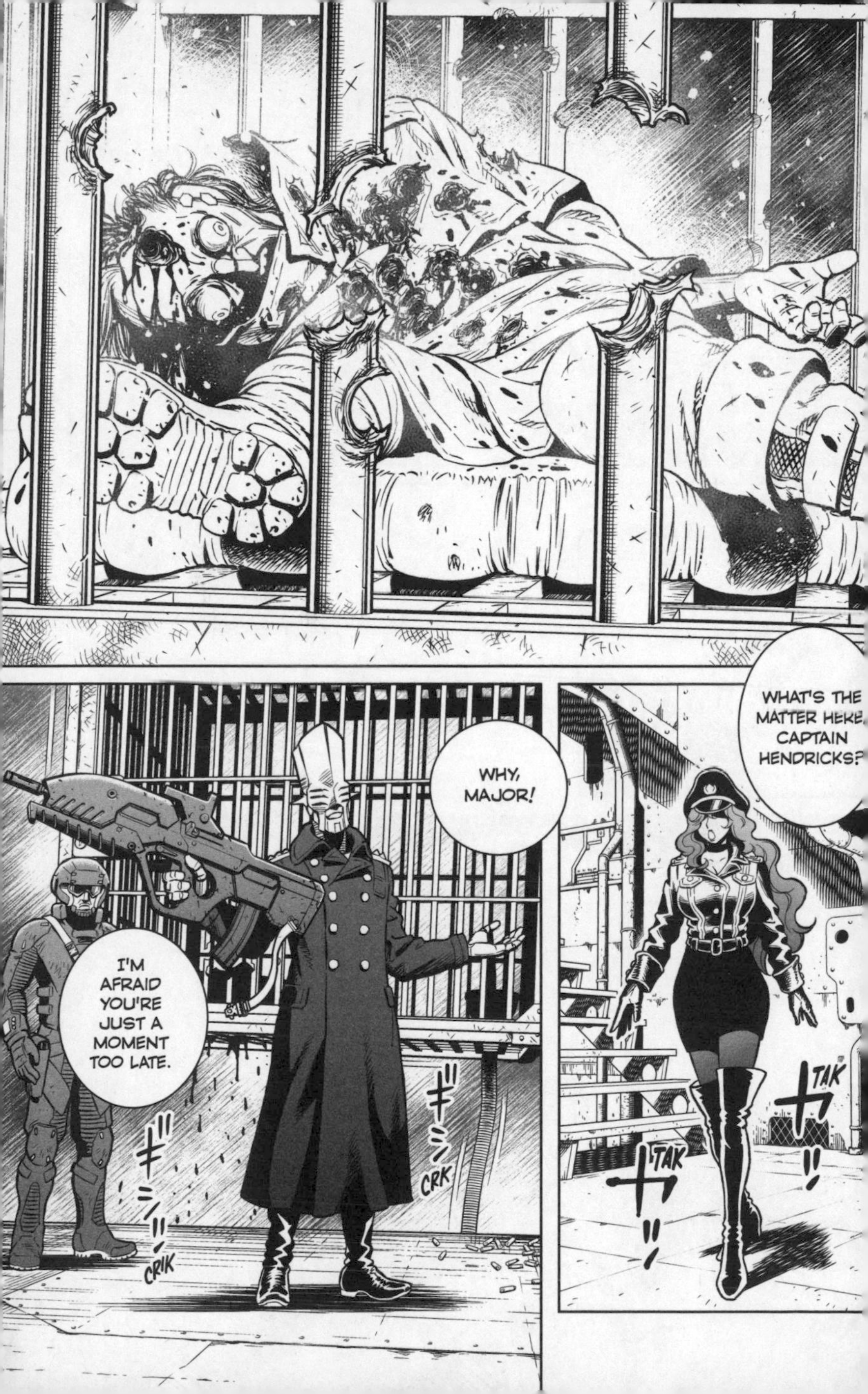
WHAT'S THE MATTER HERE, CAPTAIN HENDRICKS?
TAK
TAK
WHY, MAJOR!
I'M AFRAID YOU'RE JUST A MOMENT TOO LATE.
CRK
CRIK

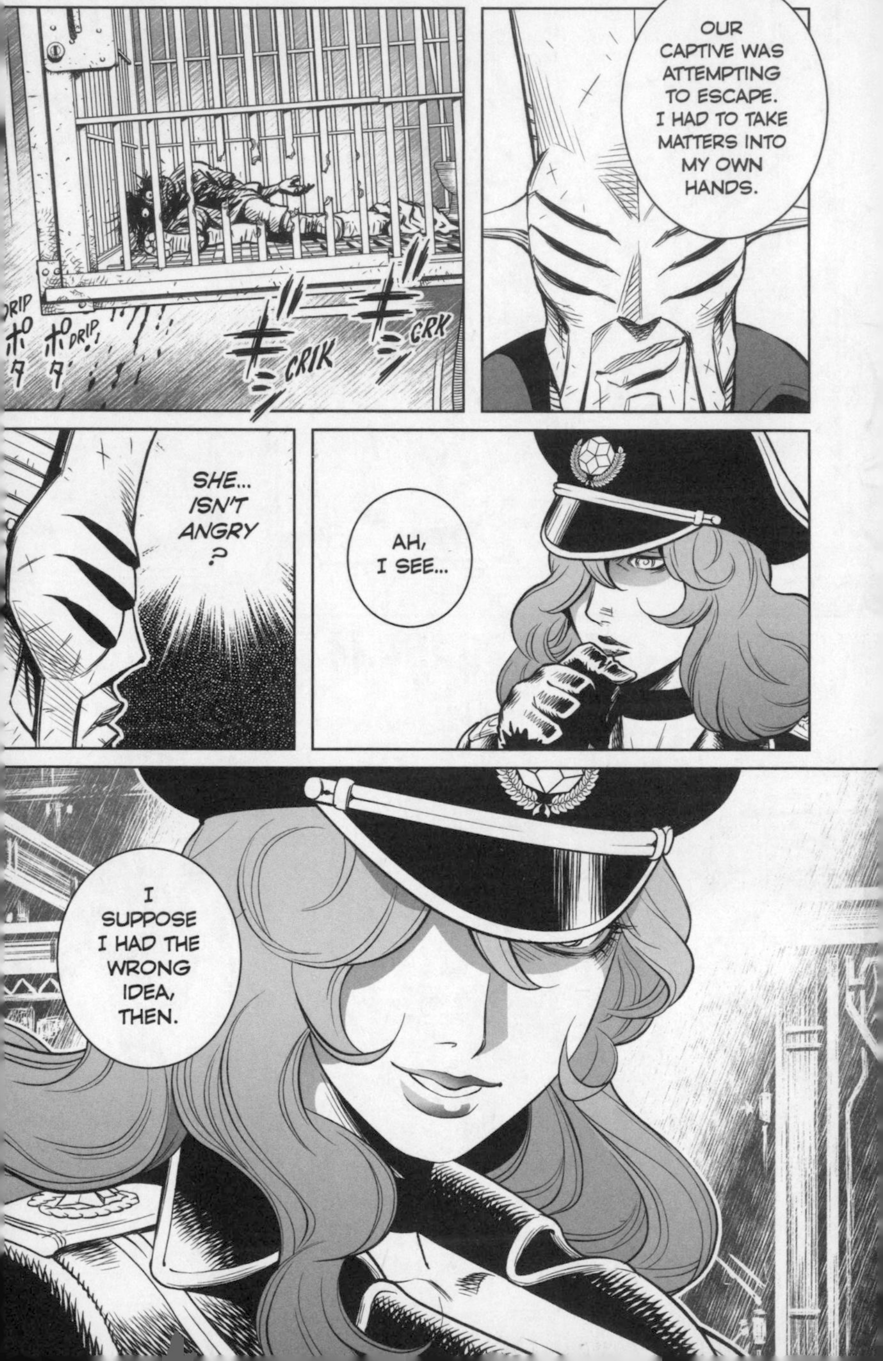
OUR CAPTIVE WAS ATTEMPTING TO ESCAPE. I HAD TO TAKE MATTERS INTO MY OWN HANDS.
CRK
CRIK
DRIP
ポタ
DRIP
ポタ
AH, I SEE...
SHE... ISN'T ANGRY?
I SUPPOSE I HAD THE WRONG IDEA, THEN.

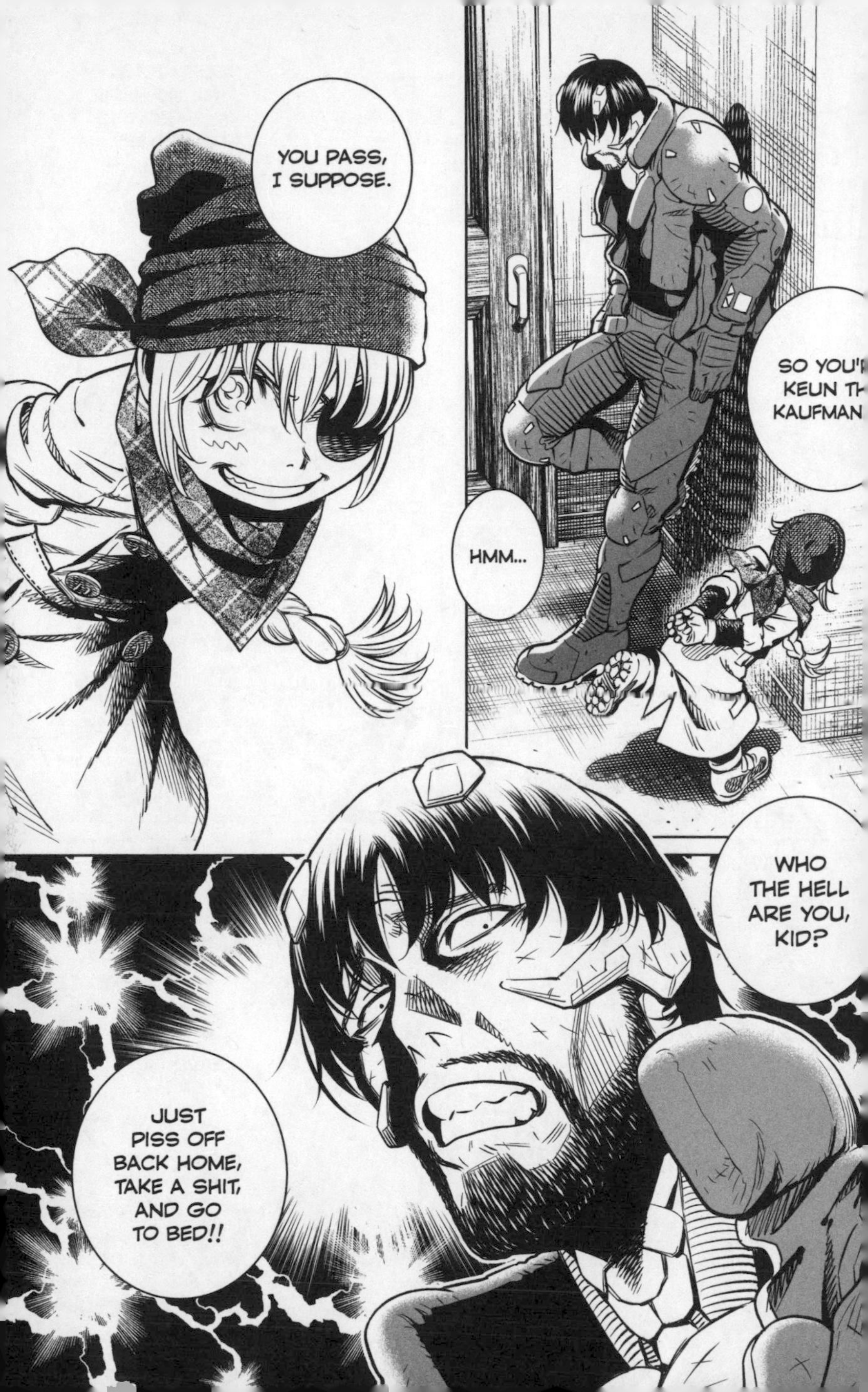
SO YOU' KEUN TH KAUFMAN
HMM...
YOU PASS, I SUPPOSE.
WHO THE HELL ARE YOU, KID?
JUST PISS OFF BACK HOME, TAKE A SHIT, AND GO TO BED!!

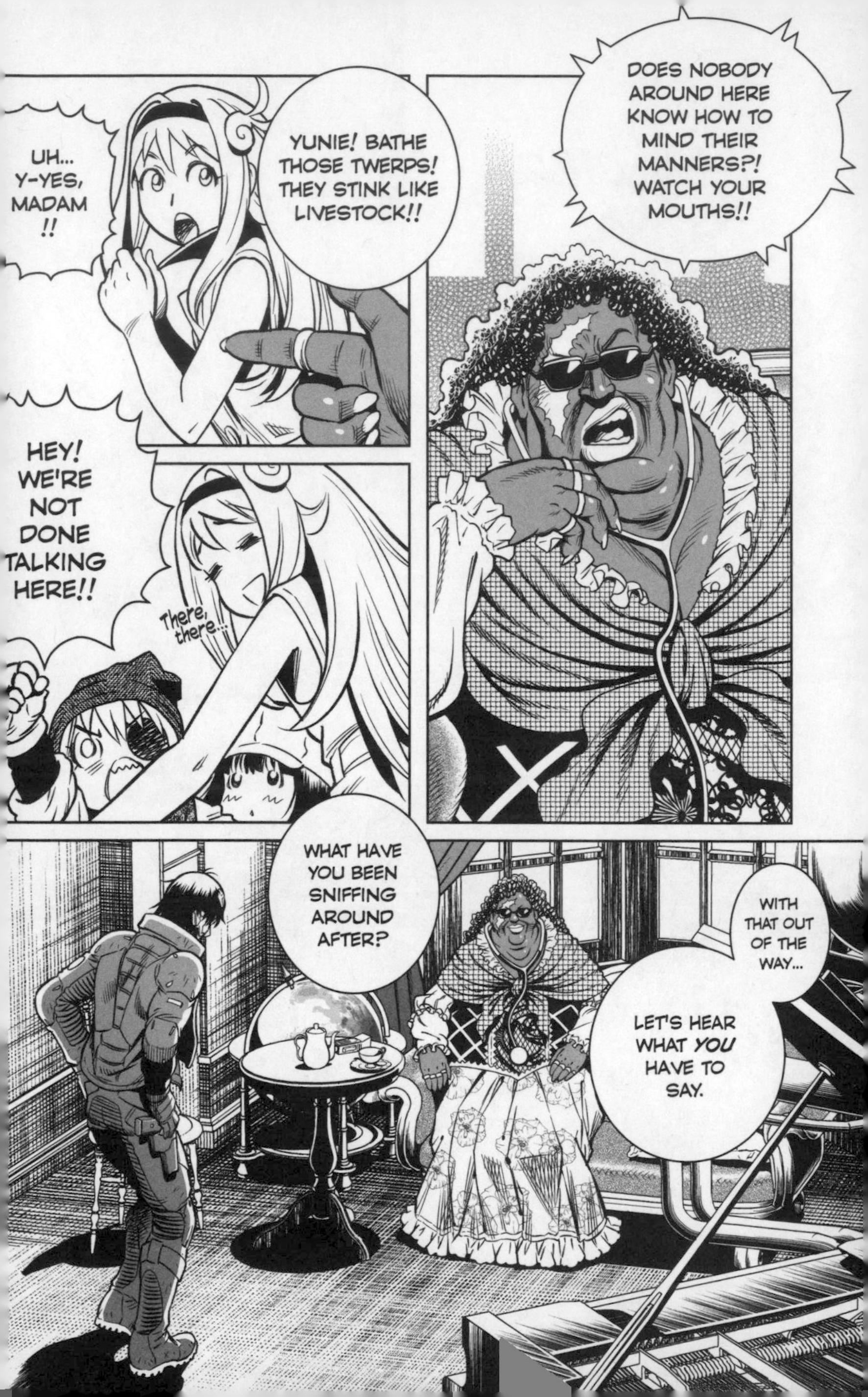
DOES NOBODY AROUND HERE KNOW HOW TO MIND THEIR MANNERS?! WATCH YOUR MOUTHS!!
YUNIE! BATHE THOSE TWERPS! THEY STINK LIKE LIVESTOCK!!
UH... Y-YES, MADAM!!
HEY! WE'RE NOT DONE TALKING HERE!!
There, there...
WITH THAT OUT OF THE WAY...
LET'S HEAR WHAT *YOU* HAVE TO SAY.
WHAT HAVE YOU BEEN SNIFFING AROUND AFTER?

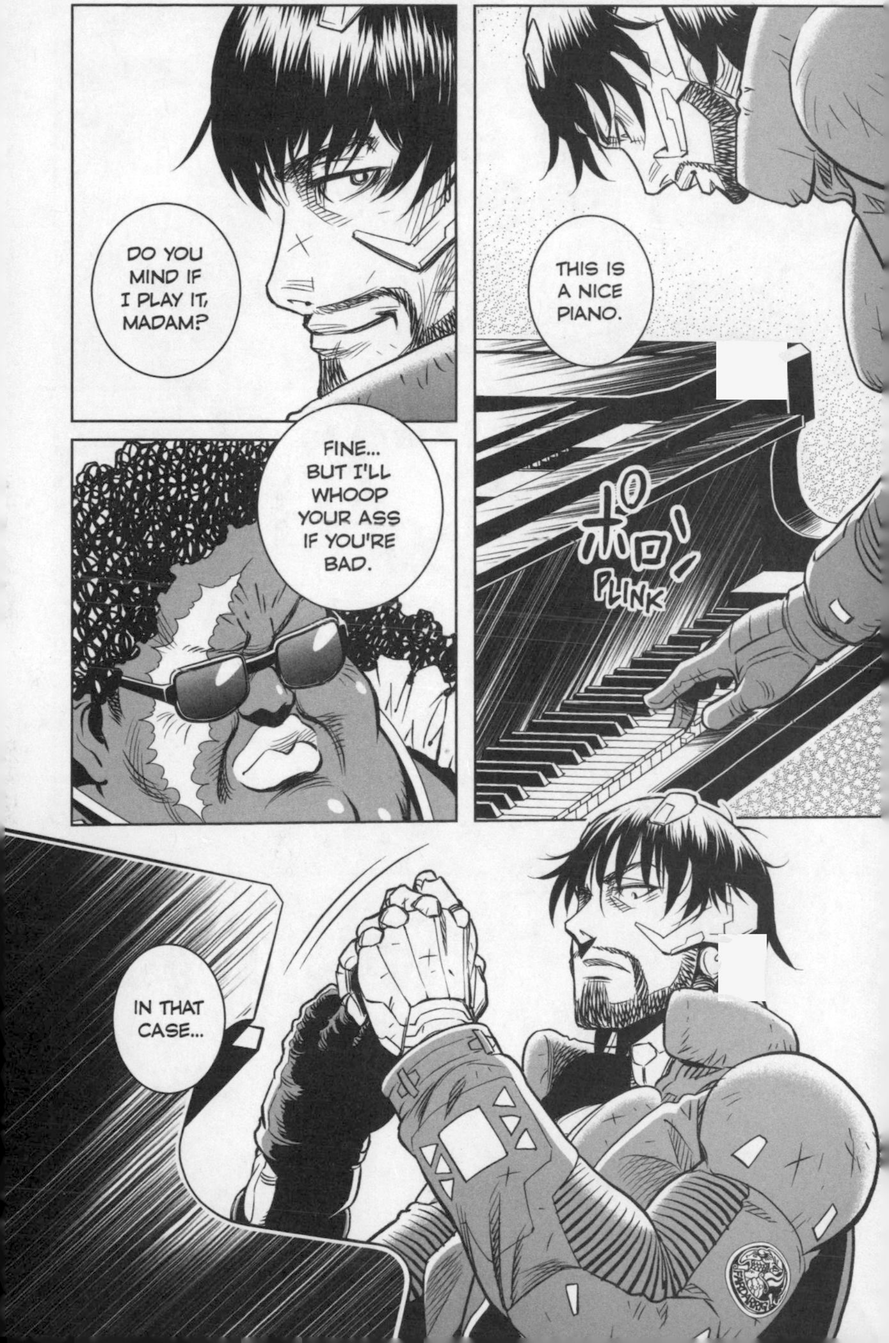
THIS IS A NICE PIANO.
ポロ
PLINK
DO YOU MIND IF I PLAY IT, MADAM?
FINE... BUT I'LL WHOOP YOUR ASS IF YOU'RE BAD.
IN THAT CASE...

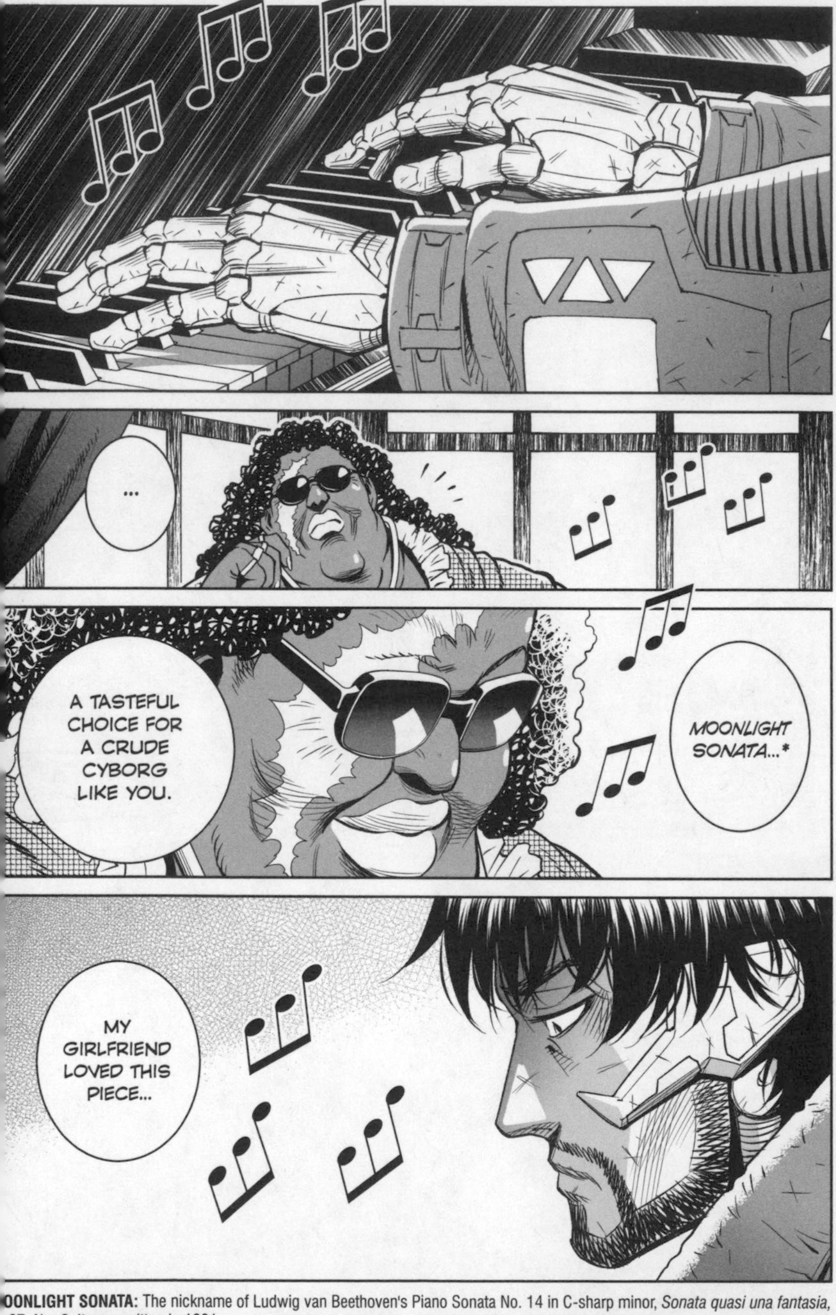
...
MOONLIGHT SONATA...*
A TASTEFUL CHOICE FOR A CRUDE CYBORG LIKE YOU.
MY GIRLFRIEND LOVED THIS PIECE...

OONLIGHT SONATA: The nickname of Ludwig van Beethoven's Piano Sonata No. 14 in C-sharp minor, *Sonata quasi una fantasia,* 27, No. 2. It was written in 1801.

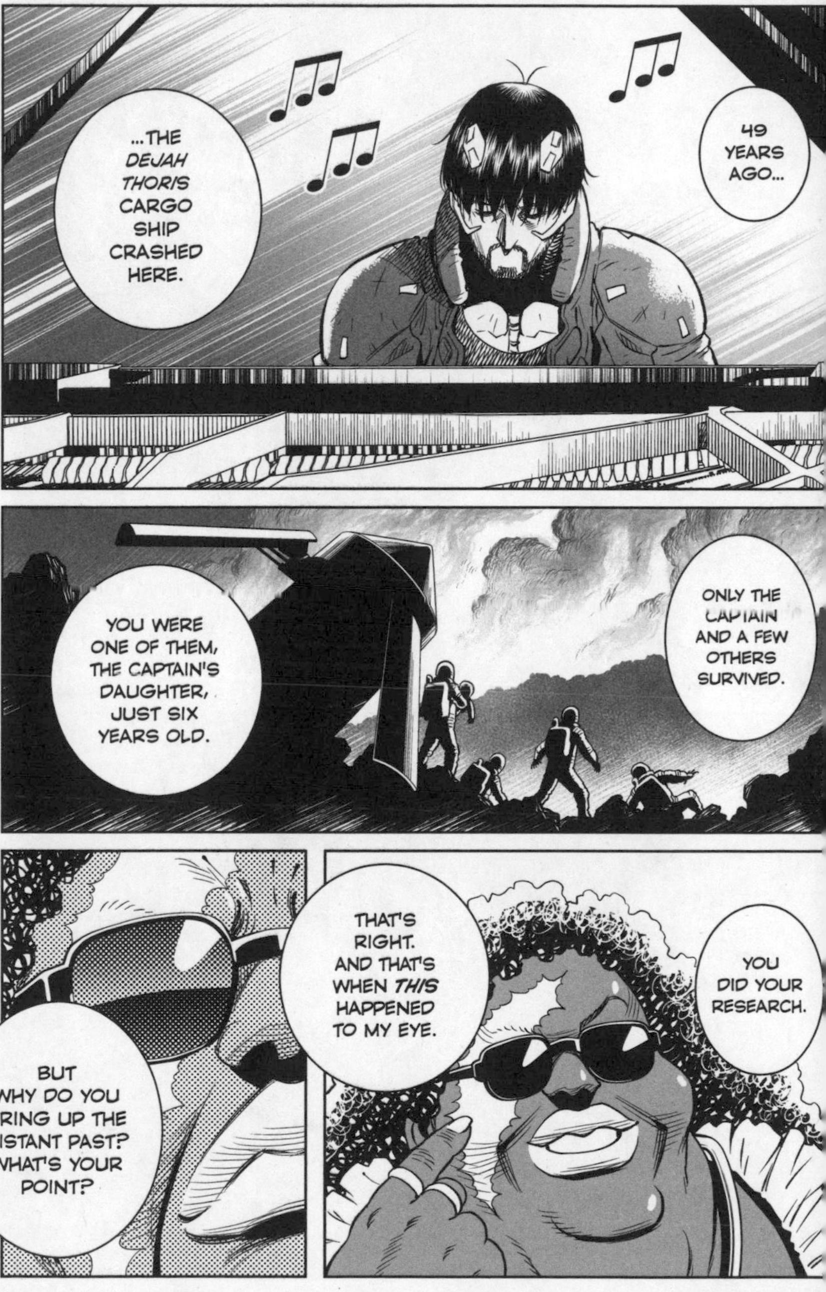
49 YEARS AGO...
...THE *DEJAH THORIS* CARGO SHIP CRASHED HERE.
ONLY THE CAPTAIN AND A FEW OTHERS SURVIVED.
YOU WERE ONE OF THEM, THE CAPTAIN'S DAUGHTER, JUST SIX YEARS OLD.
YOU DID YOUR RESEARCH.
THAT'S RIGHT. AND THAT'S WHEN *THIS* HAPPENED TO MY EYE.
BUT WHY DO YOU BRING UP THE DISTANT PAST? WHAT'S YOUR POINT?

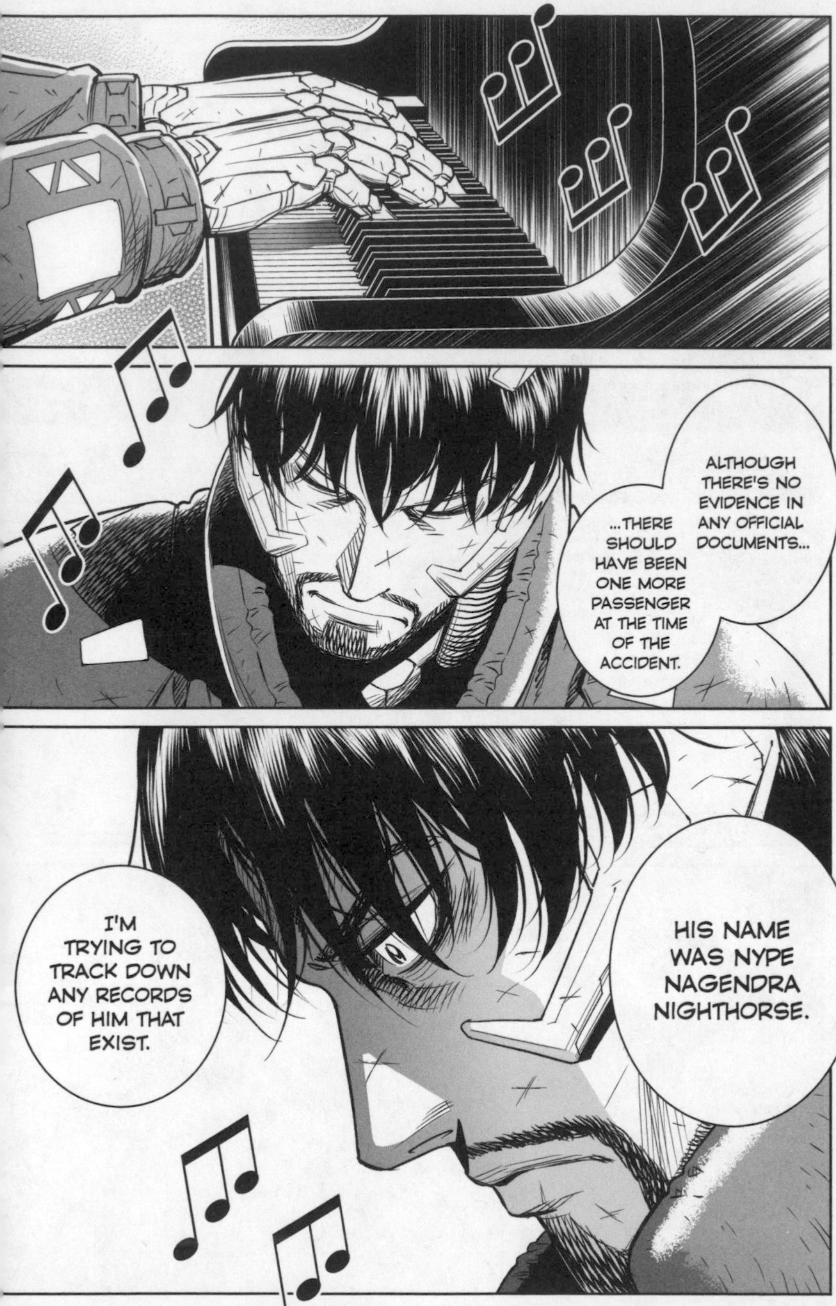
ALTHOUGH THERE'S NO EVIDENCE IN ANY OFFICIAL DOCUMENTS...
...THERE SHOULD HAVE BEEN ONE MORE PASSENGER AT THE TIME OF THE ACCIDENT.
HIS NAME WAS NYPE NAGENDRA NIGHTHORSE.
I'M TRYING TO TRACK DOWN ANY RECORDS OF HIM THAT EXIST.

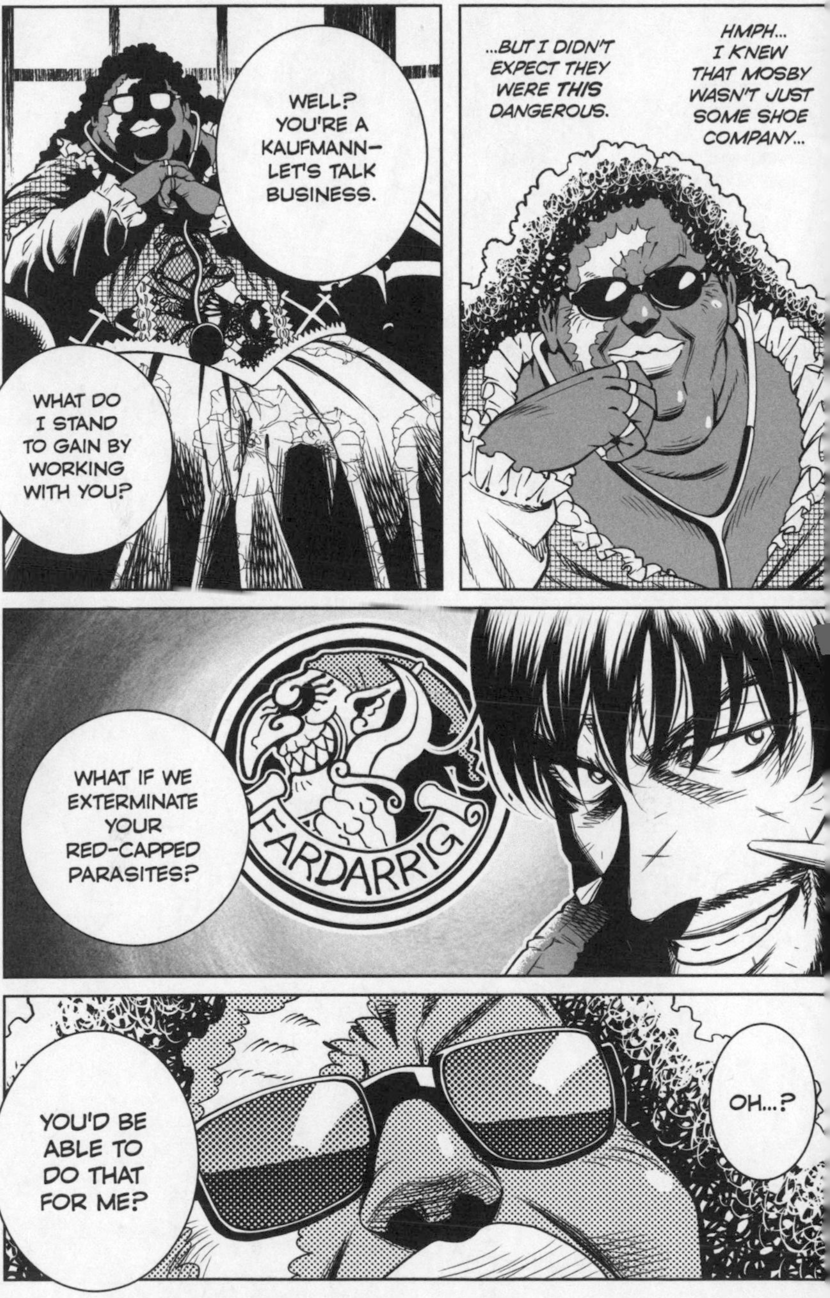
HMPH... I KNEW THAT MOSBY WASN'T JUST SOME SHOE COMPANY...
...BUT I DIDN'T EXPECT THEY WERE THIS DANGEROUS.
WELL? YOU'RE A KAUFMANN— LET'S TALK BUSINESS.
WHAT DO I STAND TO GAIN BY WORKING WITH YOU?
FARDARRIG
WHAT IF WE EXTERMINATE YOUR RED-CAPPED PARASITES?
OH...?
YOU'D BE ABLE TO DO THAT FOR ME?

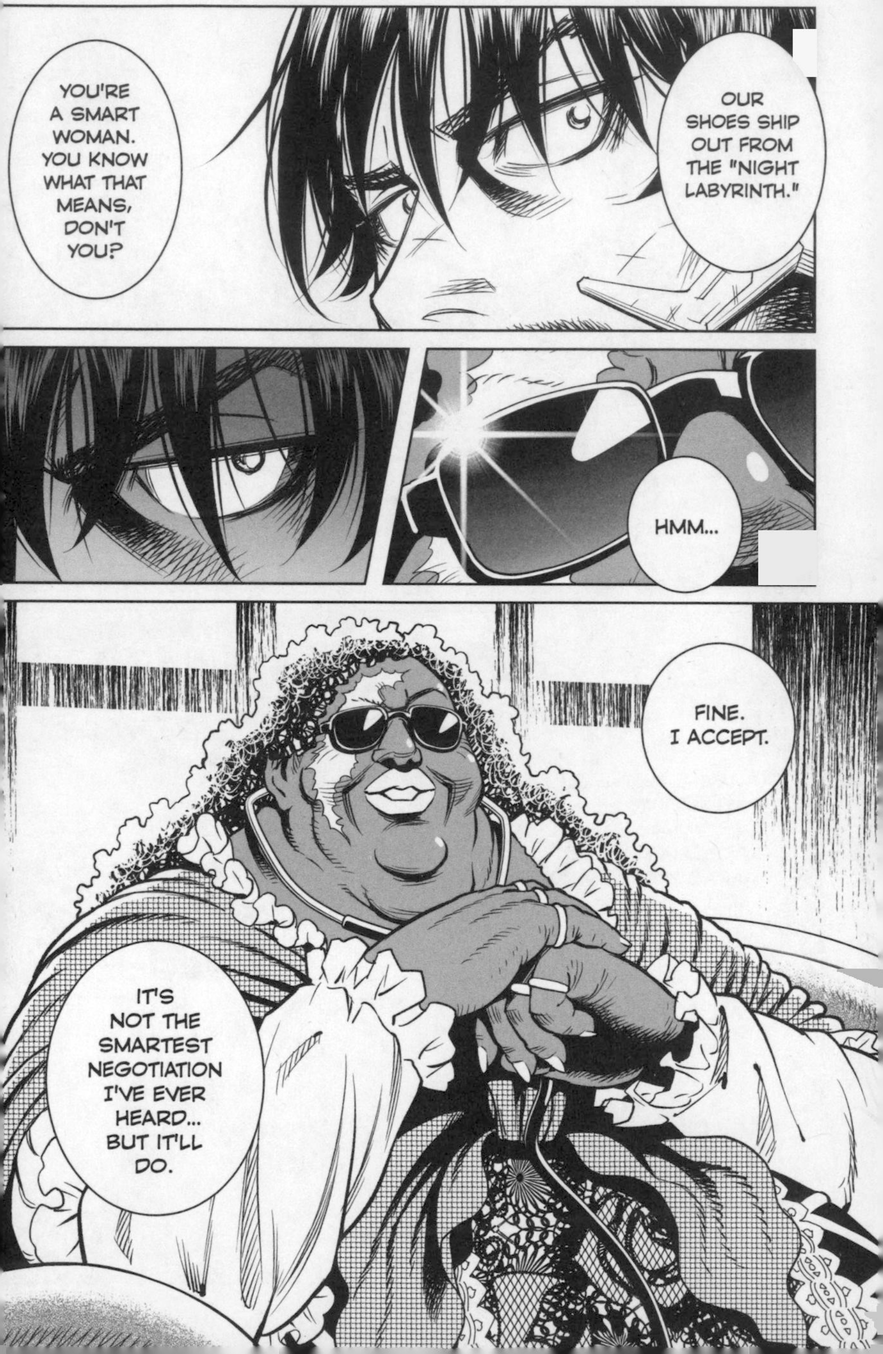
OUR SHOES SHIP OUT FROM THE "NIGHT LABYRINTH."
YOU'RE A SMART WOMAN. YOU KNOW WHAT THAT MEANS, DON'T YOU?
HMM...
FINE. I ACCEPT.
IT'S NOT THE SMARTEST NEGOTIATION I'VE EVER HEARD... BUT IT'LL DO.

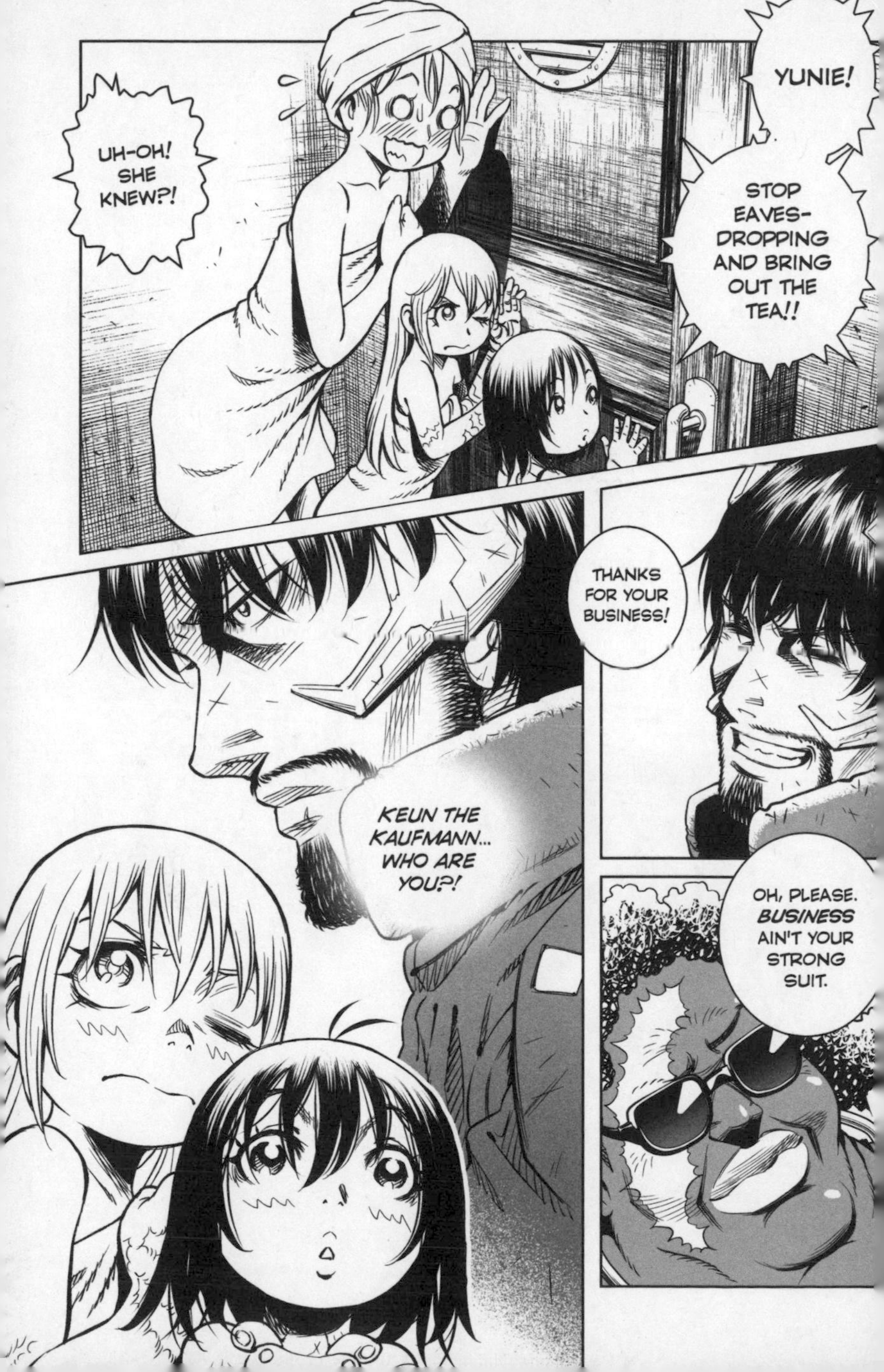
YUNIE!
STOP EAVES-DROPPING AND BRING OUT THE TEA!!
UH-OH! SHE KNEW?!
THANKS FOR YOUR BUSINESS!
OH, PLEASE. *BUSINESS* AIN'T YOUR STRONG SUIT.
KEUN THE KAUFMANN... WHO ARE YOU?!

LOG:034

THE SECRET WORKSHOP

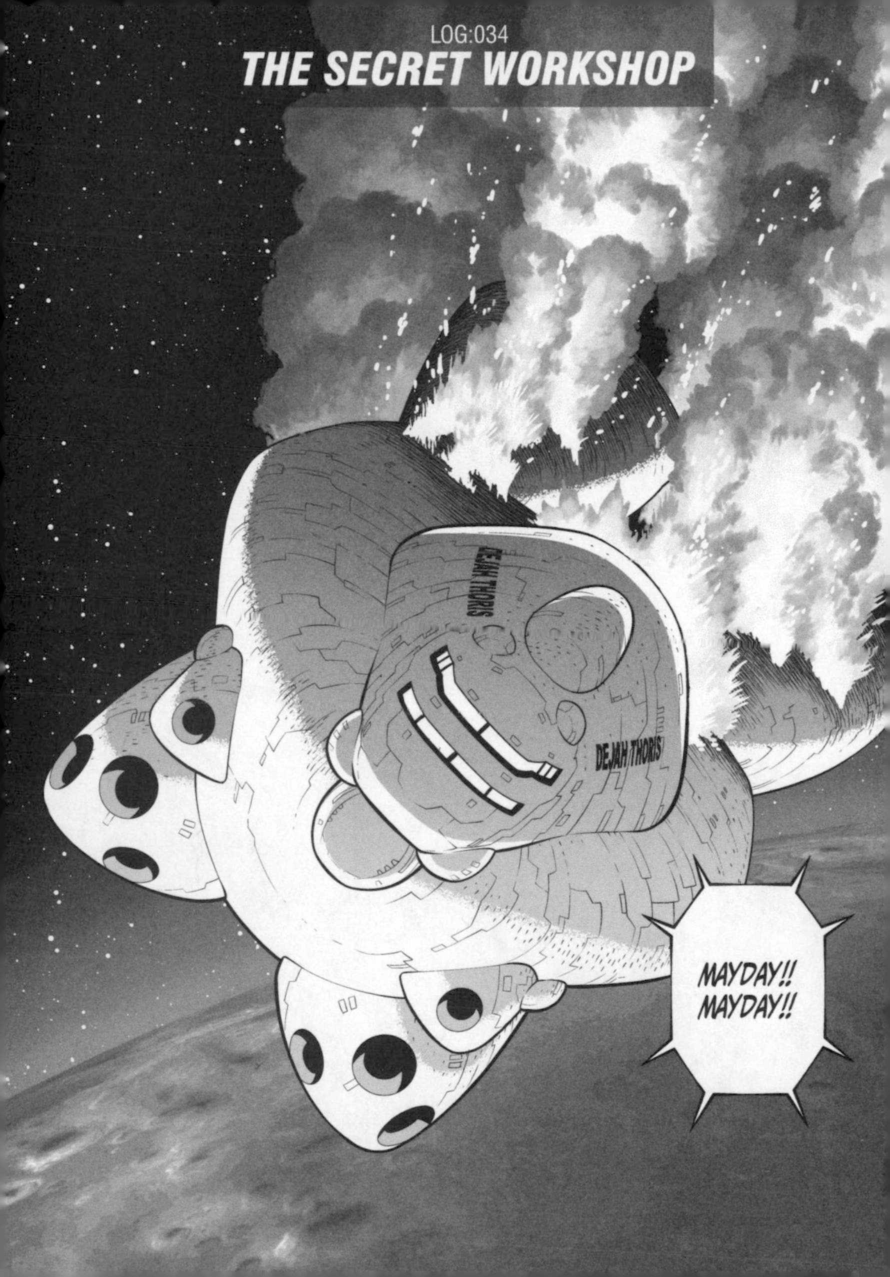
DEJAH THORIS
DEJAH THORIS
MAYDAY!! MAYDAY!!

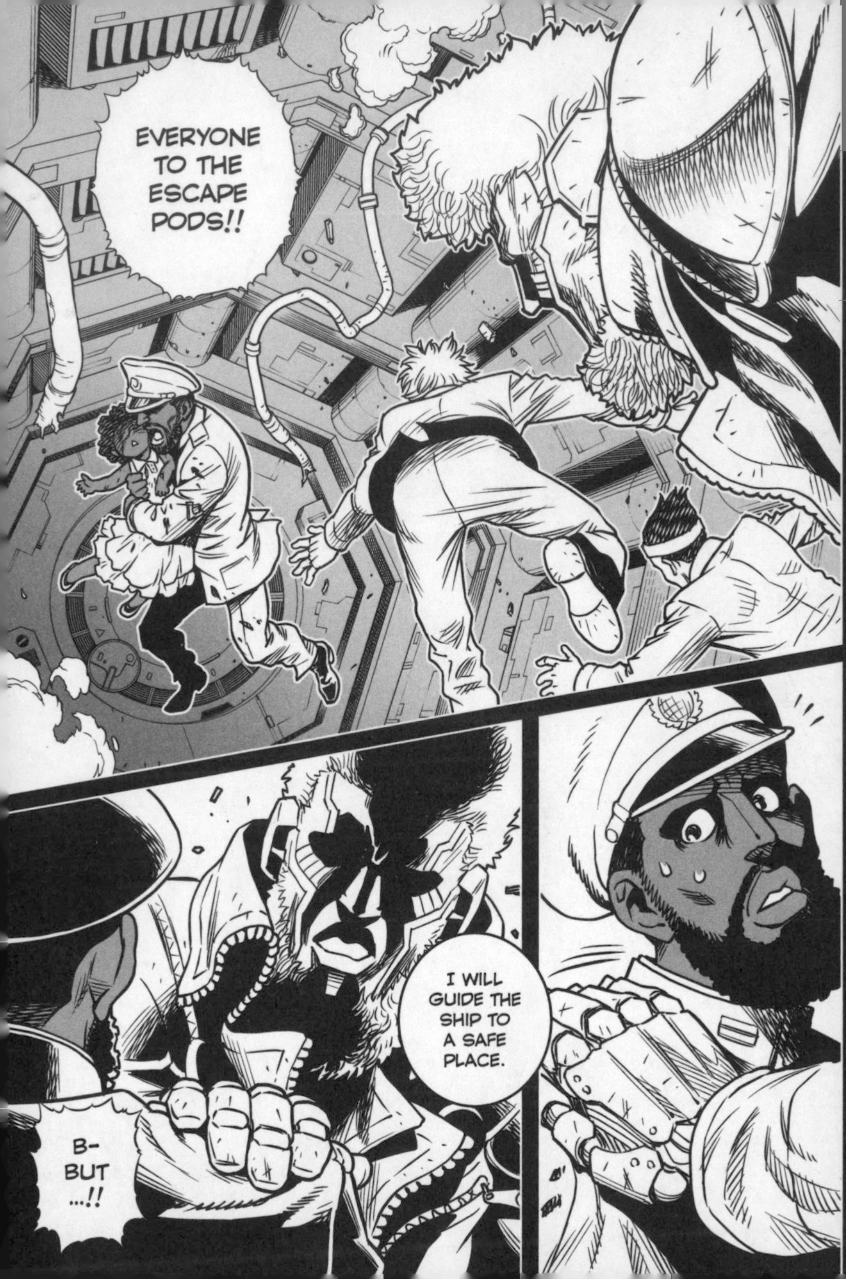
EVERYONE TO THE ESCAPE PODS!!
I WILL GUIDE THE SHIP TO A SAFE PLACE.
B-BUT ...!!

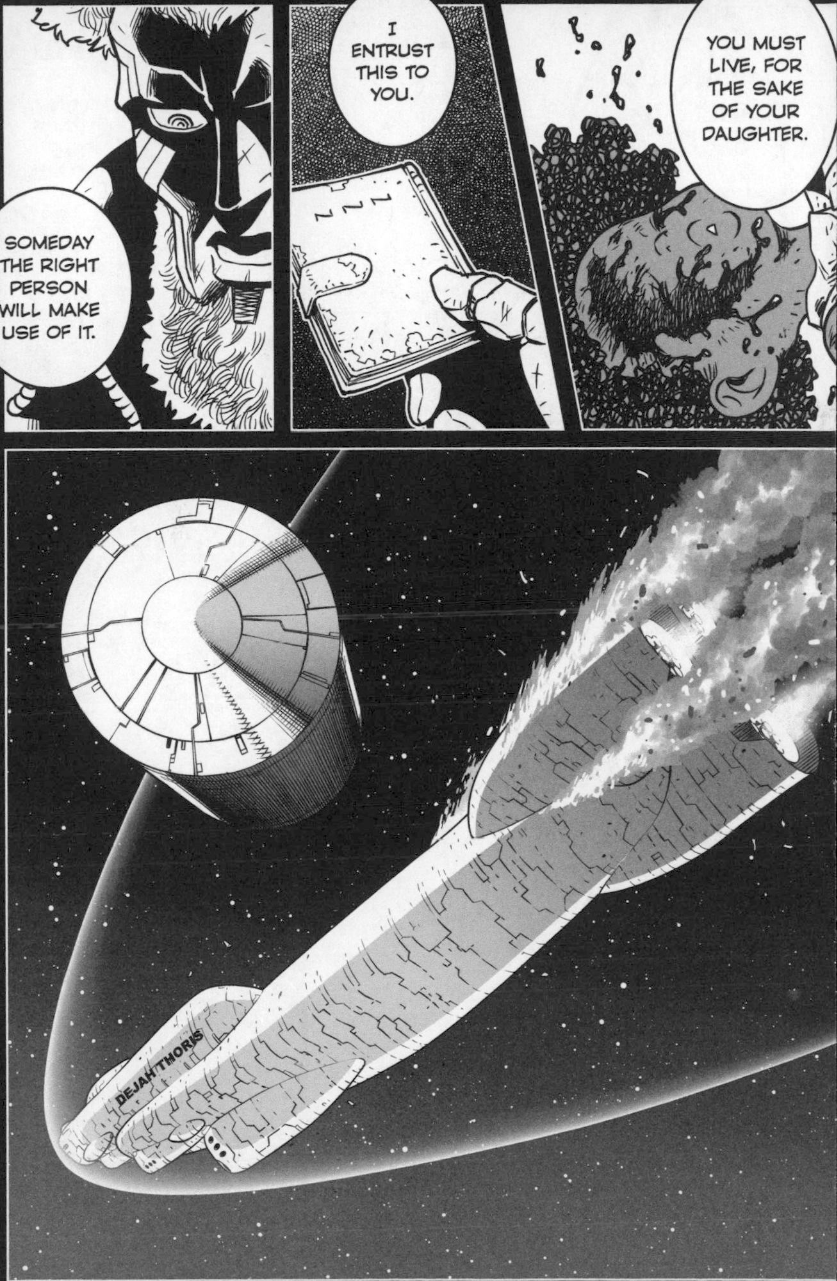
YOU MUST LIVE, FOR THE SAKE OF YOUR DAUGHTER.
I ENTRUST THIS TO YOU.
SOMEDAY THE RIGHT PERSON WILL MAKE USE OF IT.
DEJAH THORIS

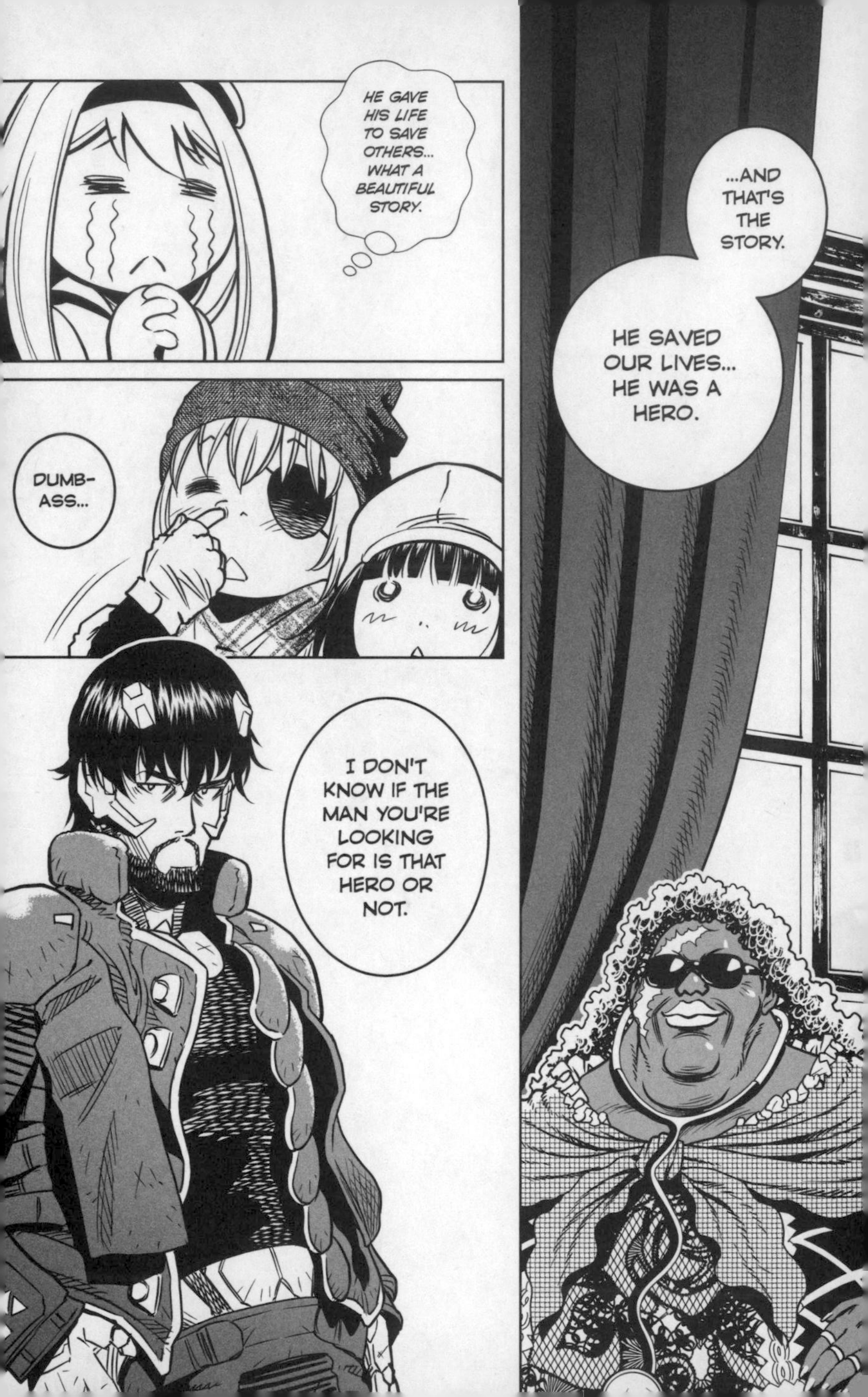
...AND THAT'S THE STORY.
HE SAVED OUR LIVES... HE WAS A HERO.
HE GAVE HIS LIFE TO SAVE OTHERS... WHAT A BEAUTIFUL STORY.
DUMB-ASS...
I DON'T KNOW IF THE MAN YOU'RE LOOKING FOR IS THAT HERO OR NOT.

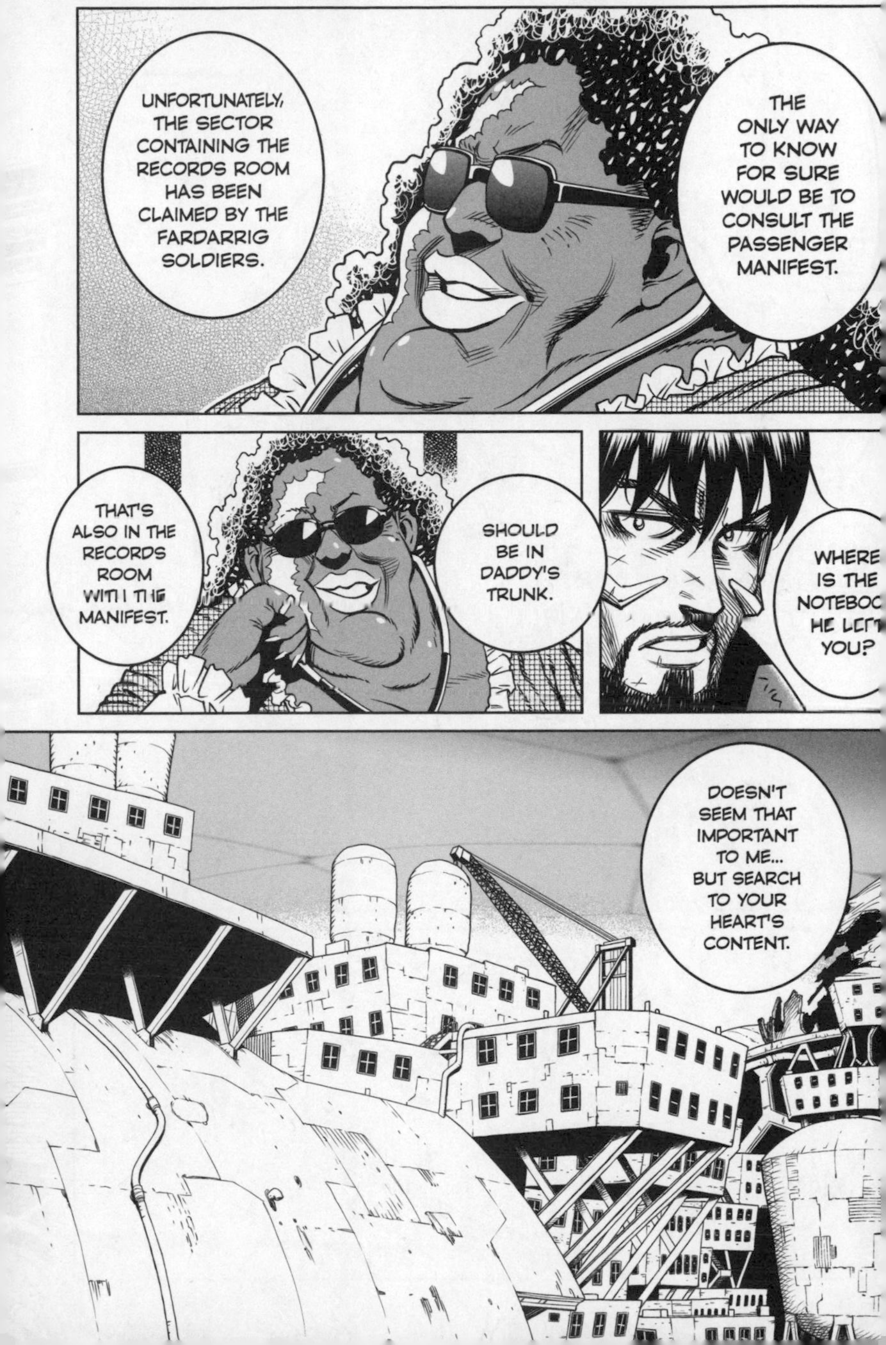
THE ONLY WAY TO KNOW FOR SURE WOULD BE TO CONSULT THE PASSENGER MANIFEST.
UNFORTUNATELY, THE SECTOR CONTAINING THE RECORDS ROOM HAS BEEN CLAIMED BY THE FARDARRIG SOLDIERS.
WHERE IS THE NOTEBOO HE LEFT YOU?
SHOULD BE IN DADDY'S TRUNK.
THAT'S ALSO IN THE RECORDS ROOM WITH THE MANIFEST.
DOESN'T SEEM THAT IMPORTANT TO ME... BUT SEARCH TO YOUR HEART'S CONTENT.

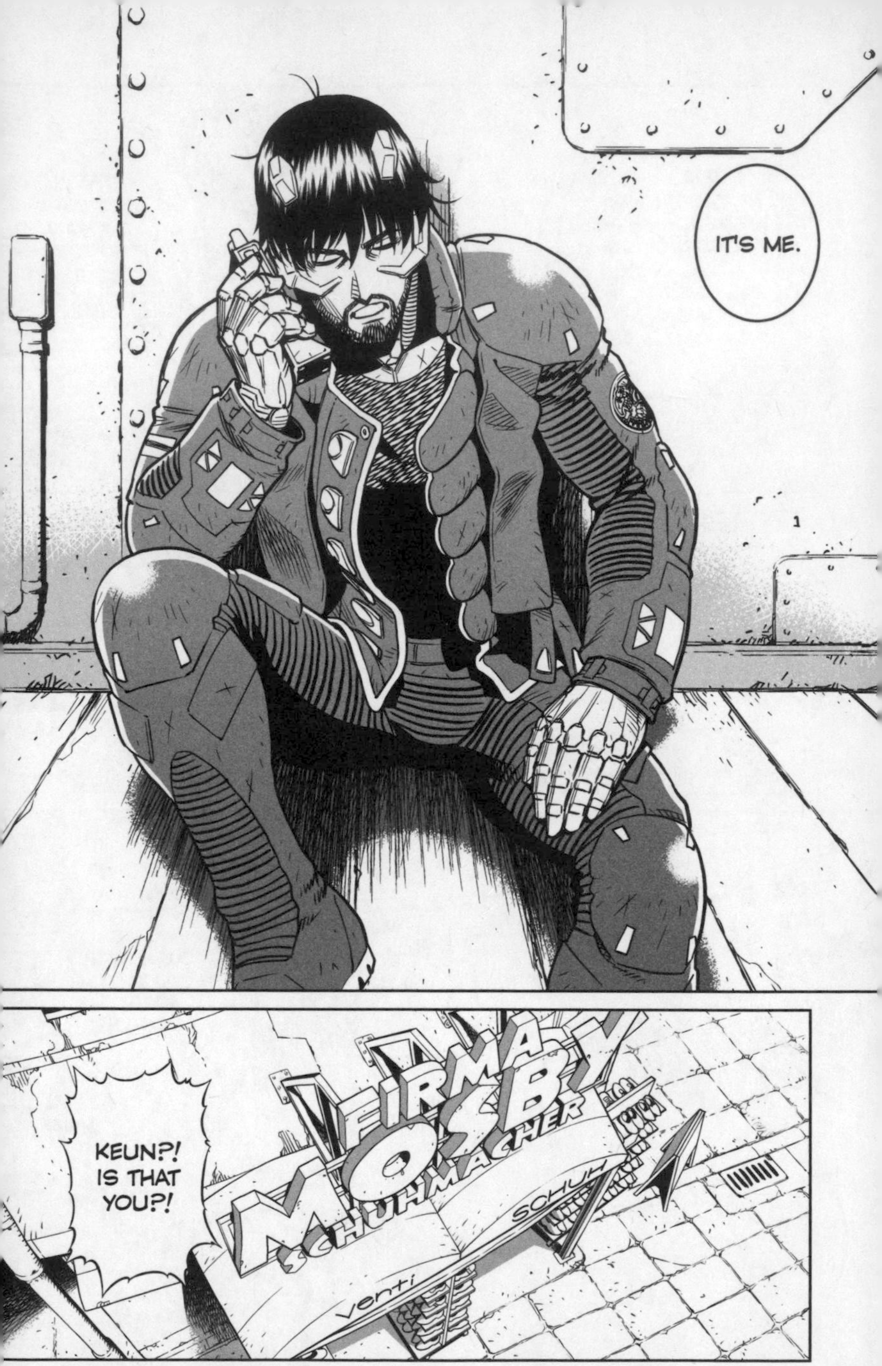
IT'S ME.
KEUN?! IS THAT YOU?!
FIRMA
SCHUHMACHER
SCHUH
venti

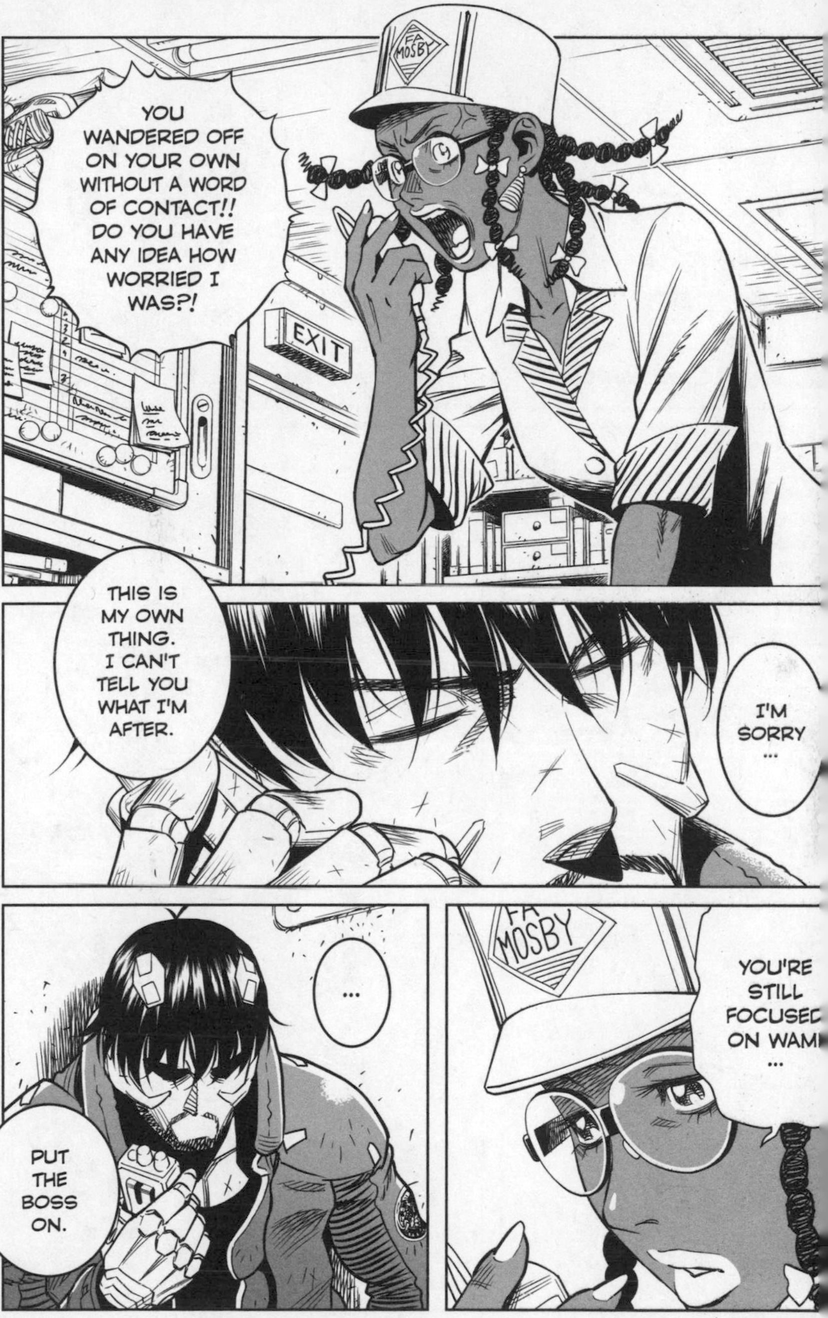
YOU WANDERED OFF ON YOUR OWN WITHOUT A WORD OF CONTACT!! DO YOU HAVE ANY IDEA HOW WORRIED I WAS?!
EXIT
FA MOSBY
I'M SORRY ...
THIS IS MY OWN THING. I CAN'T TELL YOU WHAT I'M AFTER.
FA MOSBY
YOU'RE STILL FOCUSED ON WAM ...
...
PUT THE BOSS ON.

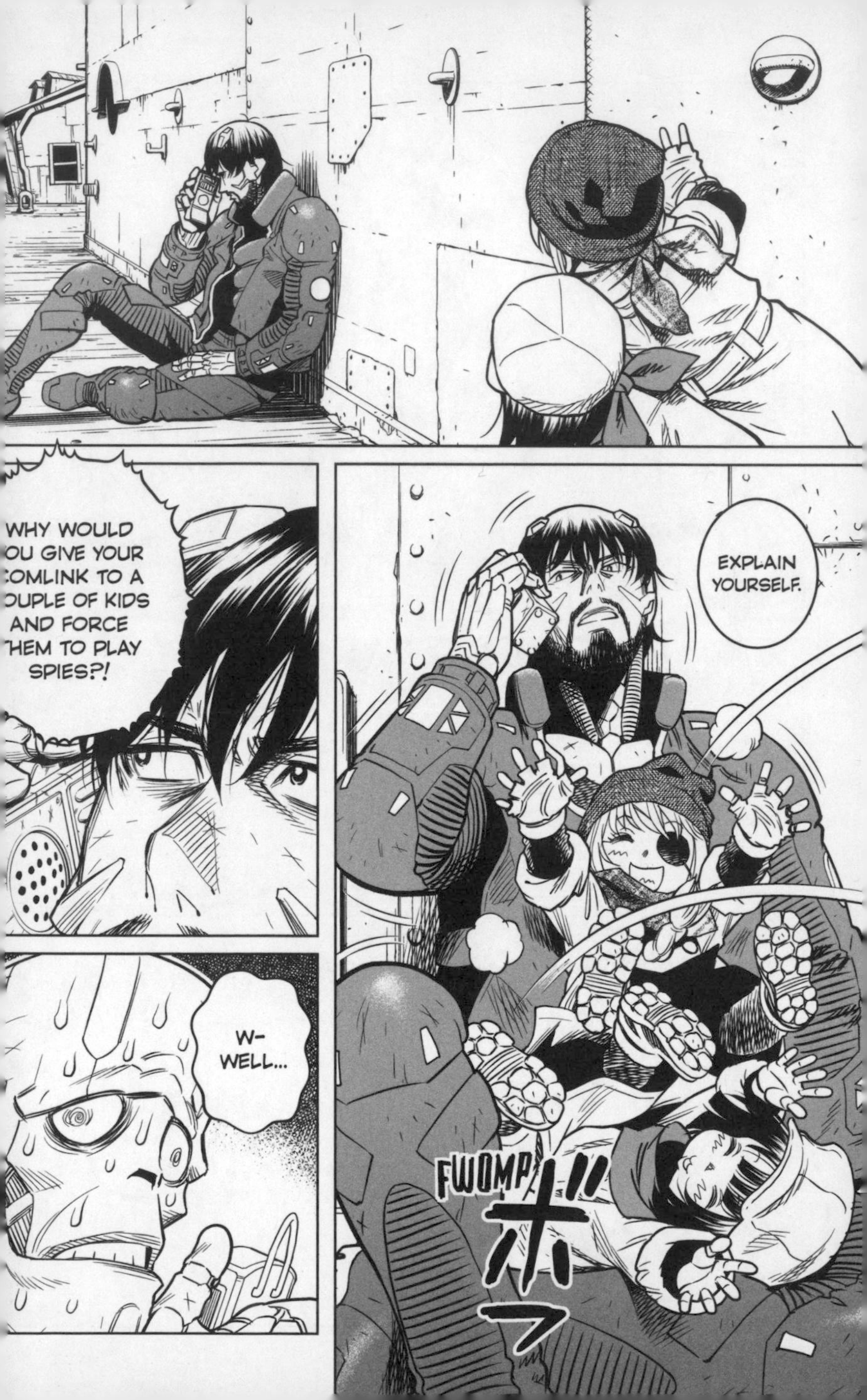
EXPLAIN YOURSELF.
FWOMP
WHY WOULD OU GIVE YOUR COMLINK TO A OUPLE OF KIDS AND FORCE HEM TO PLAY SPIES?!
W- WELL...

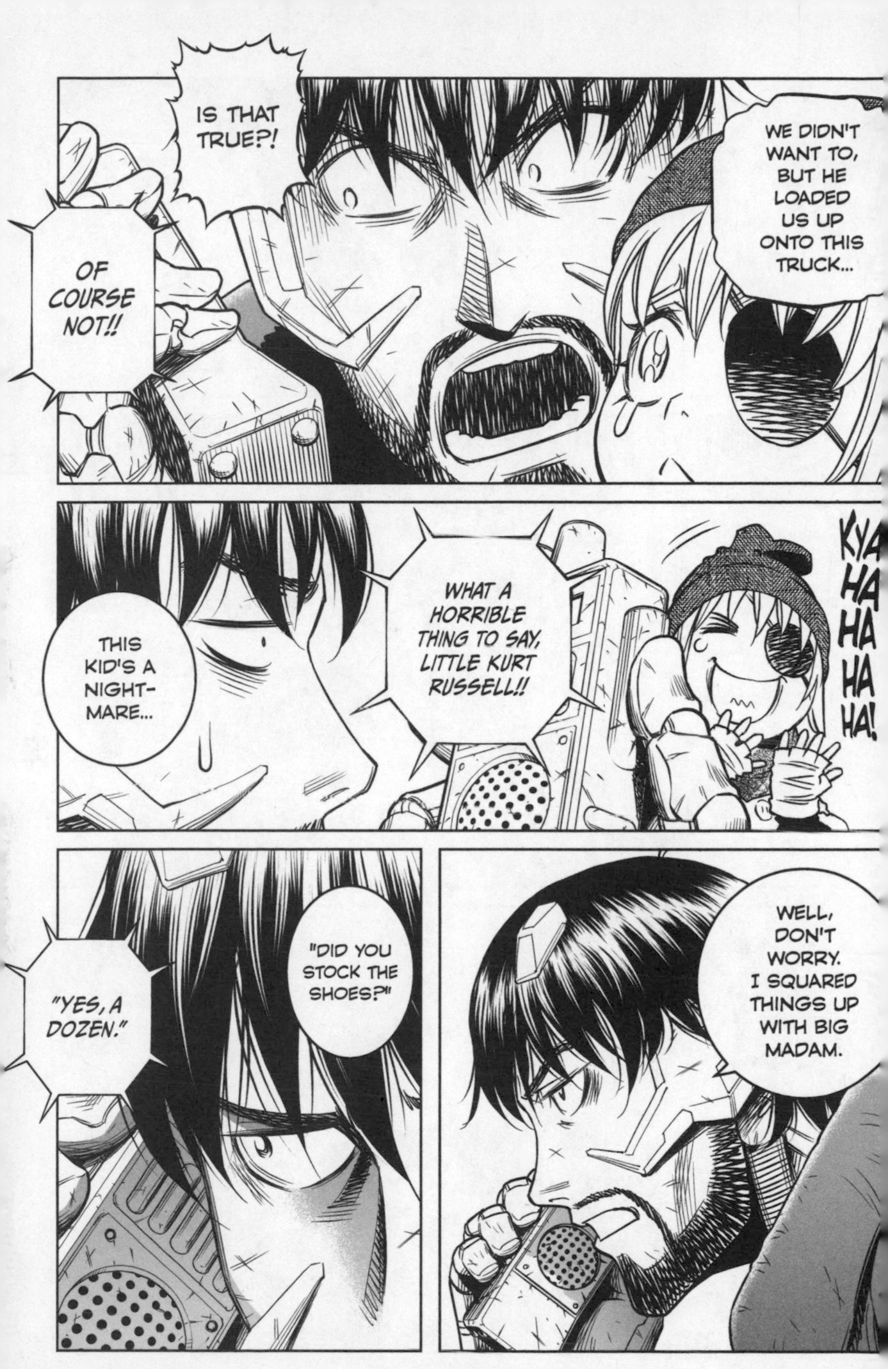
WE DIDN'T WANT TO, BUT HE LOADED US UP ONTO THIS TRUCK...
IS THAT TRUE?!
OF COURSE NOT!!
KYAHAHAHAHAHA!
WHAT A HORRIBLE THING TO SAY, LITTLE KURT RUSSELL!!
THIS KID'S A NIGHT-MARE...
WELL, DON'T WORRY. I SQUARED THINGS UP WITH BIG MADAM.
"DID YOU STOCK THE SHOES?"
"YES, A DOZEN."

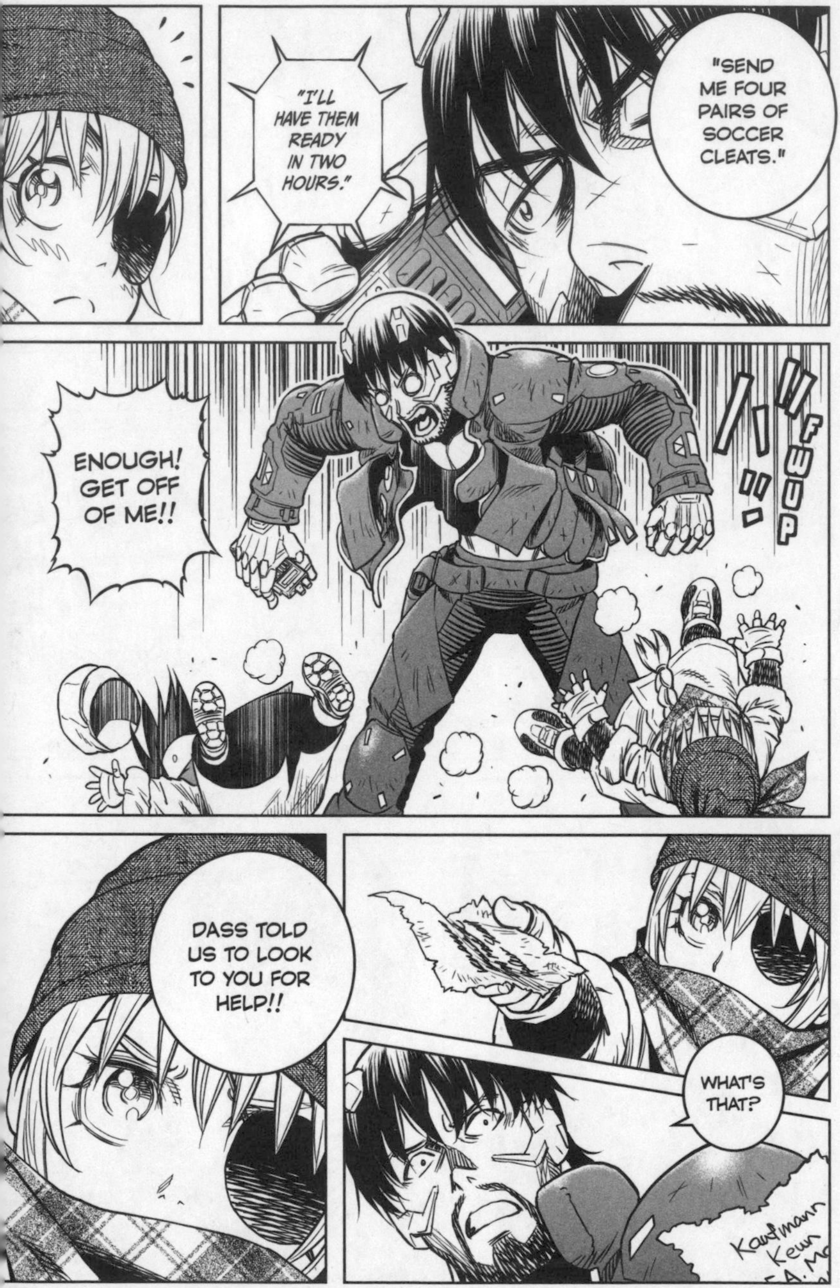
"SEND ME FOUR PAIRS OF SOCCER CLEATS."
"I'LL HAVE THEM READY IN TWO HOURS."
FWUP
ENOUGH! GET OFF OF ME!!
WHAT'S THAT?
DASS TOLD US TO LOOK TO YOU FOR HELP!!
Kaufmann
Keun

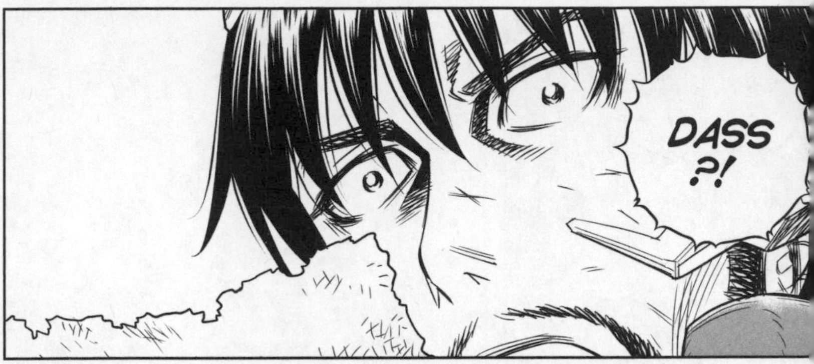
DASS ?!
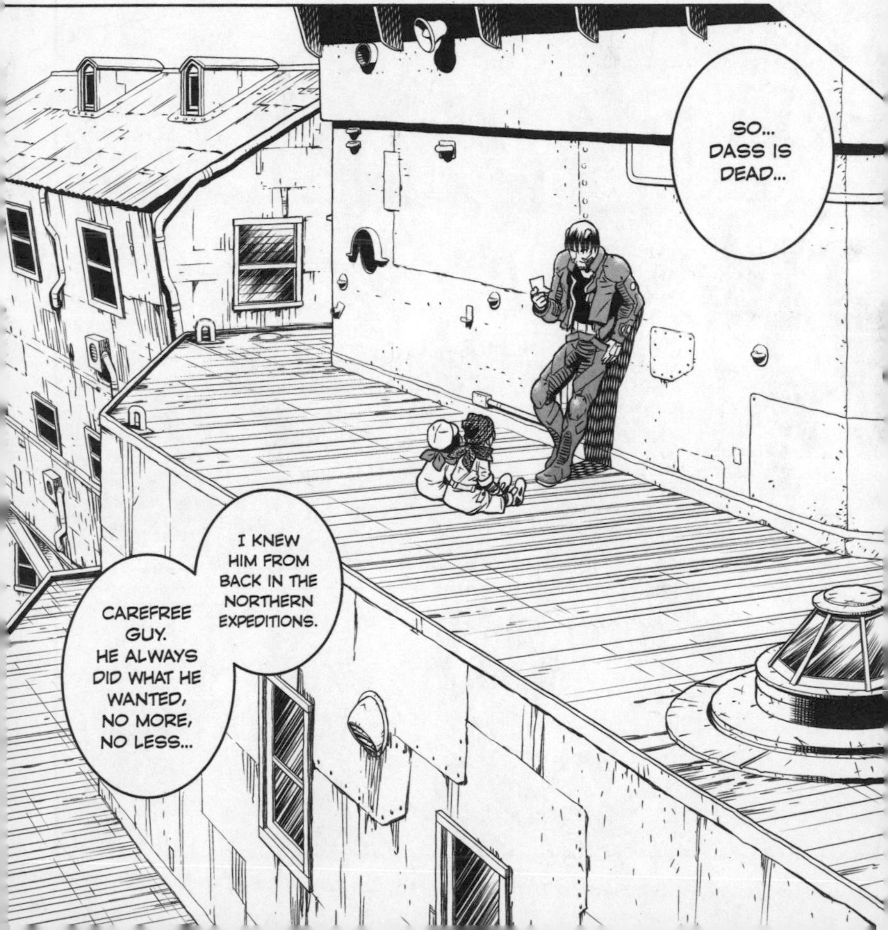
SO... DASS IS DEAD...
I KNEW HIM FROM BACK IN THE NORTHERN EXPEDITIONS.
CAREFREE GUY. HE ALWAYS DID WHAT HE WANTED, NO MORE, NO LESS...

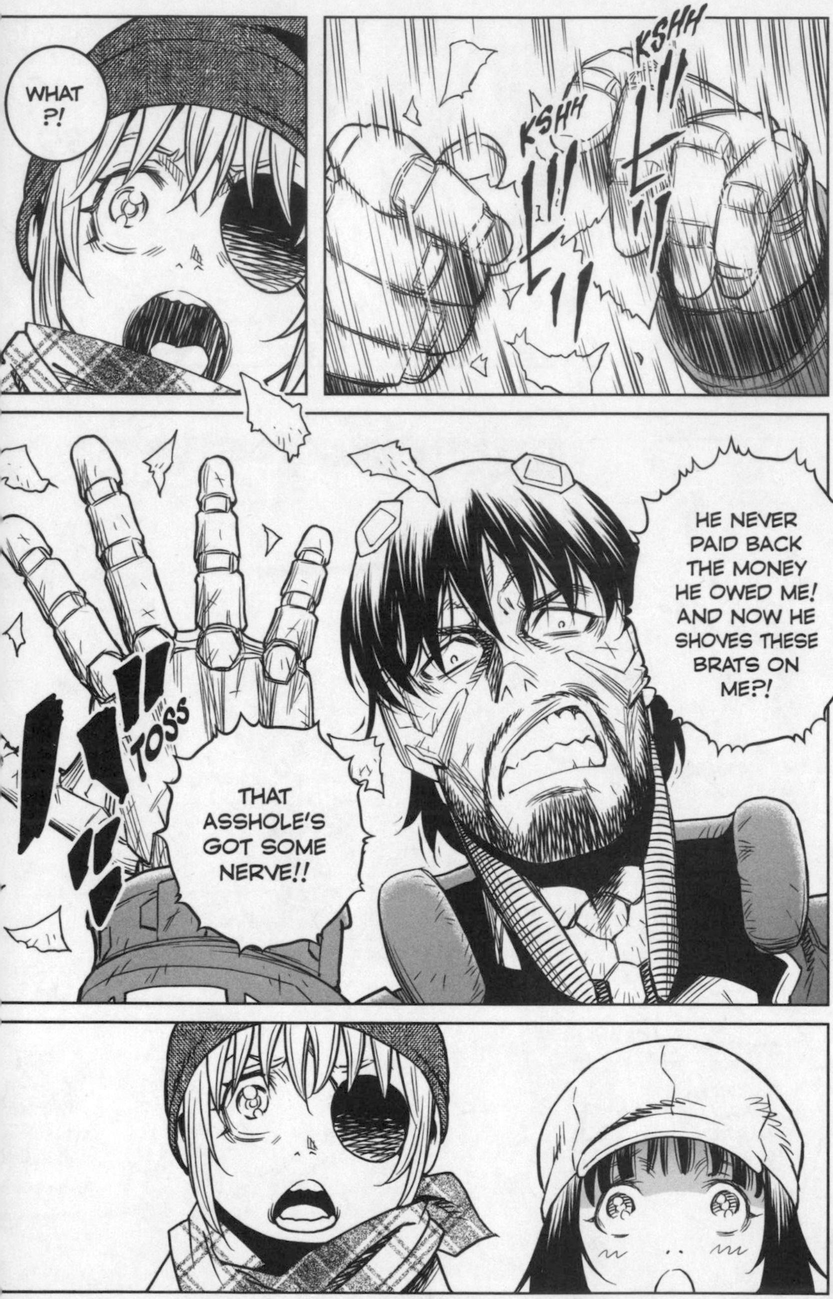
KSHH
KSHH
WHAT ?!
HE NEVER PAID BACK THE MONEY HE OWED ME! AND NOW HE SHOVES THESE BRATS ON ME?!
TOSS
THAT ASSHOLE'S GOT SOME NERVE!!

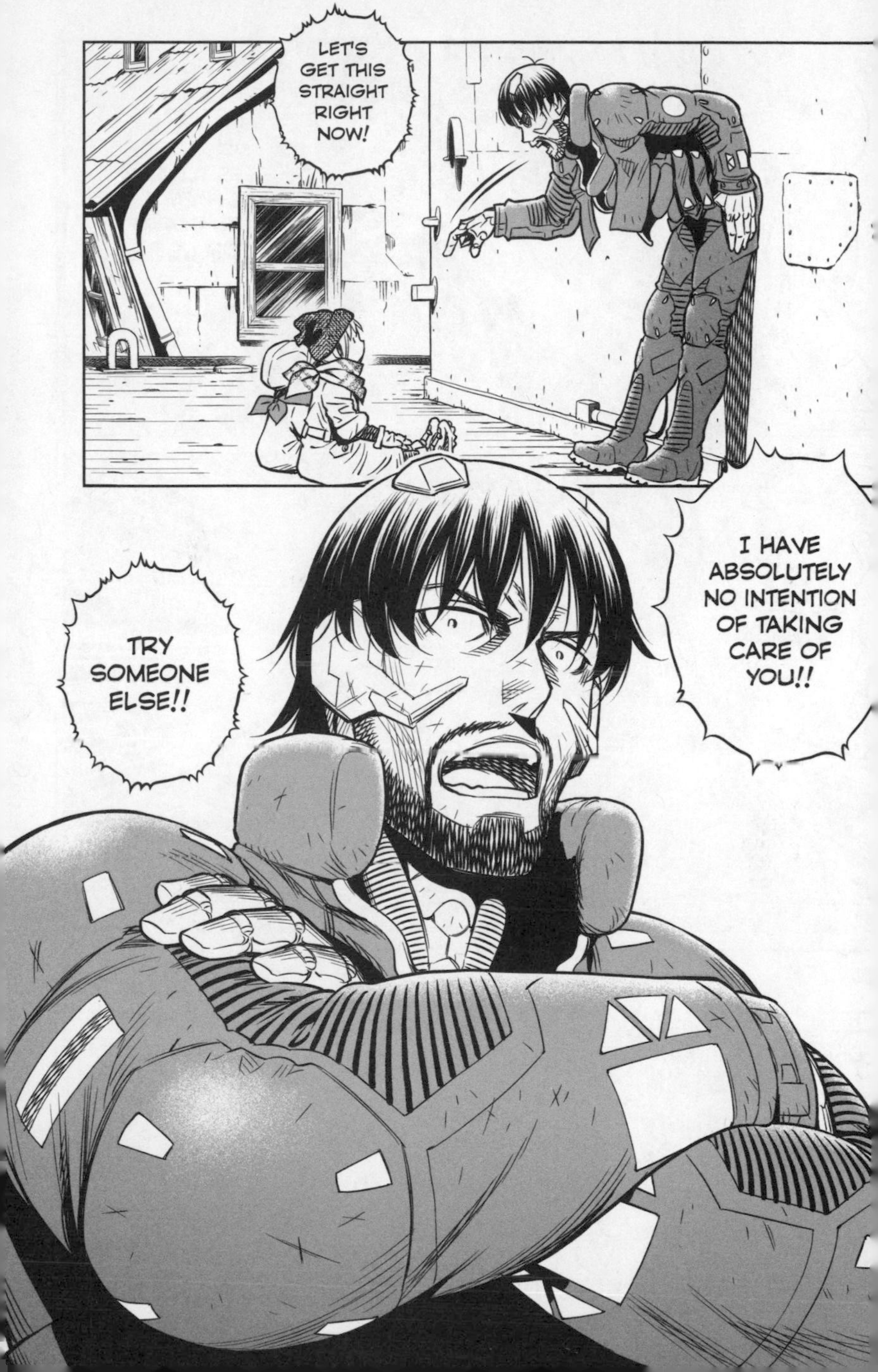
LET'S GET THIS STRAIGHT RIGHT NOW!
I HAVE ABSOLUTELY NO INTENTION OF TAKING CARE OF YOU!!
TRY SOMEONE ELSE!!

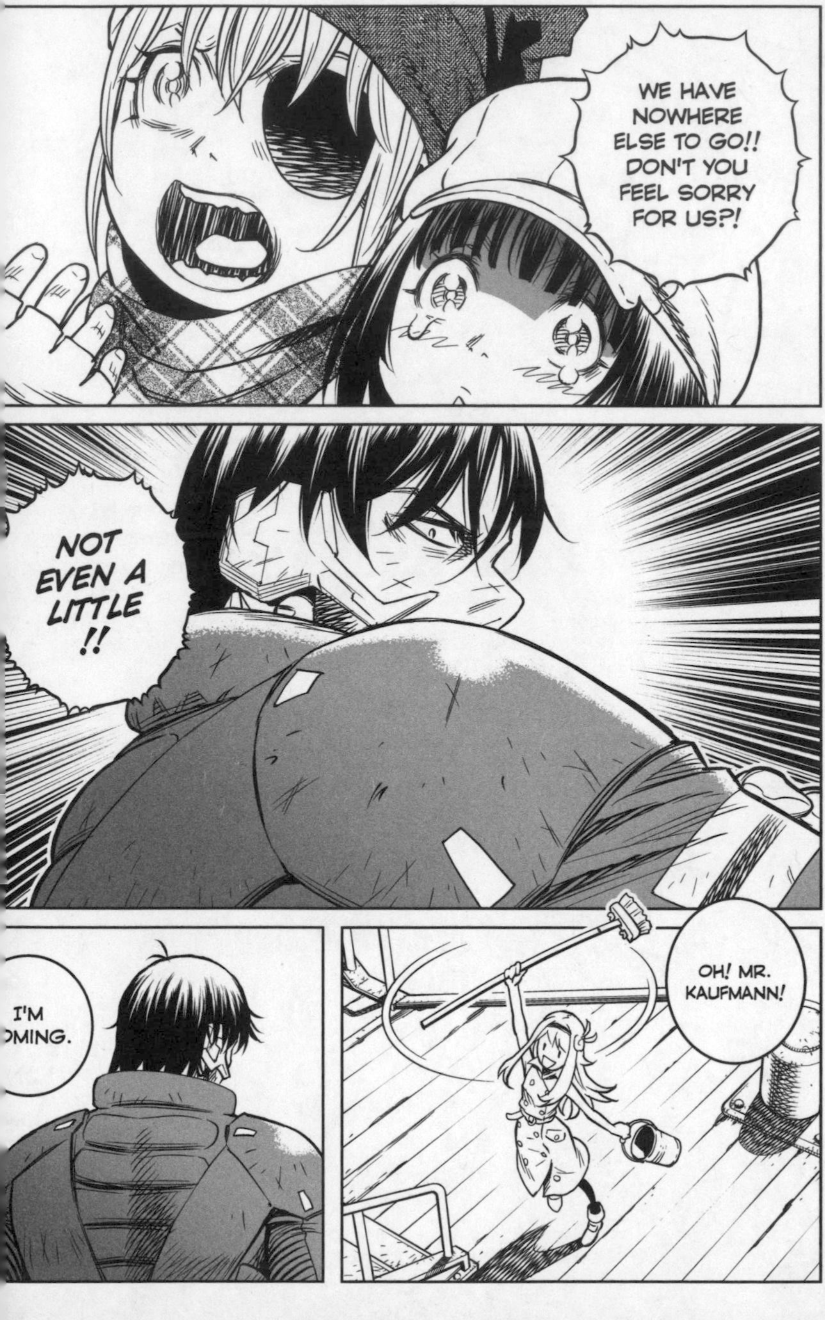
WE HAVE NOWHERE ELSE TO GO!! DON'T YOU FEEL SORRY FOR US?!
NOT EVEN A LITTLE !!
OH! MR. KAUFMANN!
I'M
OMING.

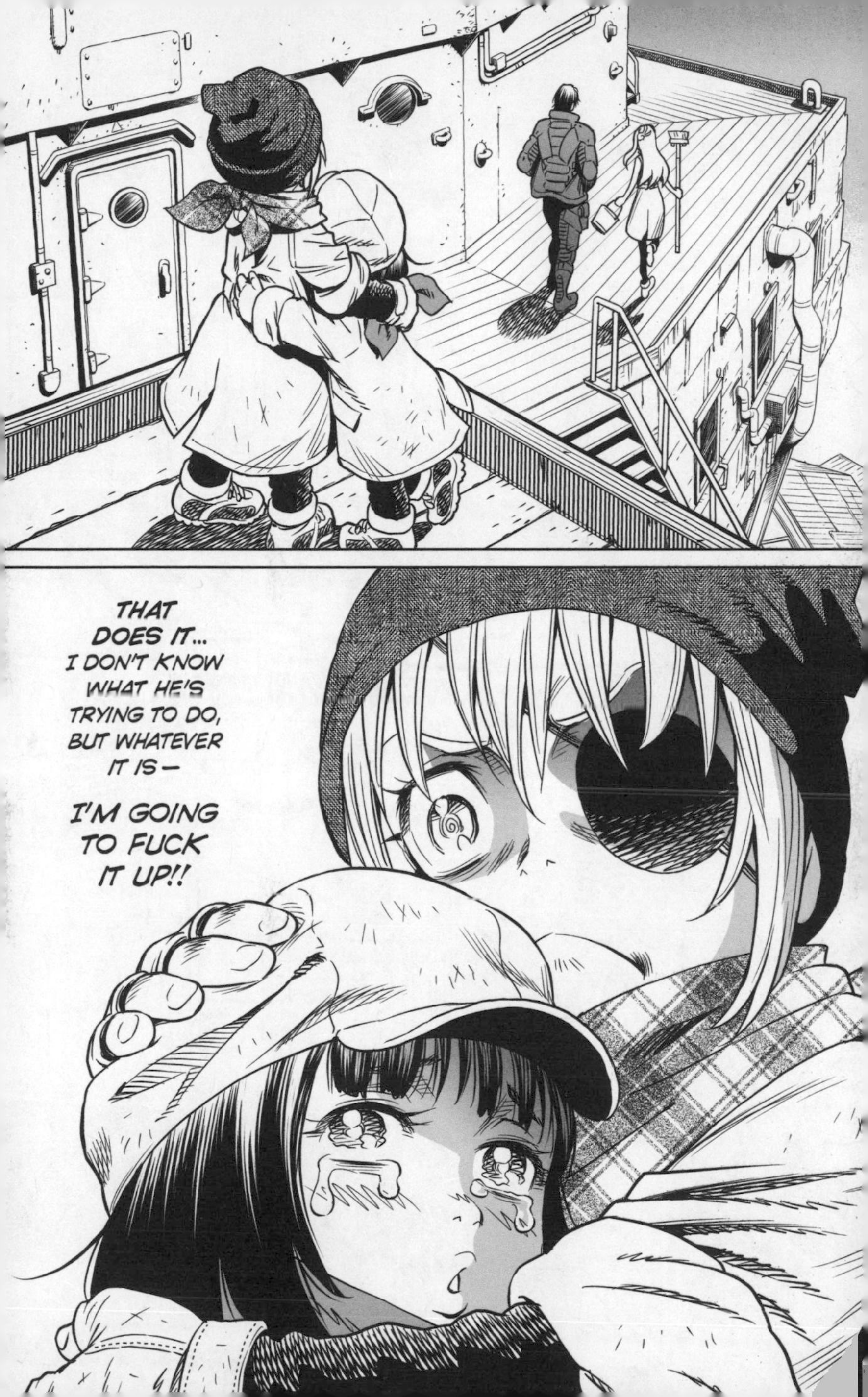
THAT DOES IT... I DON'T KNOW WHAT HE'S TRYING TO DO, BUT WHATEVER IT IS—
I'M GOING TO FUCK IT UP!!

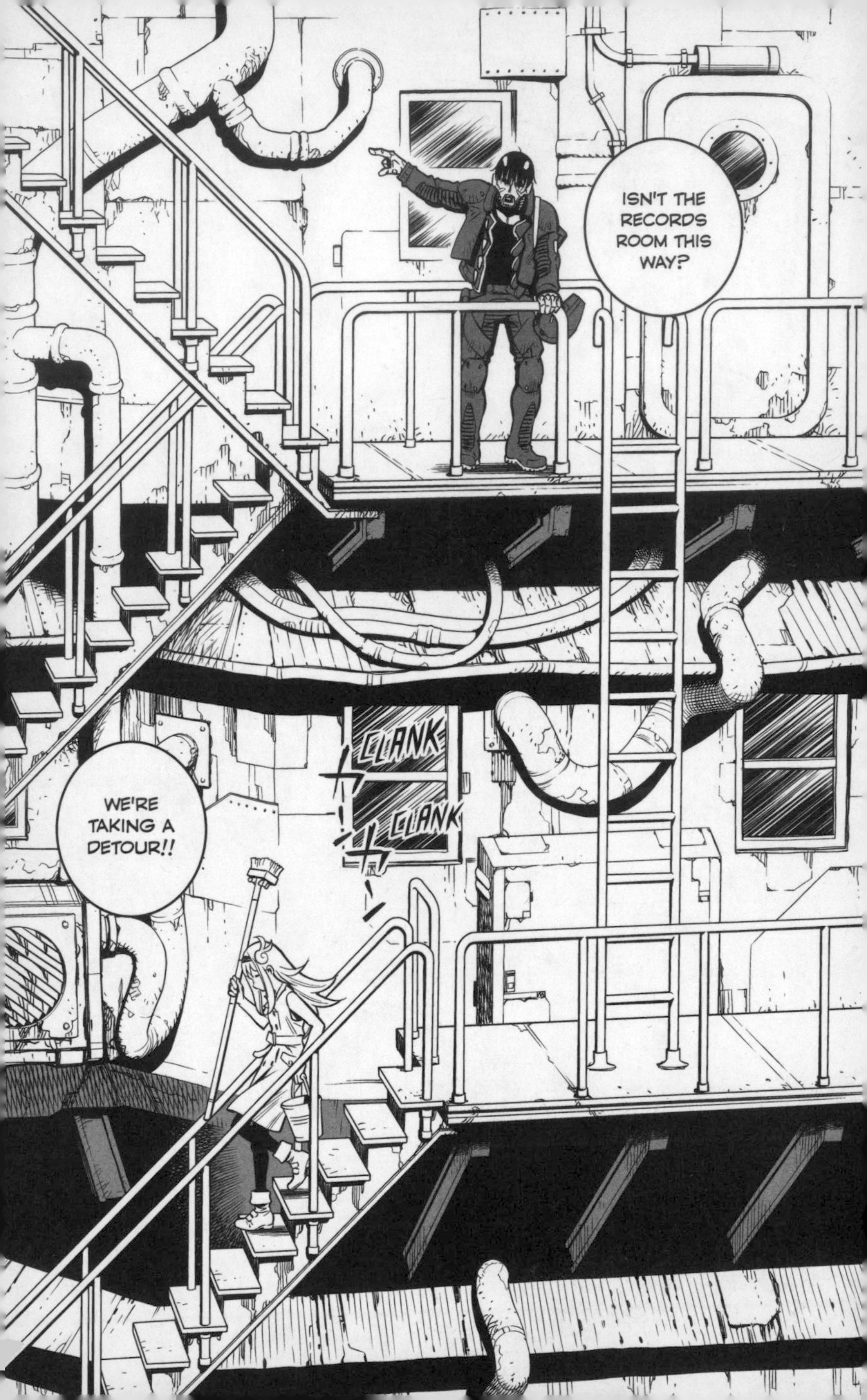
ISN'T THE RECORDS ROOM THIS WAY?
CLANK
CLANK
WE'RE TAKING A DETOUR!!

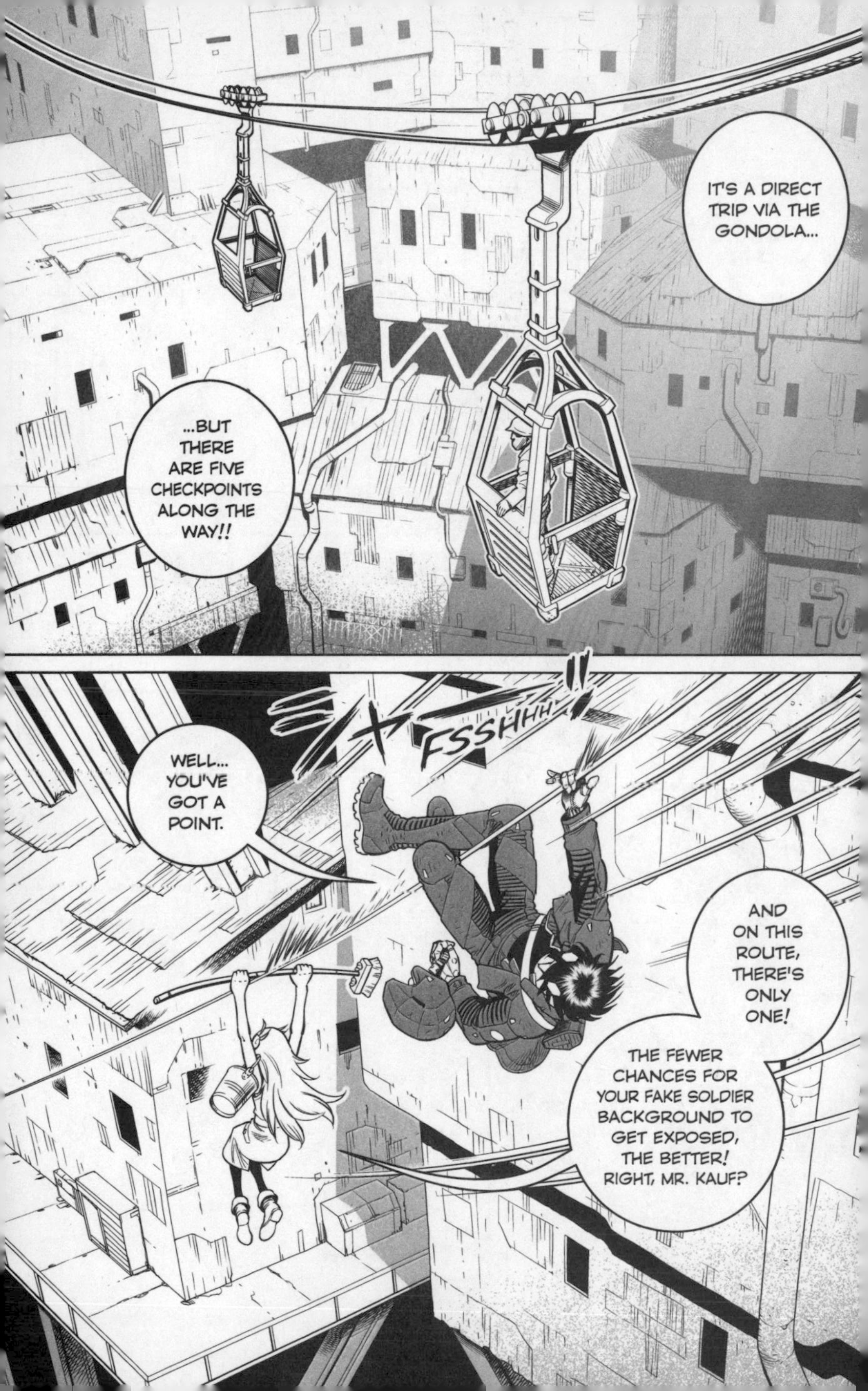
IT'S A DIRECT TRIP VIA THE GONDOLA...
...BUT THERE ARE FIVE CHECKPOINTS ALONG THE WAY!!
FSSHHH!!
AND ON THIS ROUTE, THERE'S ONLY ONE!
THE FEWER CHANCES FOR YOUR FAKE SOLDIER BACKGROUND TO GET EXPOSED, THE BETTER! RIGHT, MR. KAUF?
WELL... YOU'VE GOT A POINT.

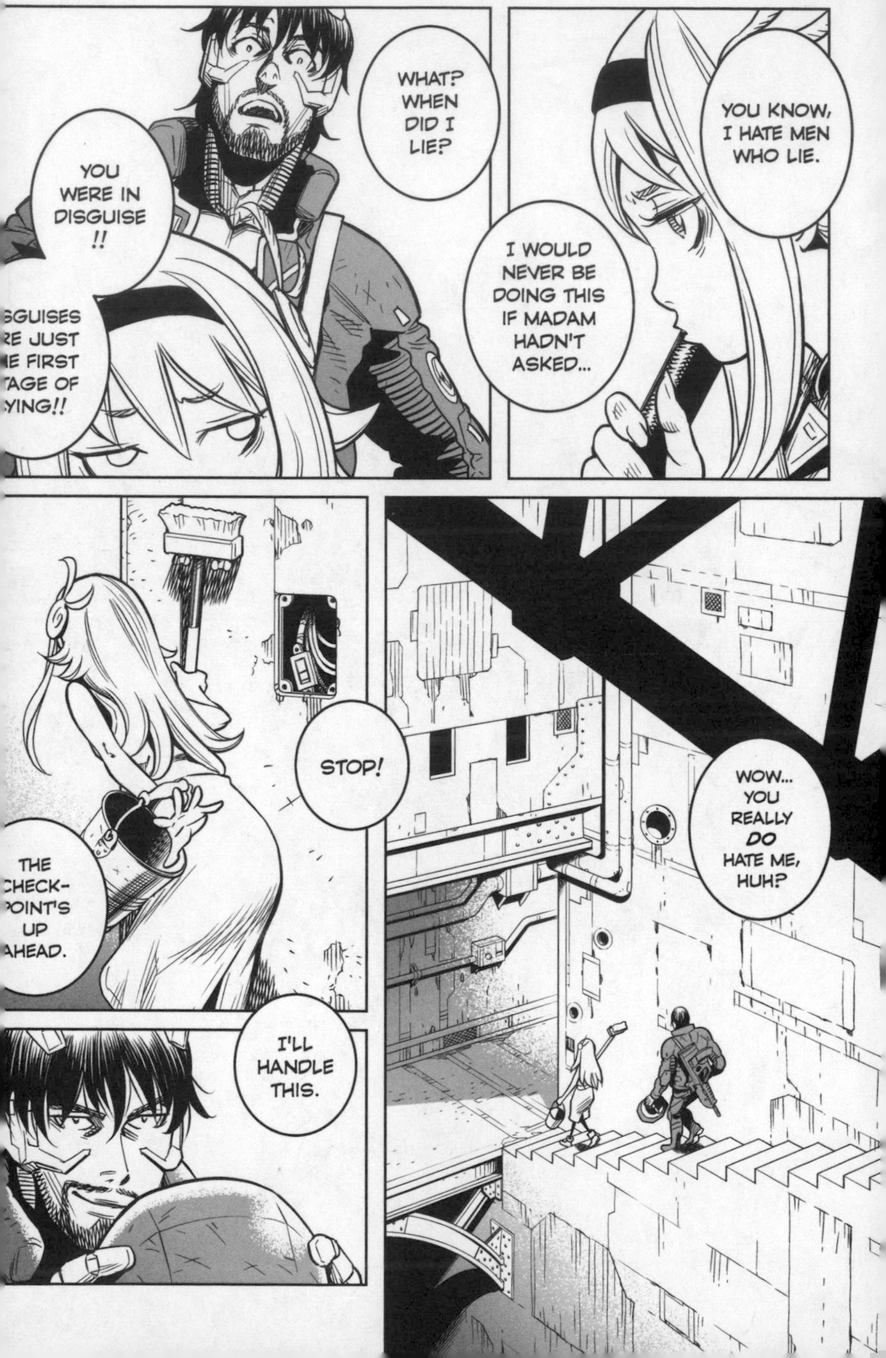
YOU KNOW, I HATE MEN WHO LIE.
I WOULD NEVER BE DOING THIS IF MADAM HADN'T ASKED...
WHAT? WHEN DID I LIE?
YOU WERE IN DISGUISE!!
SGUISES RE JUST IE FIRST TAGE OF YING!!
WOW... YOU REALLY *DO* HATE ME, HUH?
STOP!
THE HECK-OINT'S UP HEAD.
I'LL HANDLE THIS.

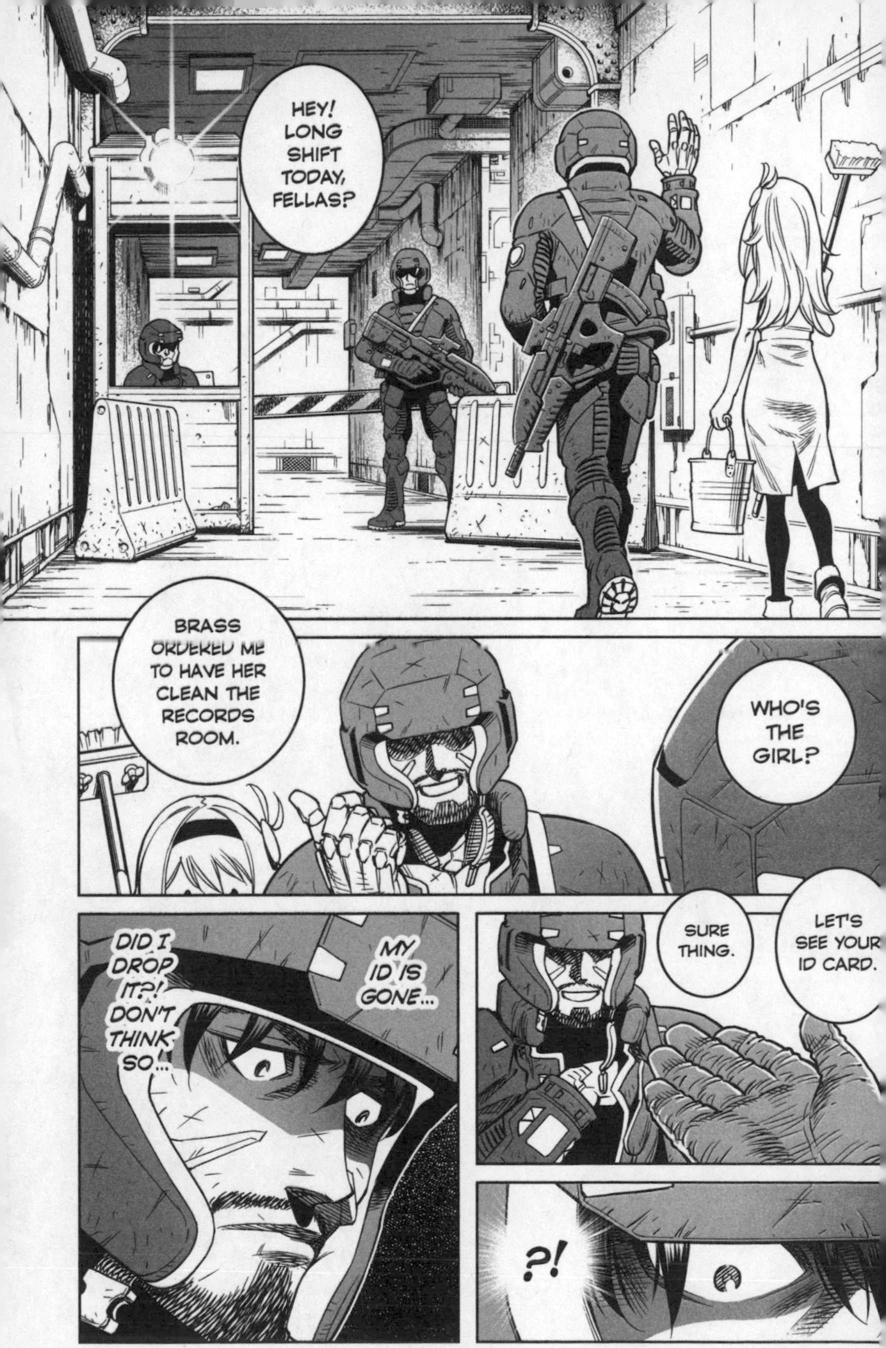
HEY! LONG SHIFT TODAY, FELLAS?
WHO'S THE GIRL?
BRASS ORDERED ME TO HAVE HER CLEAN THE RECORDS ROOM.
LET'S SEE YOUR ID CARD.
SURE THING.
?!
MY ID IS GONE...
DID I DROP IT?! DON'T THINK SO...

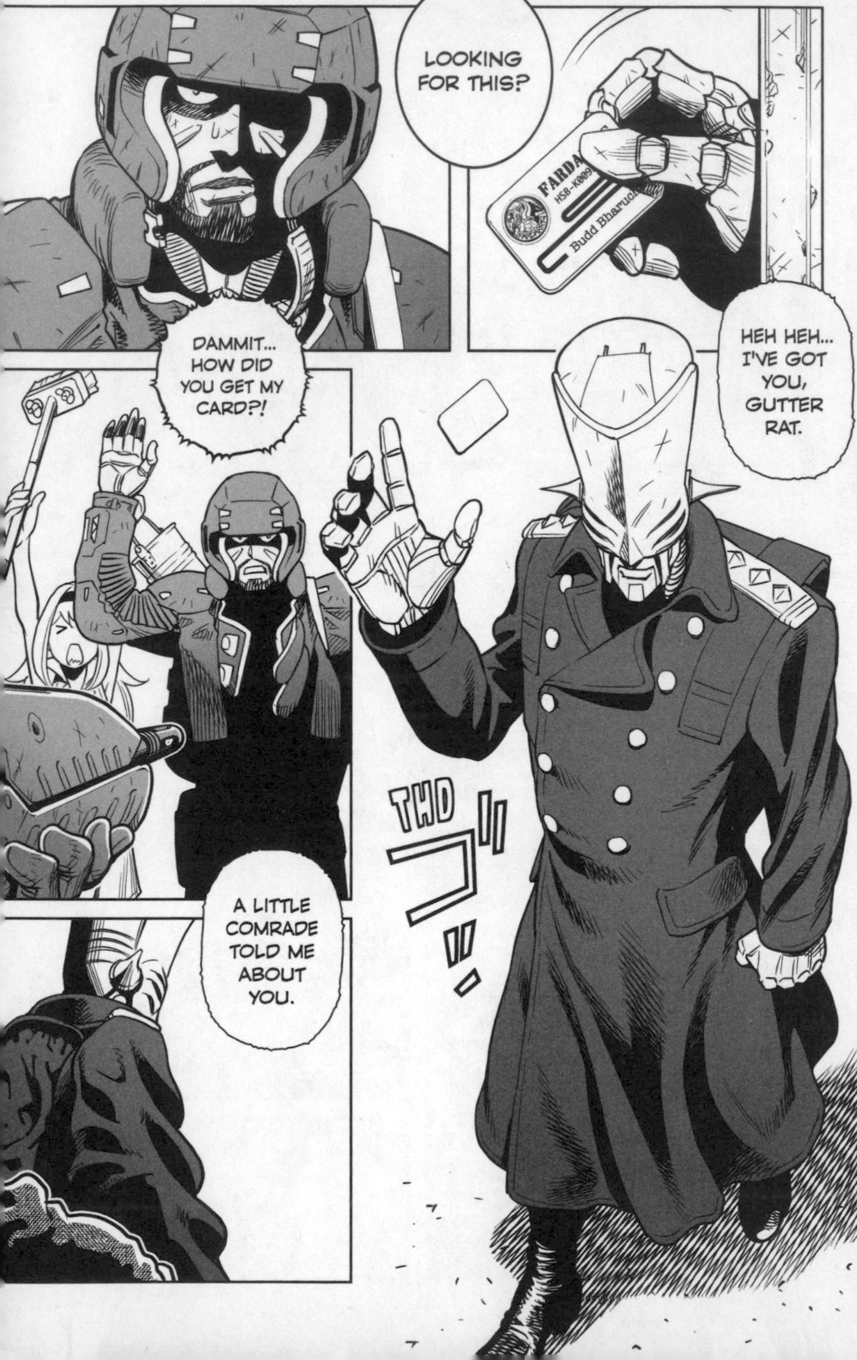
LOOKING FOR THIS?
DAMMIT... HOW DID YOU GET MY CARD?!
HEH HEH... I'VE GOT YOU, GUTTER RAT.
THD
A LITTLE COMRADE TOLD ME ABOUT YOU.

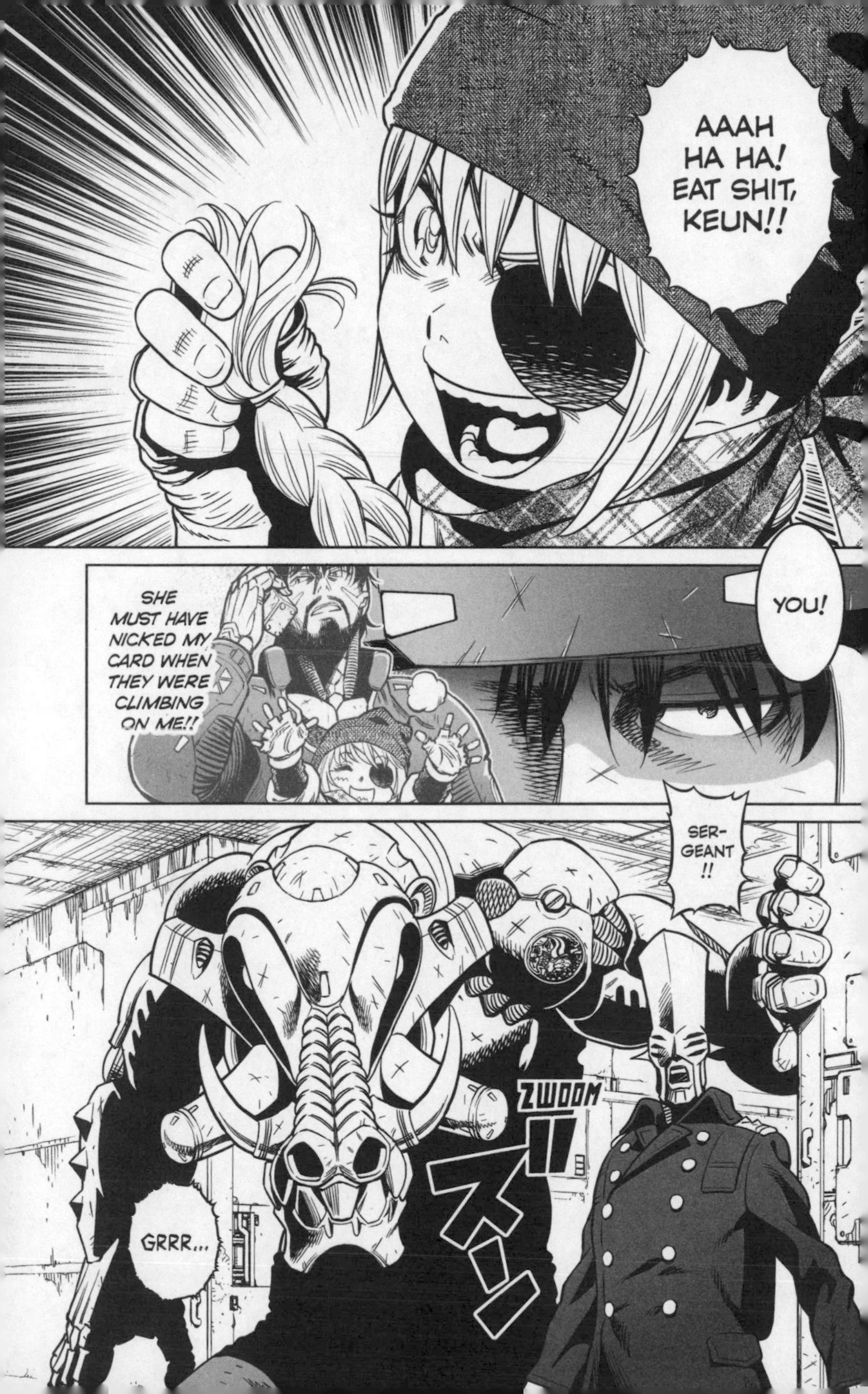
AAAH HA HA! EAT SHIT, KEUN!!
YOU!
SHE MUST HAVE NICKED MY CARD WHEN THEY WERE CLIMBING ON ME!!
SER-GEANT !!
ZWOOM
GRRR...

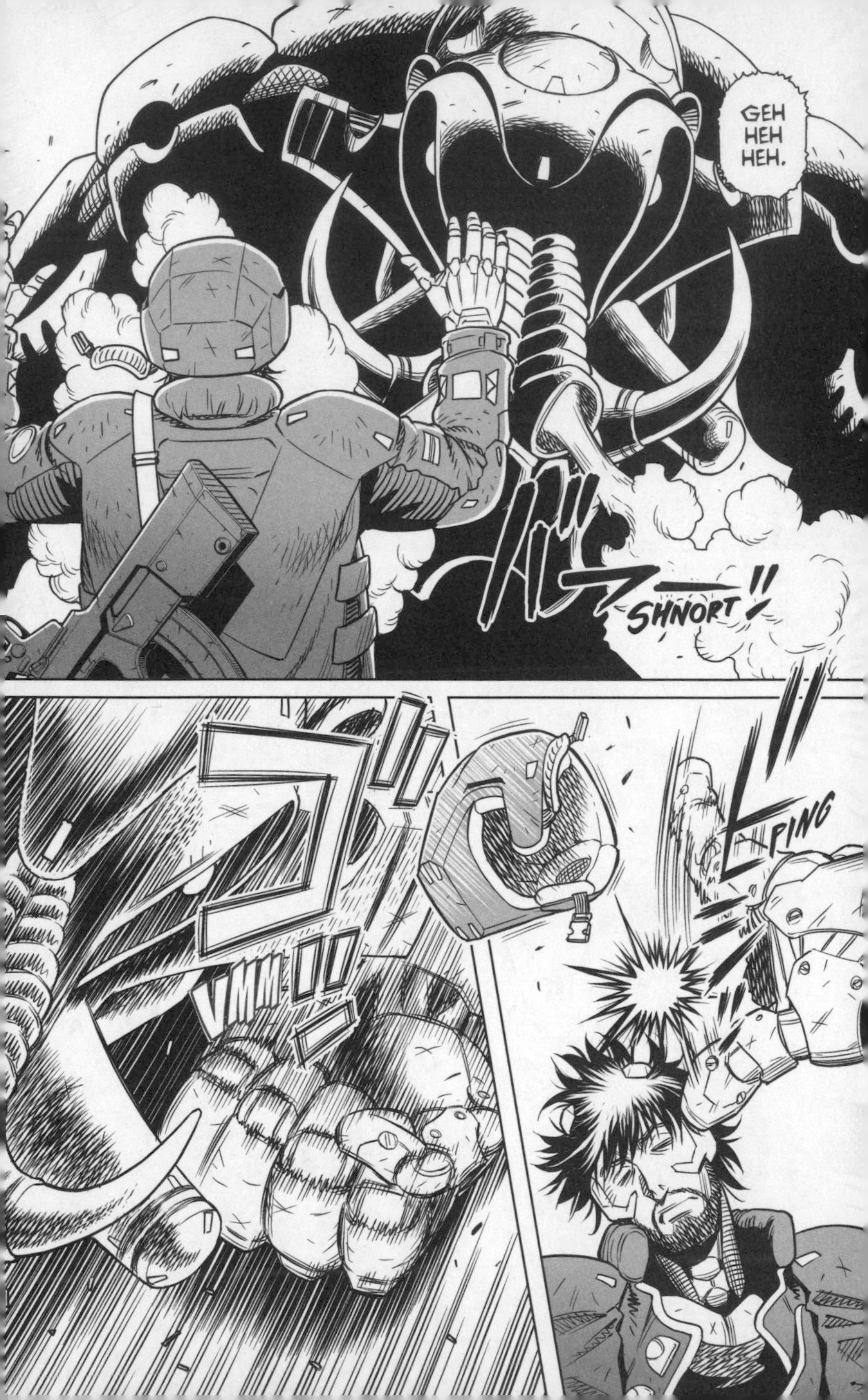
GEH HEH HEH.
SHNORT!!
PING
VMM!!

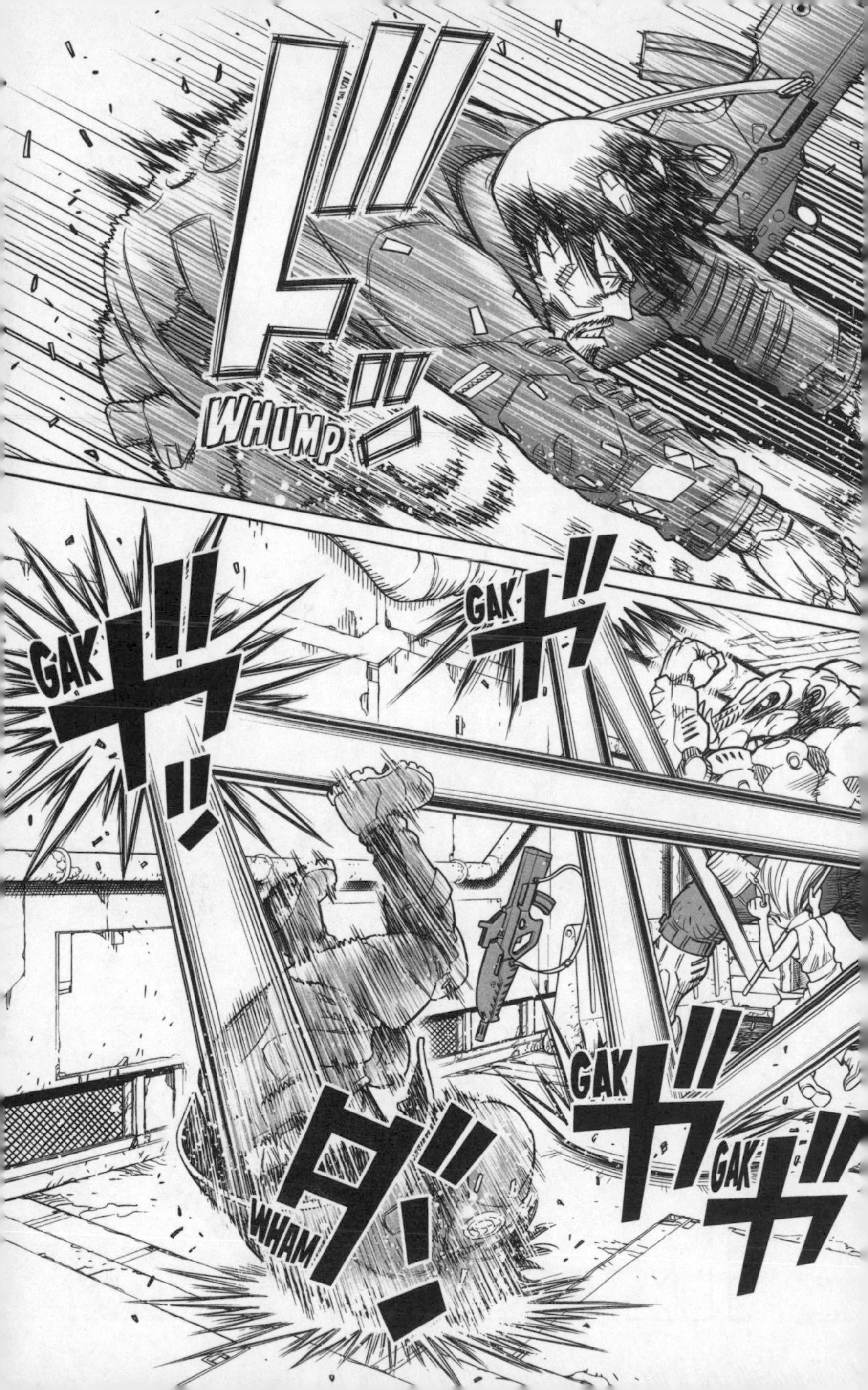
WHUMP
GAK
GAK
GAK
GAK
WHAM

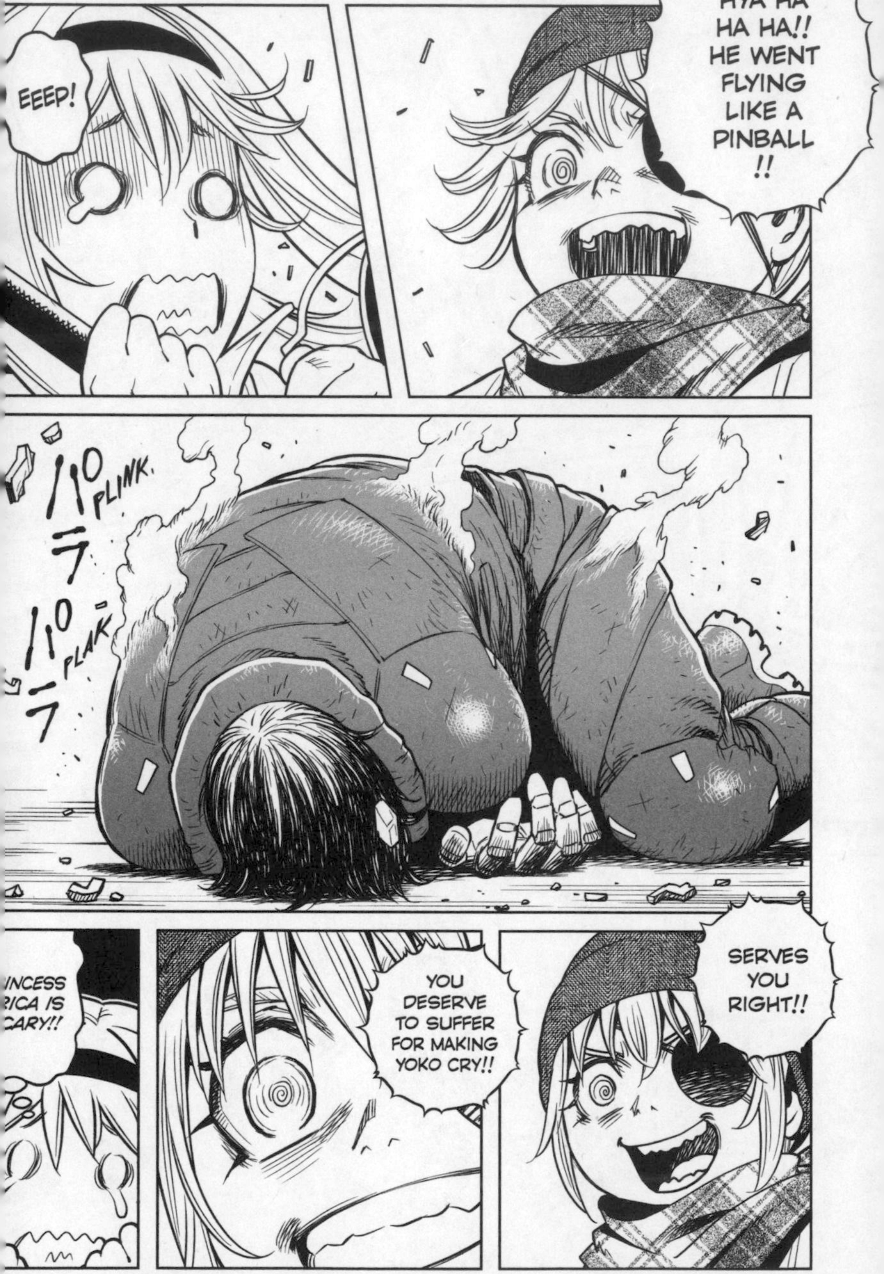
HYA HA HA HA!! HE WENT FLYING LIKE A PINBALL !!
EEEP!
パラ PLINK.
パラ PLAK
SERVES YOU RIGHT!!
YOU DESERVE TO SUFFER FOR MAKING YOKO CRY!!
INCESS RICA IS CARY!!

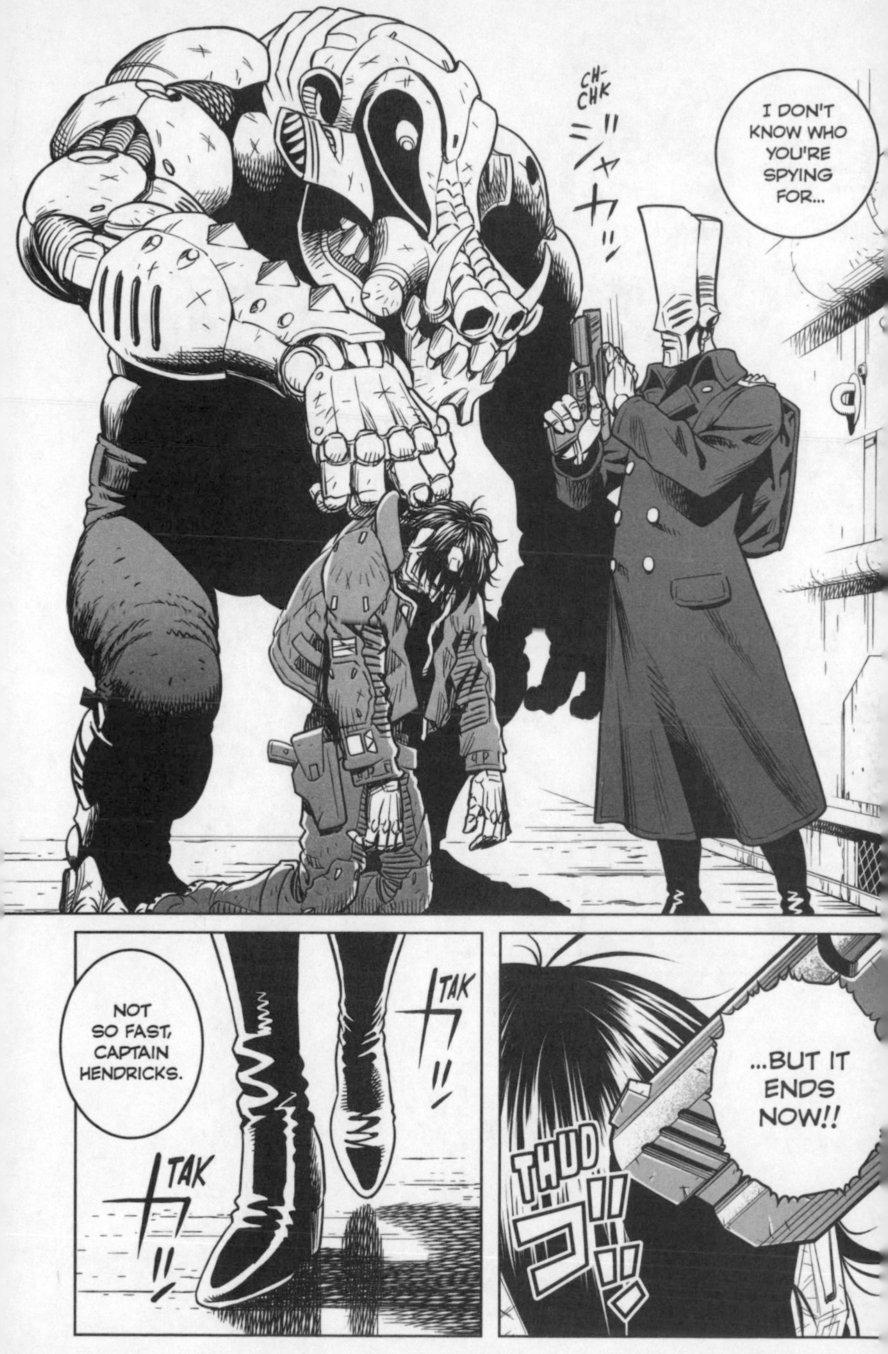
I DON'T KNOW WHO YOU'RE SPYING FOR...
CH-CHK
...BUT IT ENDS NOW!!
THUD
NOT SO FAST, CAPTAIN HENDRICKS.
TAK
TAK

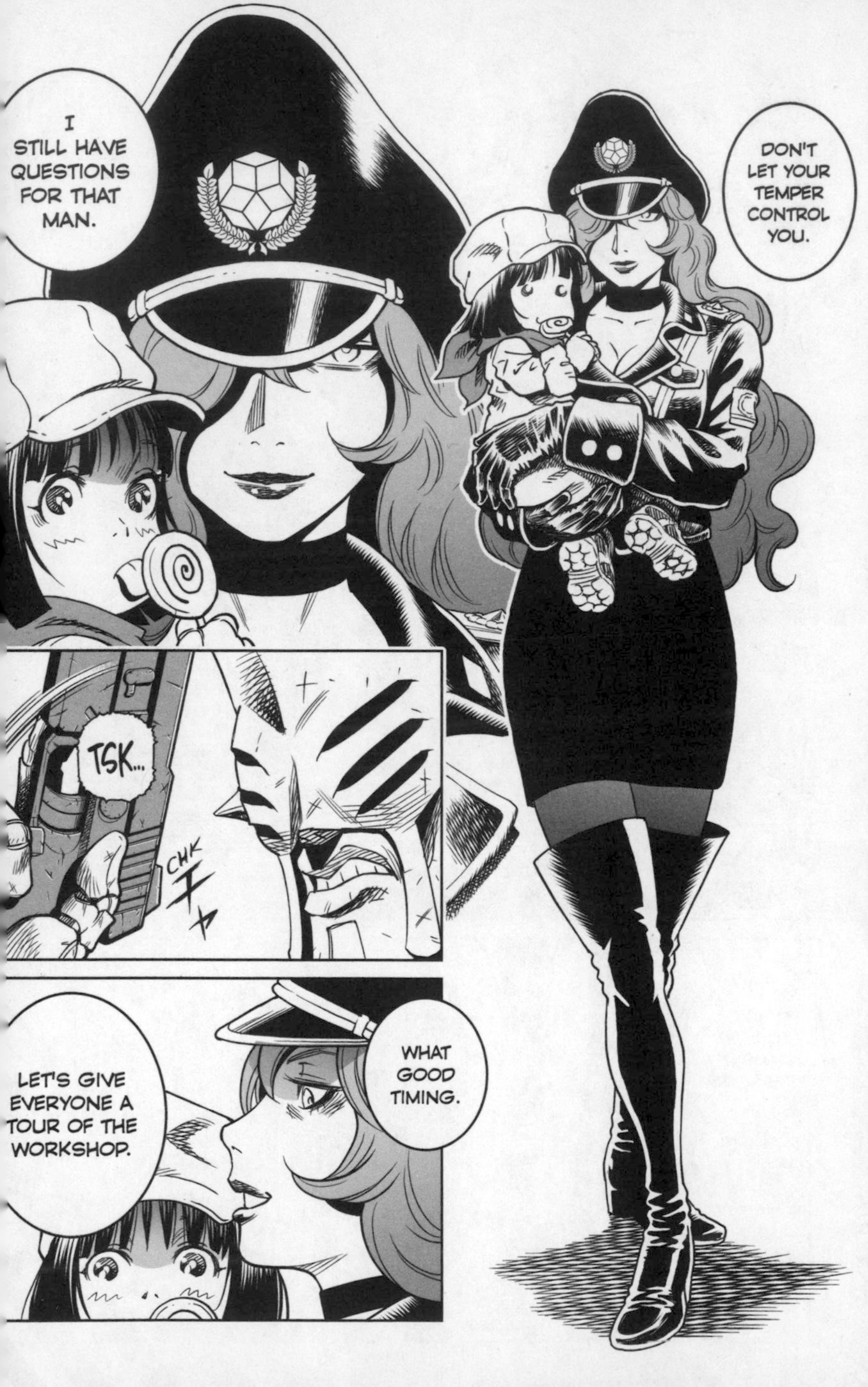
DON'T LET YOUR TEMPER CONTROL YOU.
I STILL HAVE QUESTIONS FOR THAT MAN.
TSK...
CHK
WHAT GOOD TIMING.
LET'S GIVE EVERYONE A TOUR OF THE WORKSHOP.

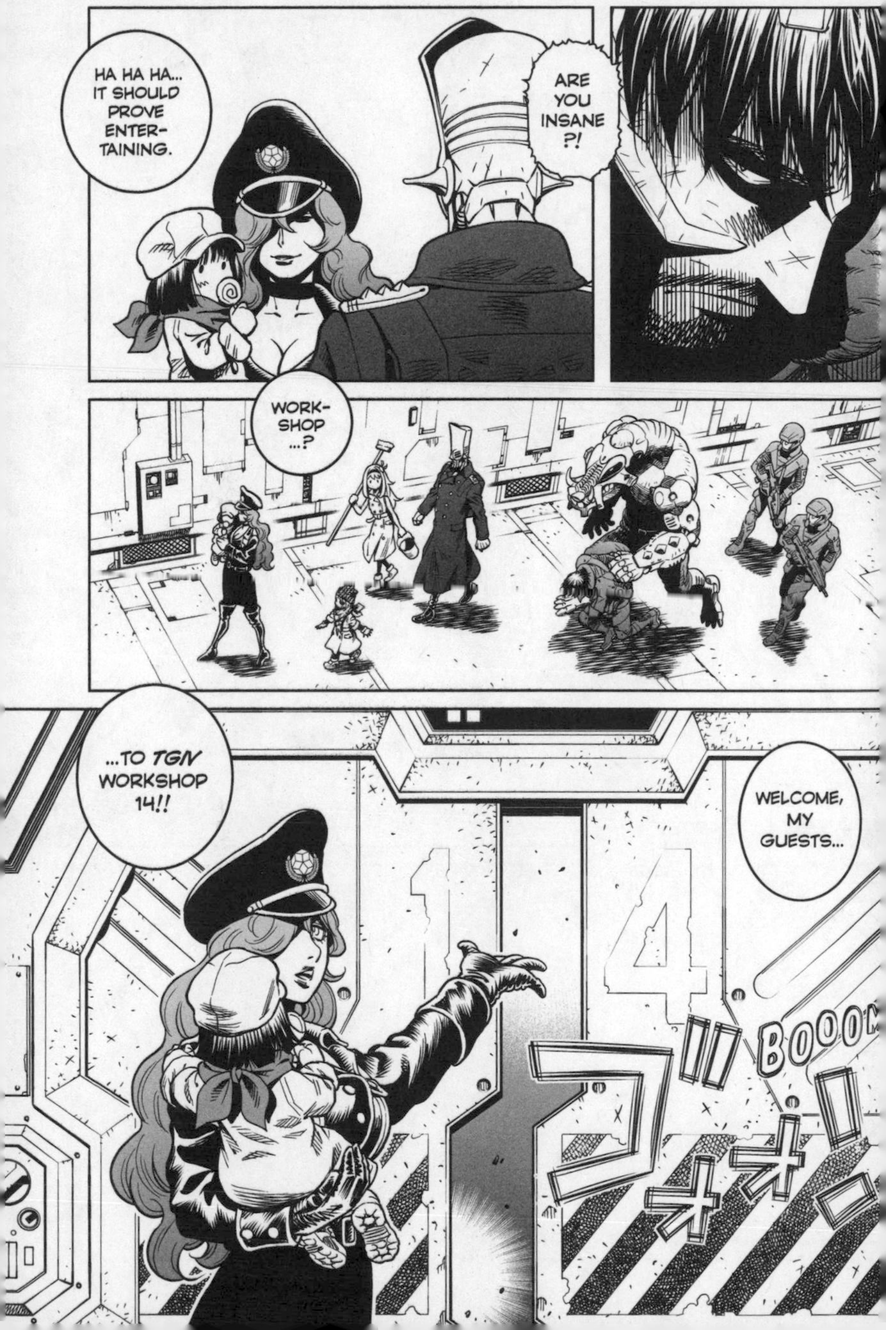
ARE YOU INSANE ?!
HA HA HA... IT SHOULD PROVE ENTER-TAINING.
WORK-SHOP ...?
WELCOME, MY GUESTS...
...TO *TGN* WORKSHOP 14!!
BOOO

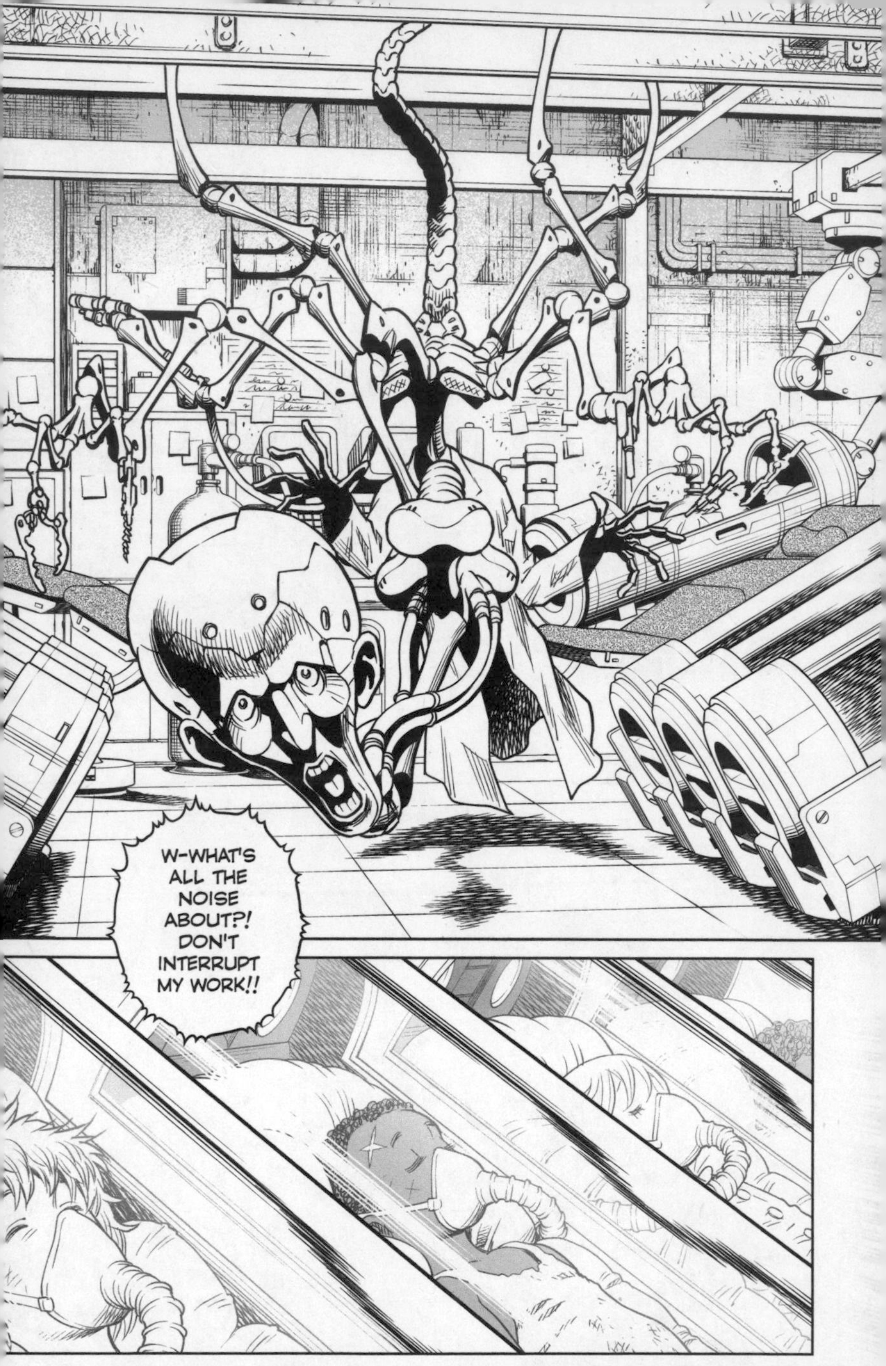
W-WHAT'S ALL THE NOISE ABOUT?! DON'T INTERRUPT MY WORK!!

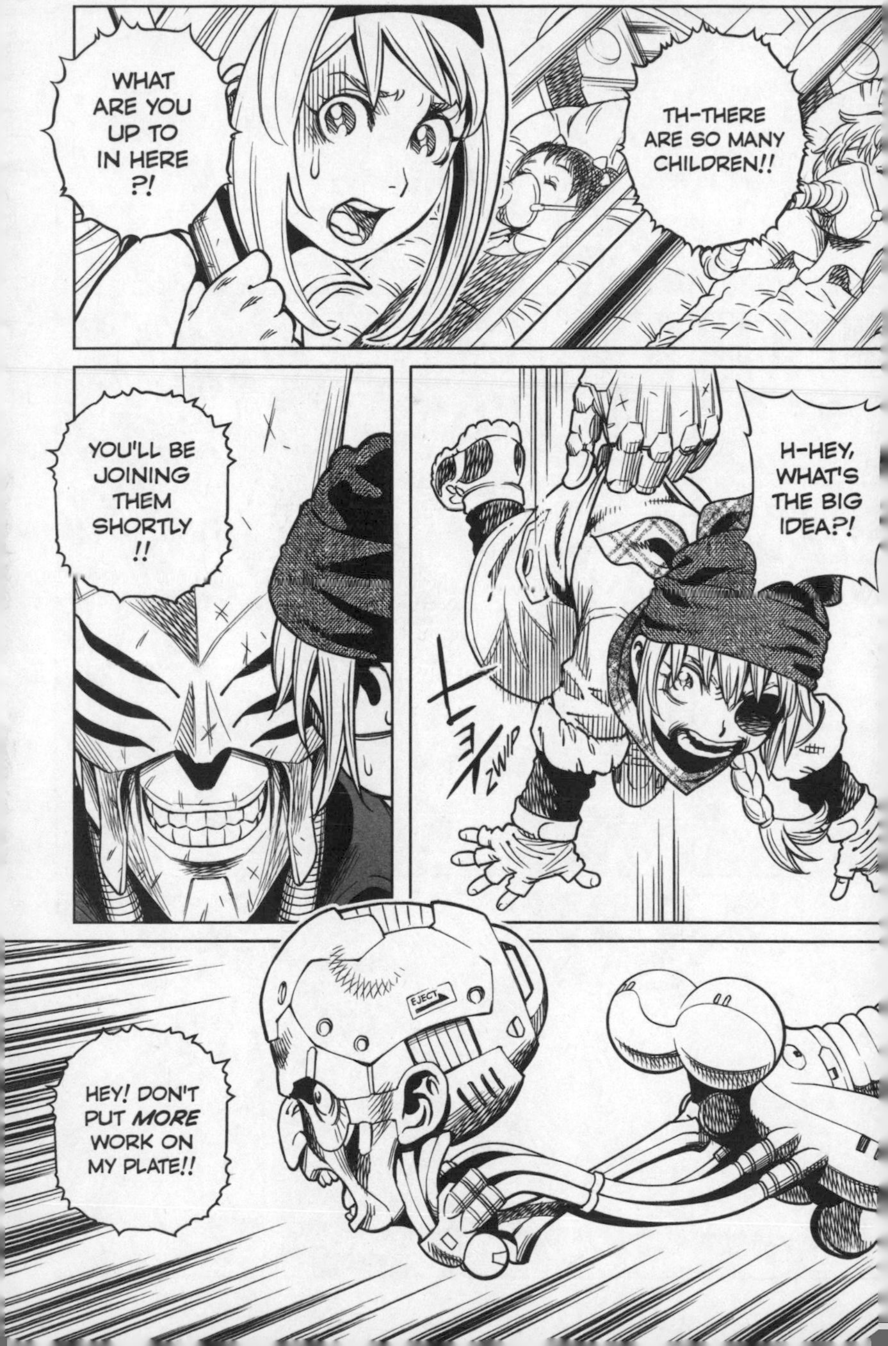
TH-THERE ARE SO MANY CHILDREN!!
WHAT ARE YOU UP TO IN HERE?!
H-HEY, WHAT'S THE BIG IDEA?!
ZWIP
YOU'LL BE JOINING THEM SHORTLY!!
EJECT
HEY! DON'T PUT *MORE* WORK ON MY PLATE!!

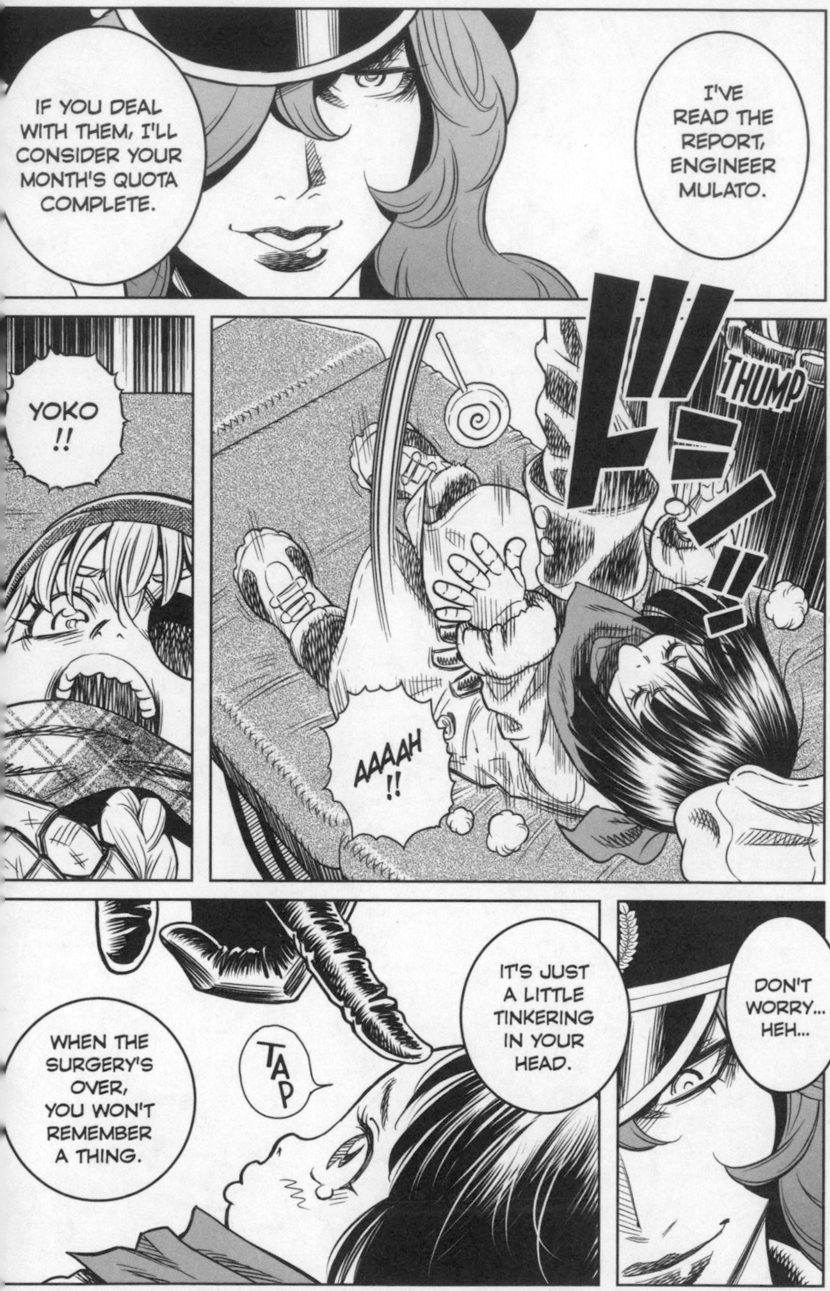
I'VE READ THE REPORT, ENGINEER MULATO.
IF YOU DEAL WITH THEM, I'LL CONSIDER YOUR MONTH'S QUOTA COMPLETE.
THUMP
AAAAH !!
YOKO !!
DON'T WORRY... HEH...
IT'S JUST A LITTLE TINKERING IN YOUR HEAD.
TAP
WHEN THE SURGERY'S OVER, YOU WON'T REMEMBER A THING.

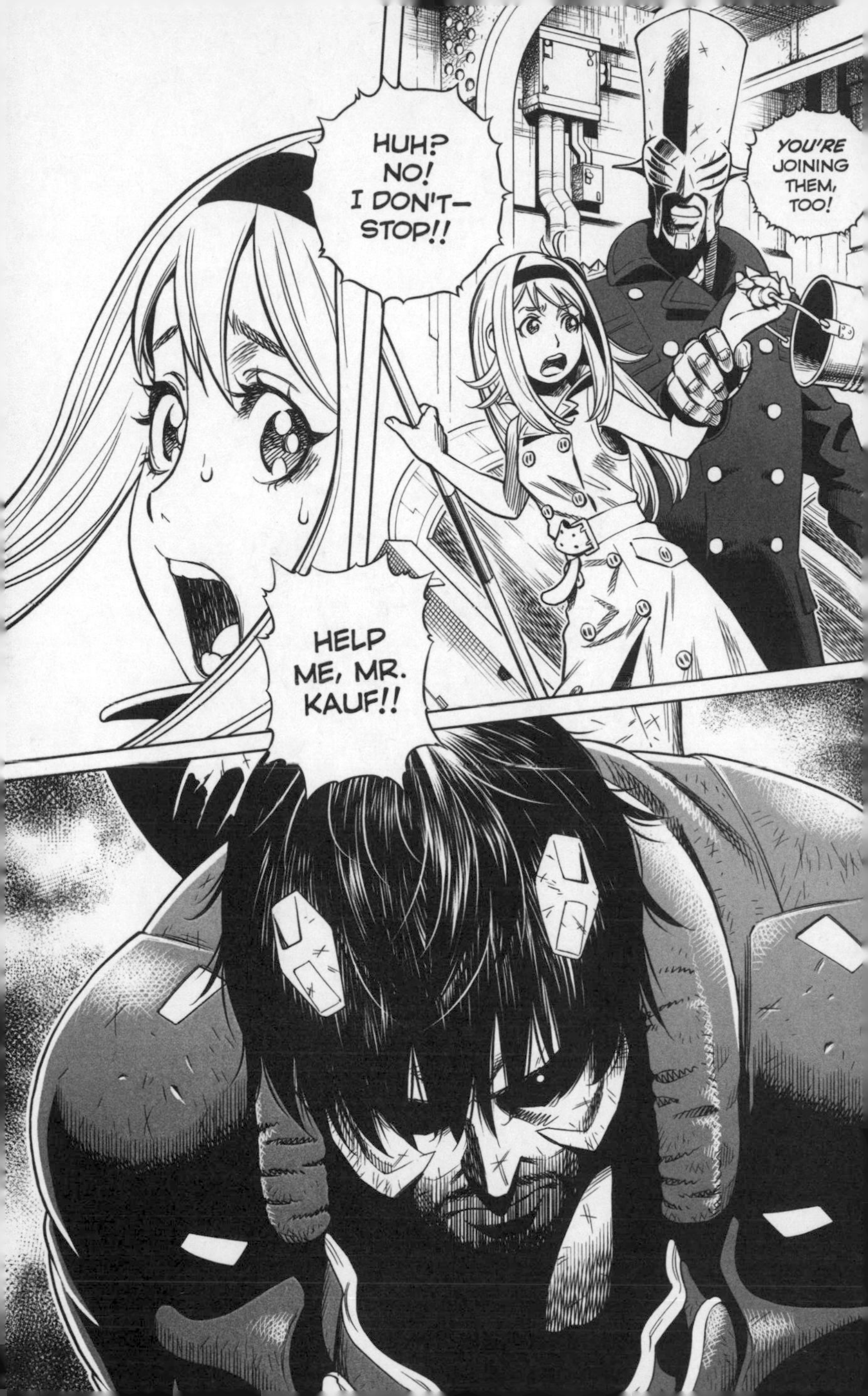
YOU'RE JOINING THEM, TOO!
HUH? NO! I DON'T— STOP!!
HELP ME, MR. KAUF!!

LOG:035
SPAKE THE MINSTRELS

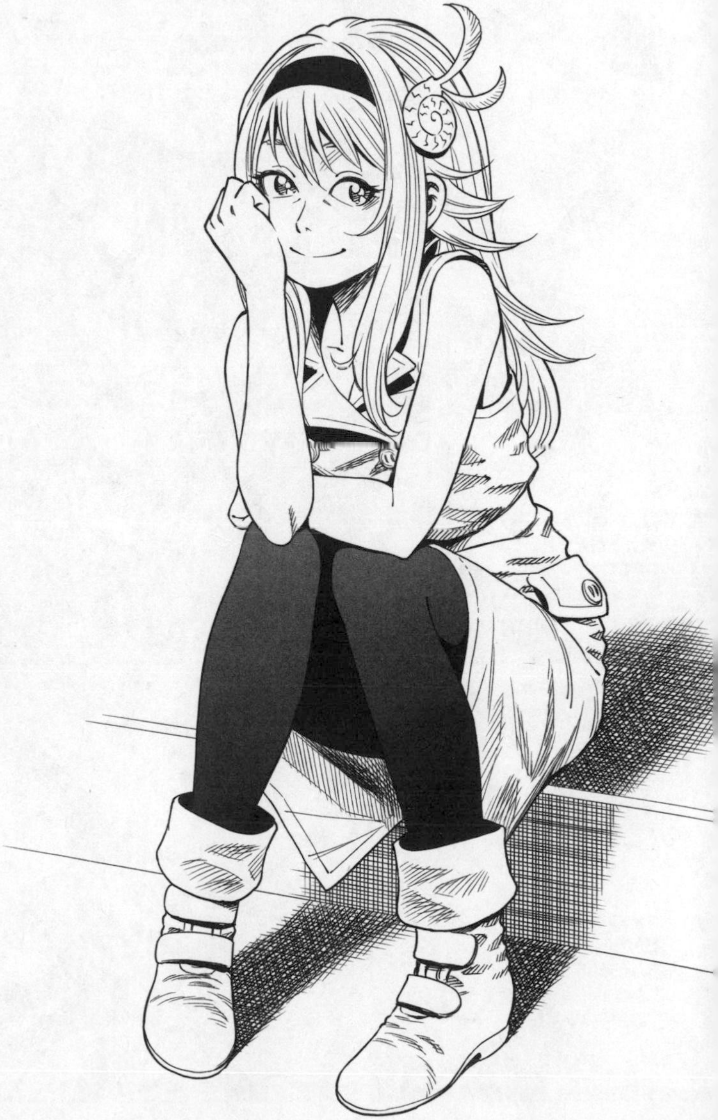

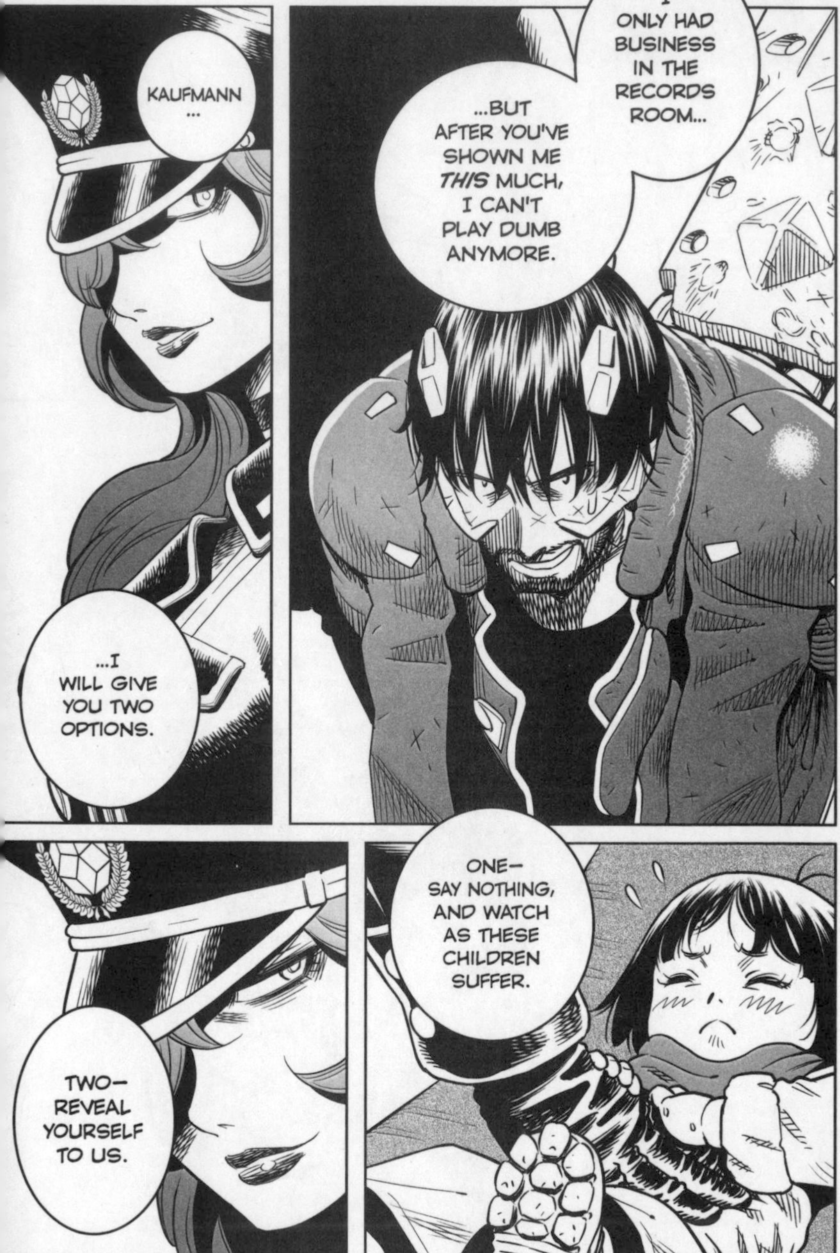
I ONLY HAD BUSINESS IN THE RECORDS ROOM...
...BUT AFTER YOU'VE SHOWN ME *THIS* MUCH, I CAN'T PLAY DUMB ANYMORE.
KAUFMANN ...
...I WILL GIVE YOU TWO OPTIONS.
ONE— SAY NOTHING, AND WATCH AS THESE CHILDREN SUFFER.
TWO— REVEAL YOURSELF TO US.

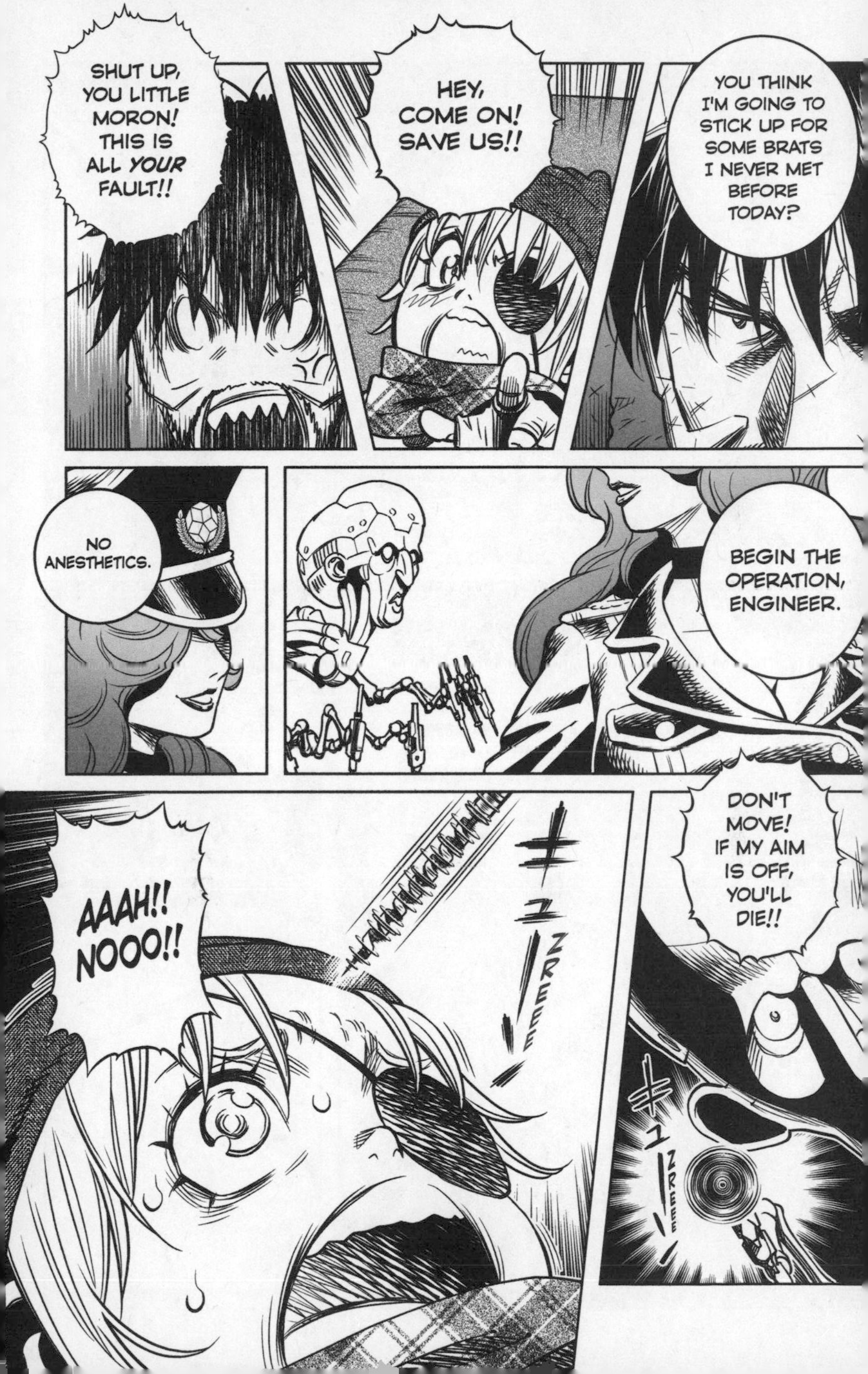
YOU THINK I'M GOING TO STICK UP FOR SOME BRATS I NEVER MET BEFORE TODAY?
HEY, COME ON! SAVE US!!
SHUT UP, YOU LITTLE MORON! THIS IS ALL *YOUR* FAULT!!
BEGIN THE OPERATION, ENGINEER.
NO ANESTHETICS.
DON'T MOVE! IF MY AIM IS OFF, YOU'LL DIE!!
ZREEE
AAAH!! NOOO!!
ZREEE

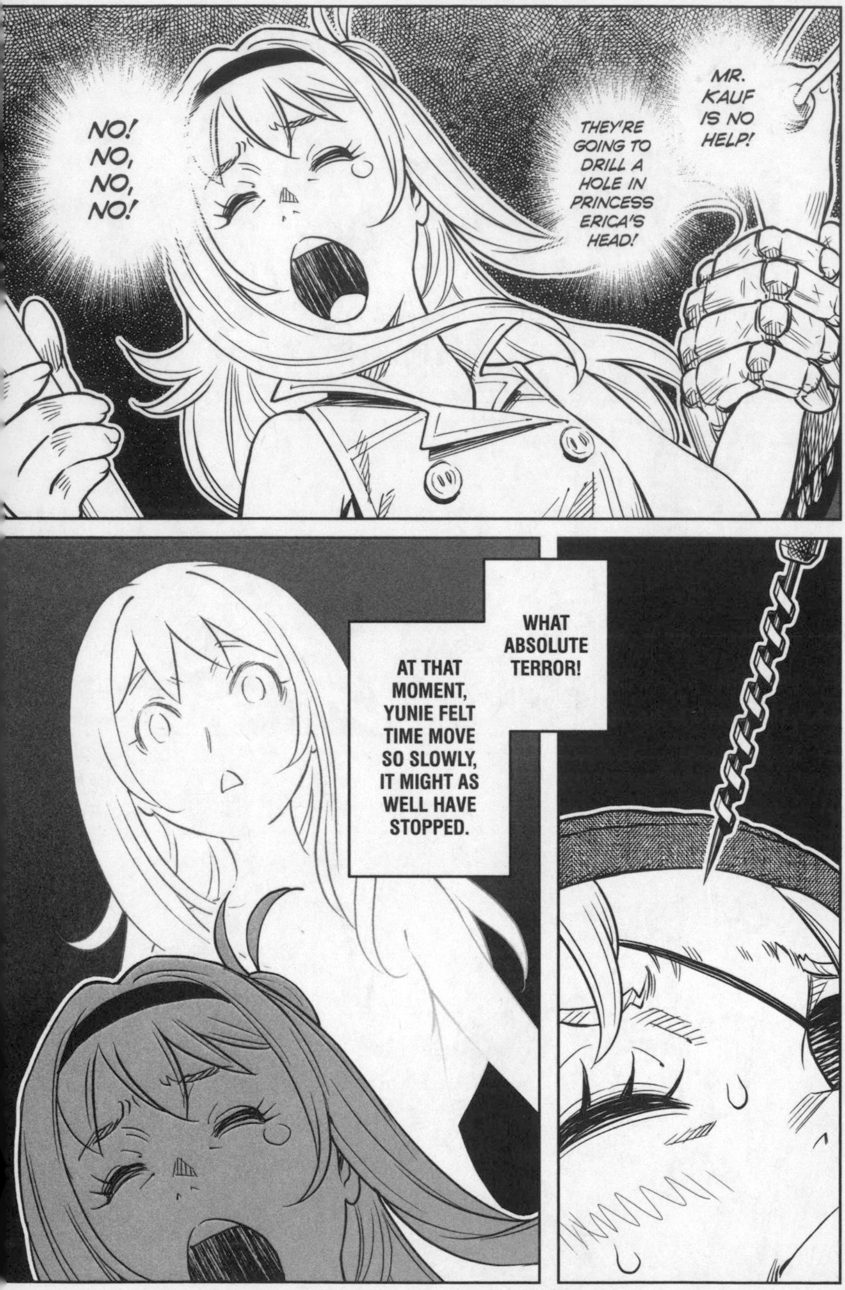
MR. KAUF IS NO HELP!
THEY'RE GOING TO DRILL A HOLE IN PRINCESS ERICA'S HEAD!
NO! NO, NO, NO, NO!
WHAT ABSOLUTE TERROR!
AT THAT MOMENT, YUNIE FELT TIME MOVE SO SLOWLY, IT MIGHT AS WELL HAVE STOPPED.

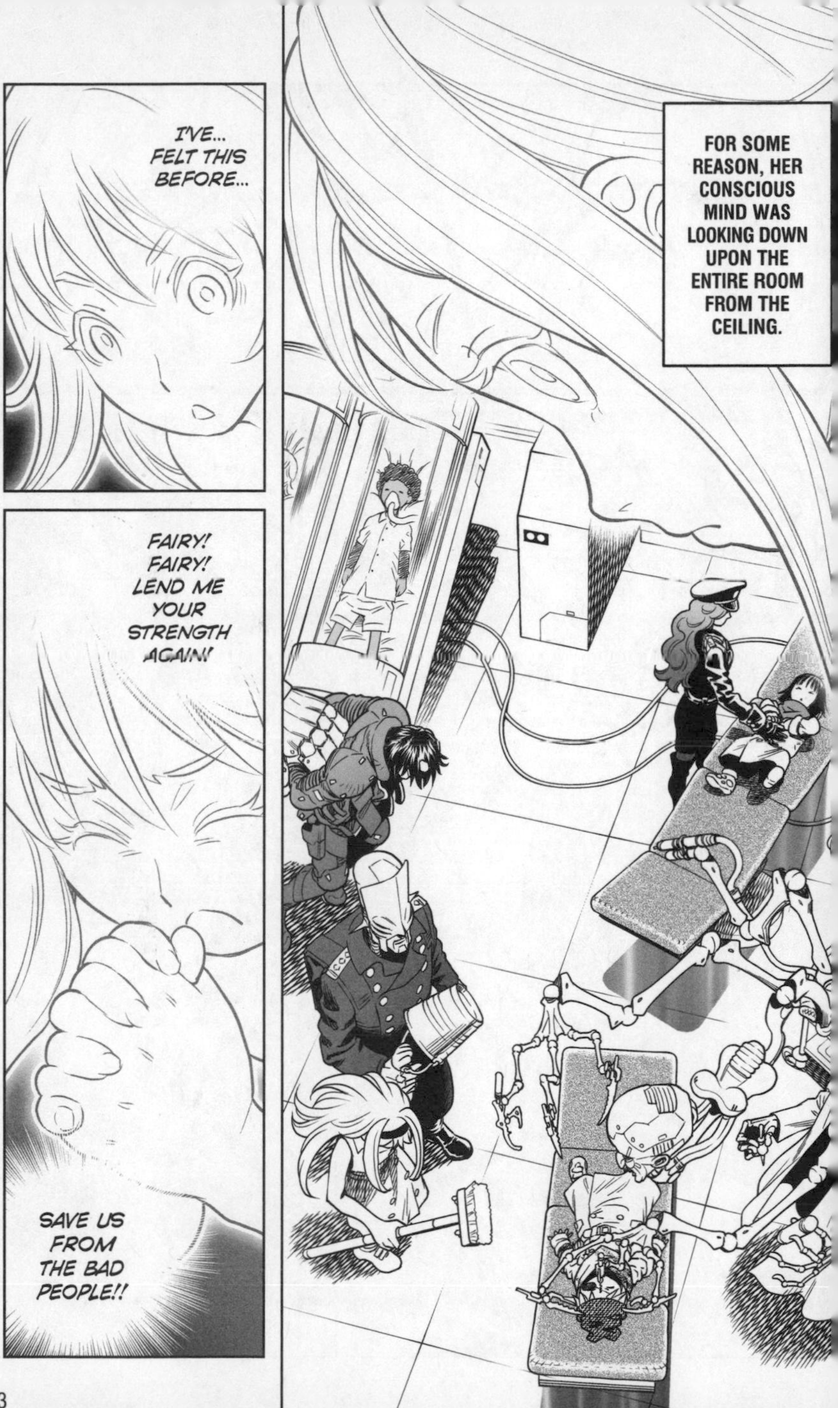
FOR SOME REASON, HER CONSCIOUS MIND WAS LOOKING DOWN UPON THE ENTIRE ROOM FROM THE CEILING.
I'VE... FELT THIS BEFORE...
FAIRY! FAIRY! LEND ME YOUR STRENGTH AGAIN!
SAVE US FROM THE BAD PEOPLE!!

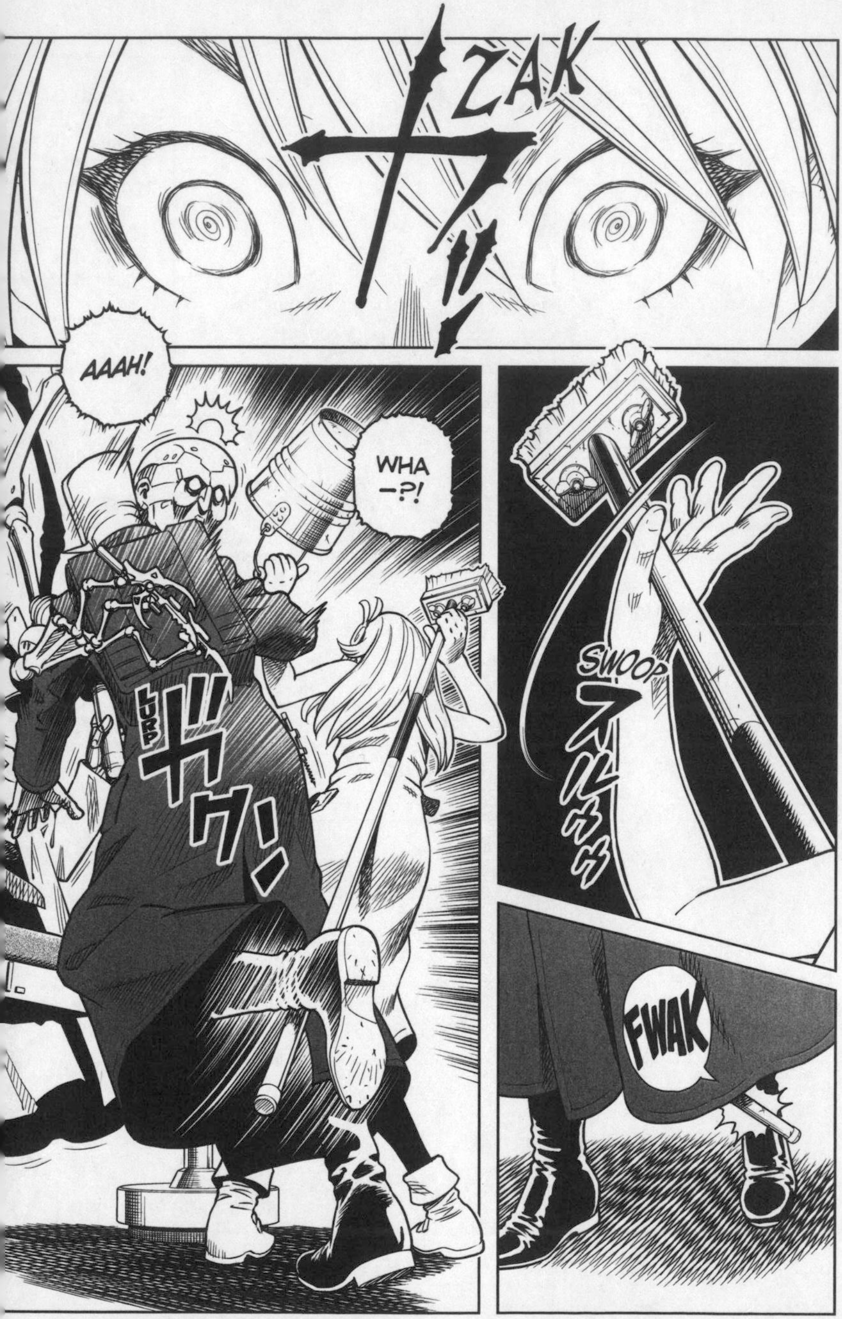
ZAK
SWOOP
FWAK
AAAH!
WHA
–?!
LURP

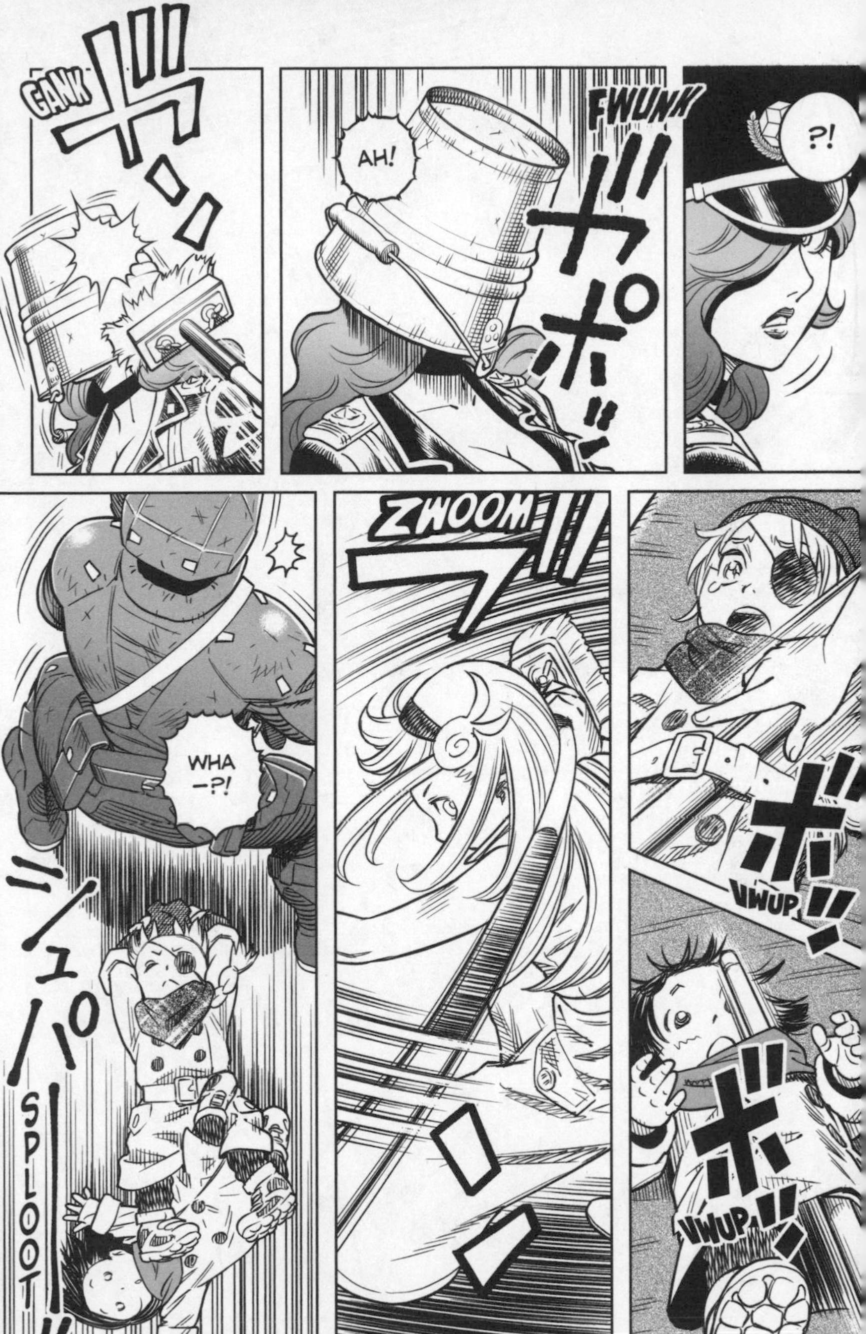
?!
FWUNK
AH!
GANK
VWUP!!
VWUP!!
ZWOOM
WHA—?!
SPLOOT!!

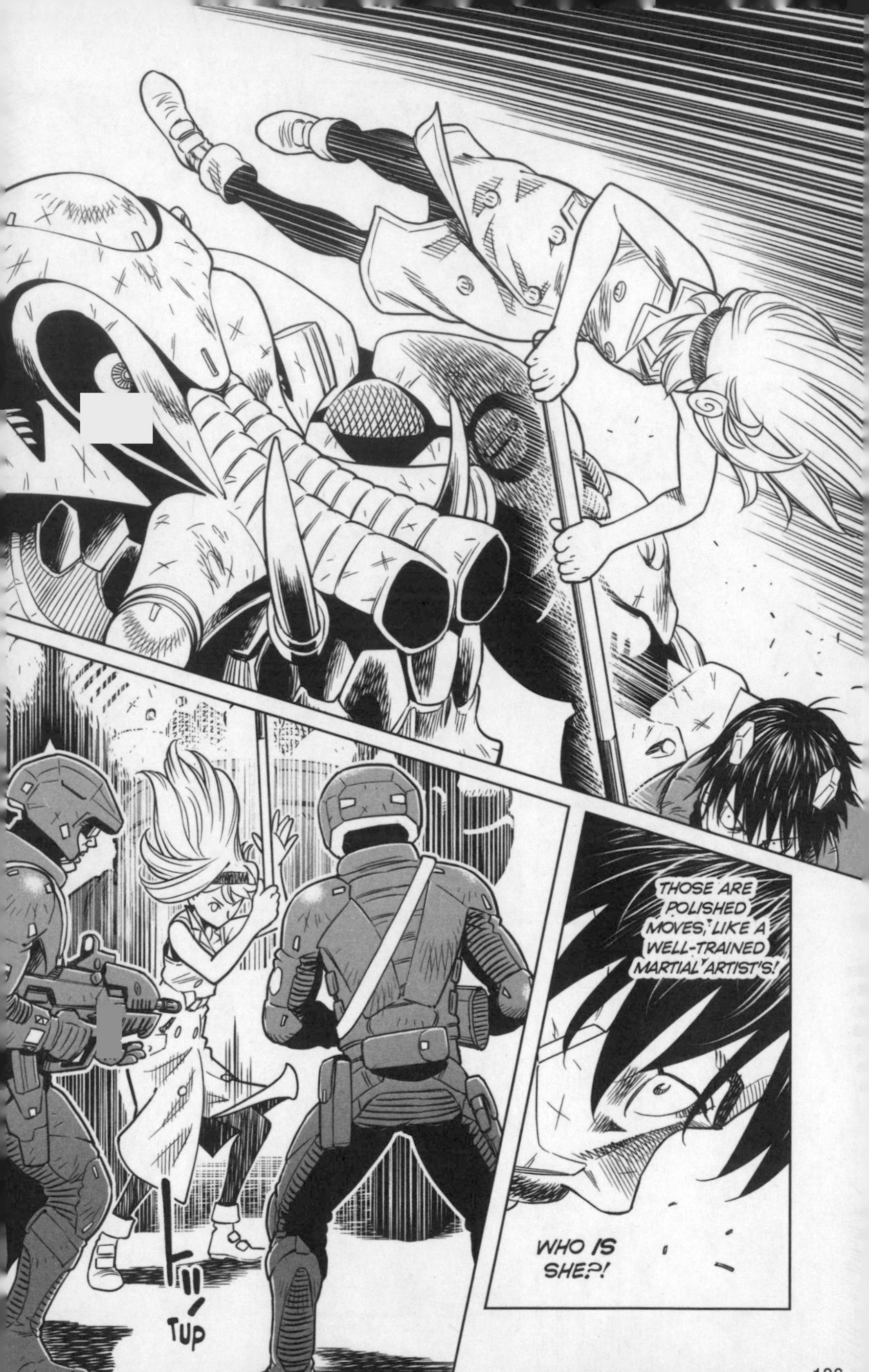
THOSE ARE POLISHED MOVES, LIKE A WELL-TRAINED MARTIAL ARTIST'S!
WHO IS SHE?!
TUP

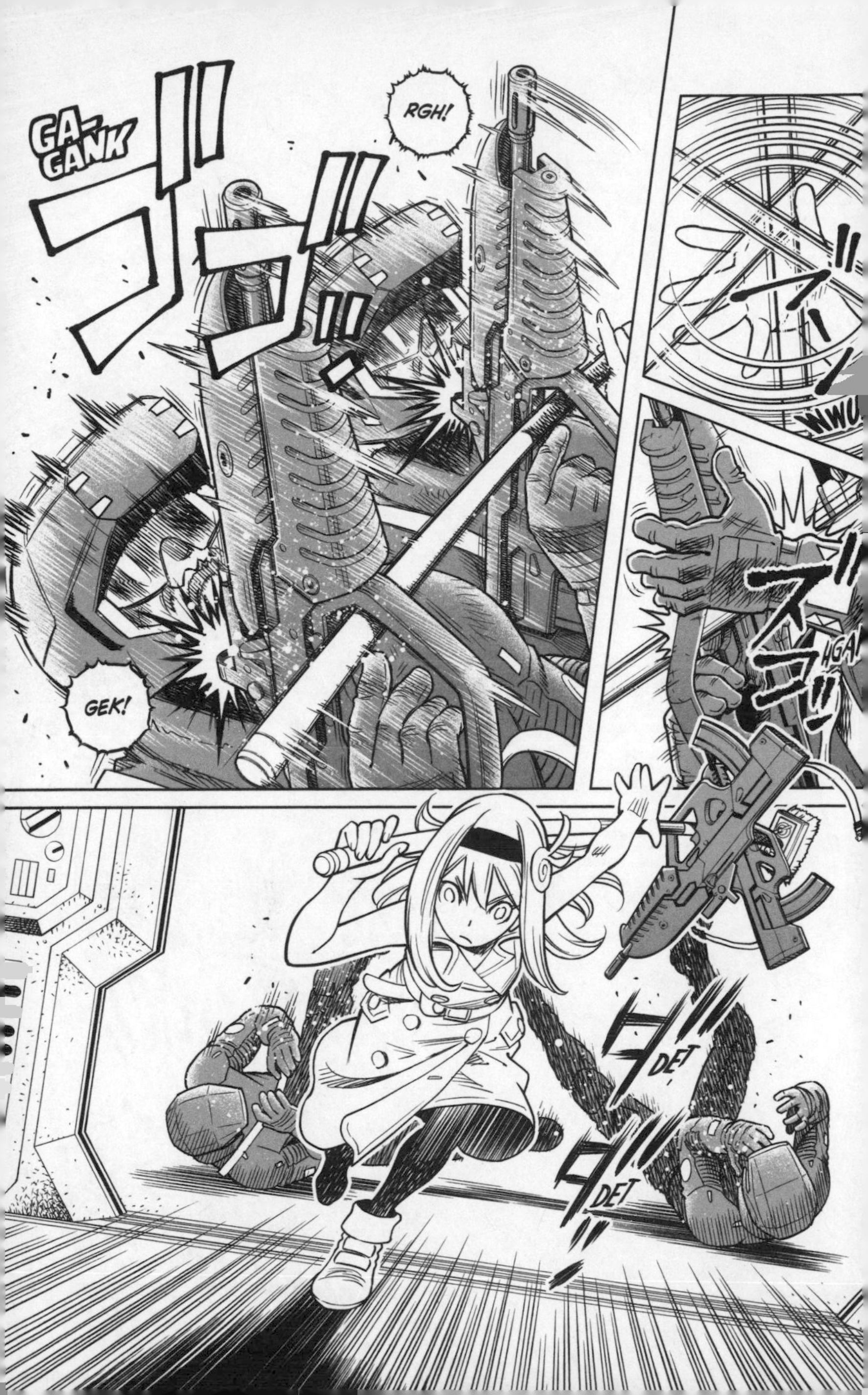
GA-GANK
RGH!
GEK!
DET
DET

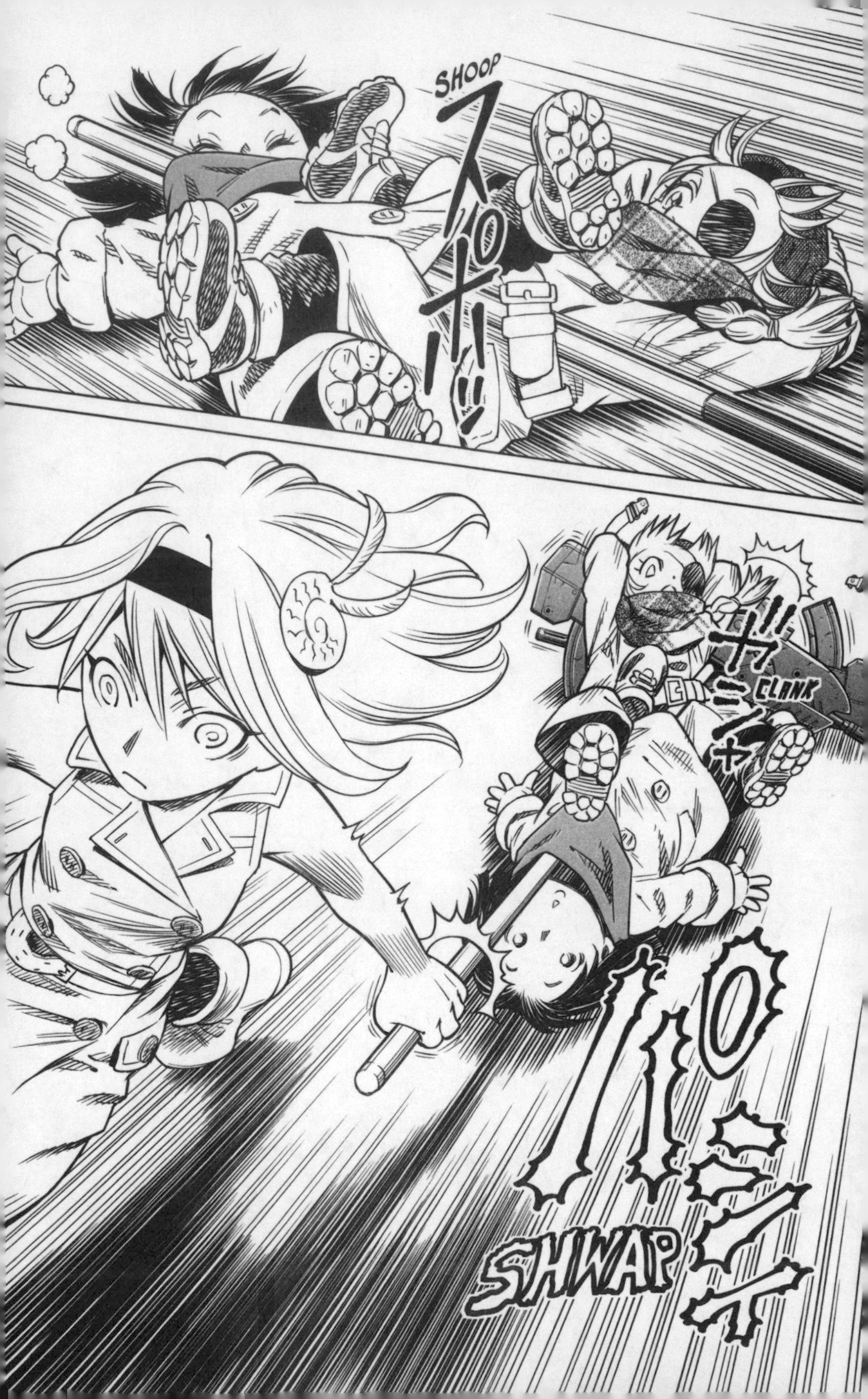
SHOOP
CLANK
SHWAP

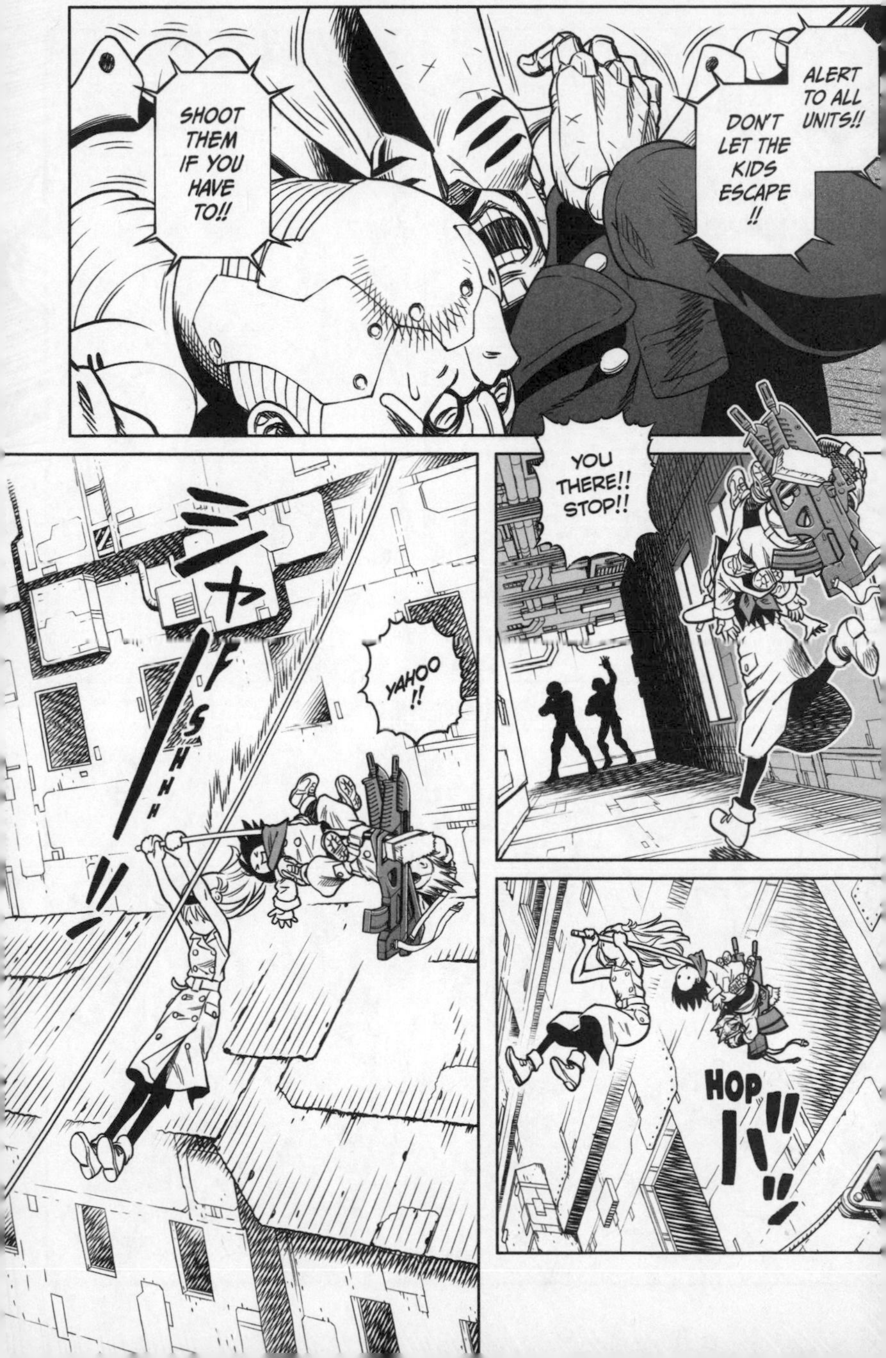
ALERT TO ALL UNITS!!
DON'T LET THE KIDS ESCAPE !!
SHOOT THEM IF YOU HAVE TO!!
YOU THERE!! STOP!!
HOP
FSHHH
YAHOO !!

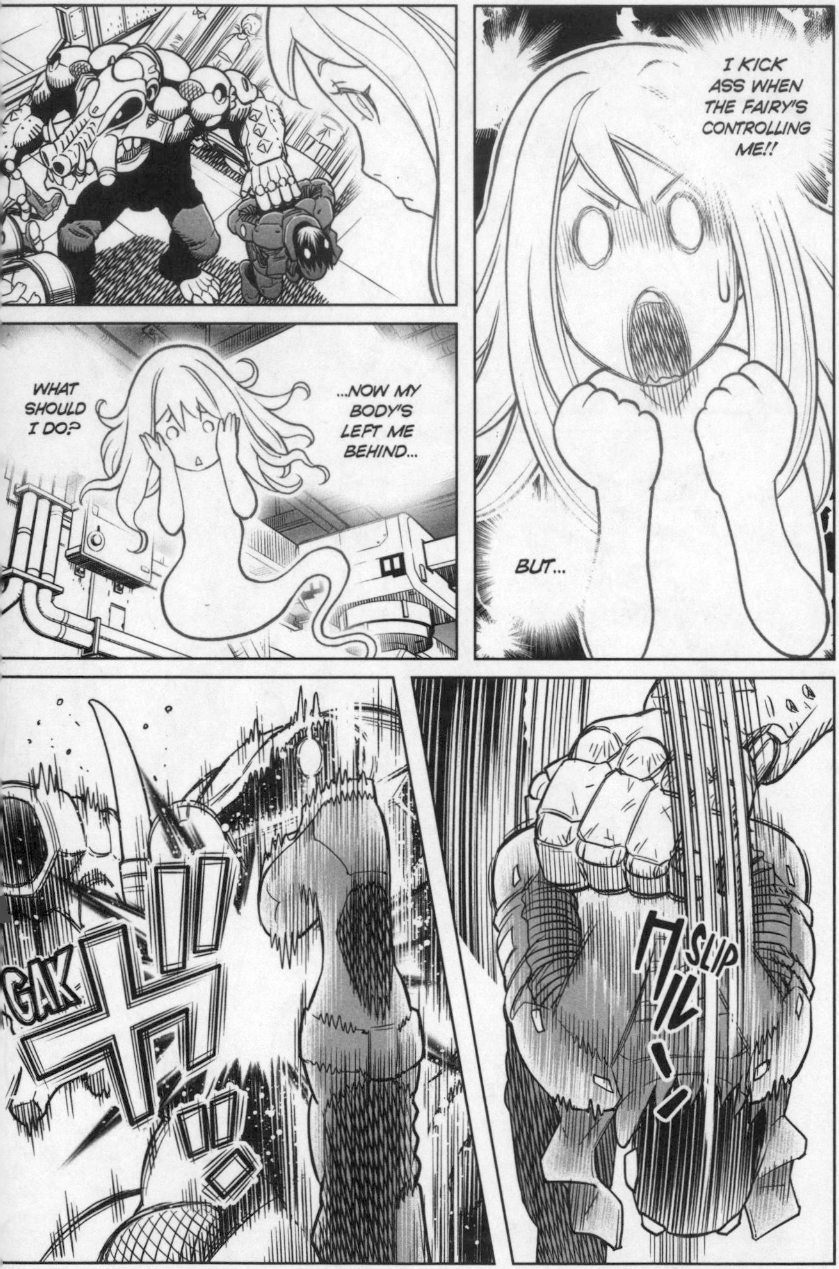
I KICK ASS WHEN THE FAIRY'S CONTROLLING ME!!
BUT...
...NOW MY BODY'S LEFT ME BEHIND...
WHAT SHOULD I DO?
SLIP
GAK

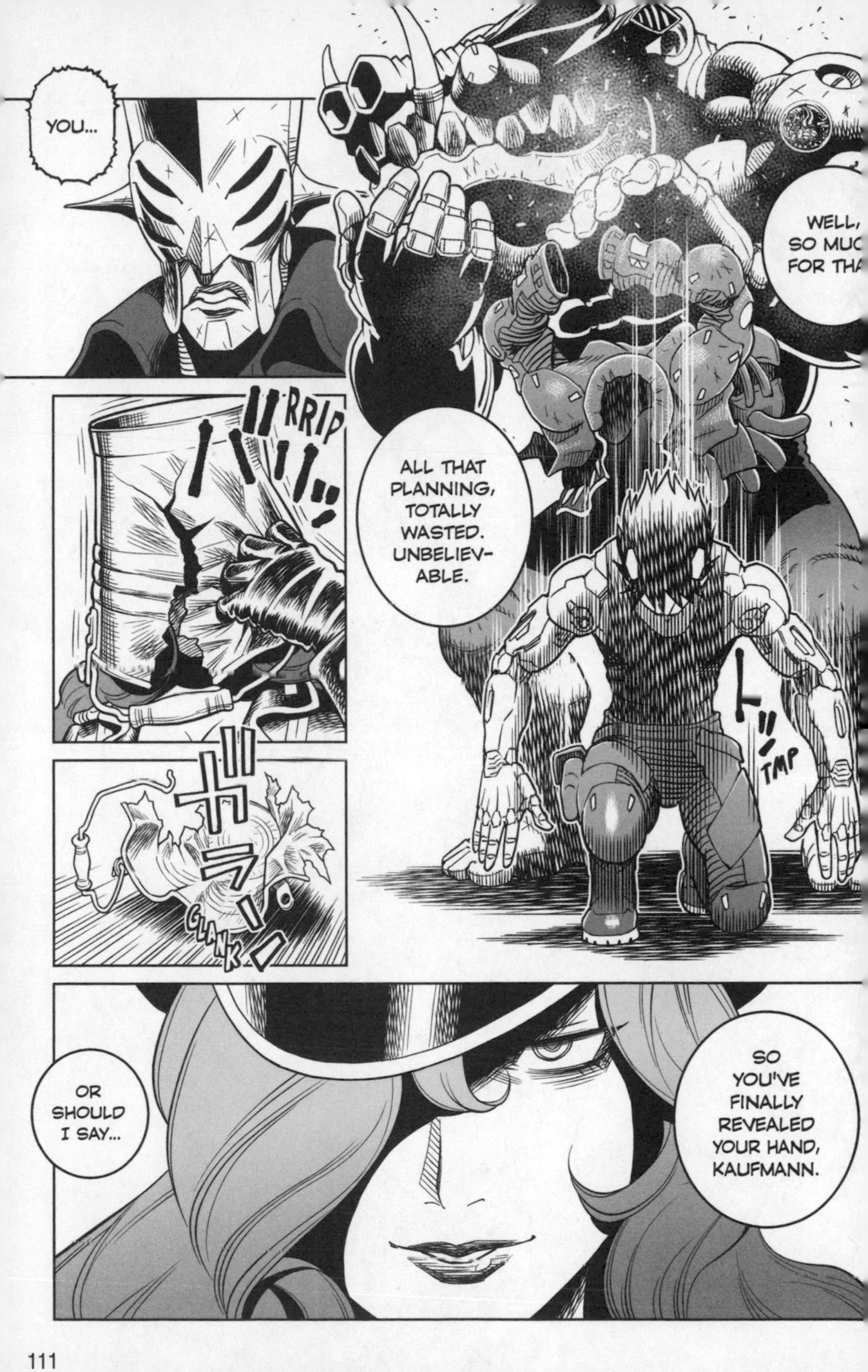
WELL, SO MUC FOR THA
ALL THAT PLANNING, TOTALLY WASTED. UNBELIEV-ABLE.
TMP
YOU...
RRIP
GLANK
SO YOU'VE FINALLY REVEALED YOUR HAND, KAUFMANN.
OR SHOULD I SAY...

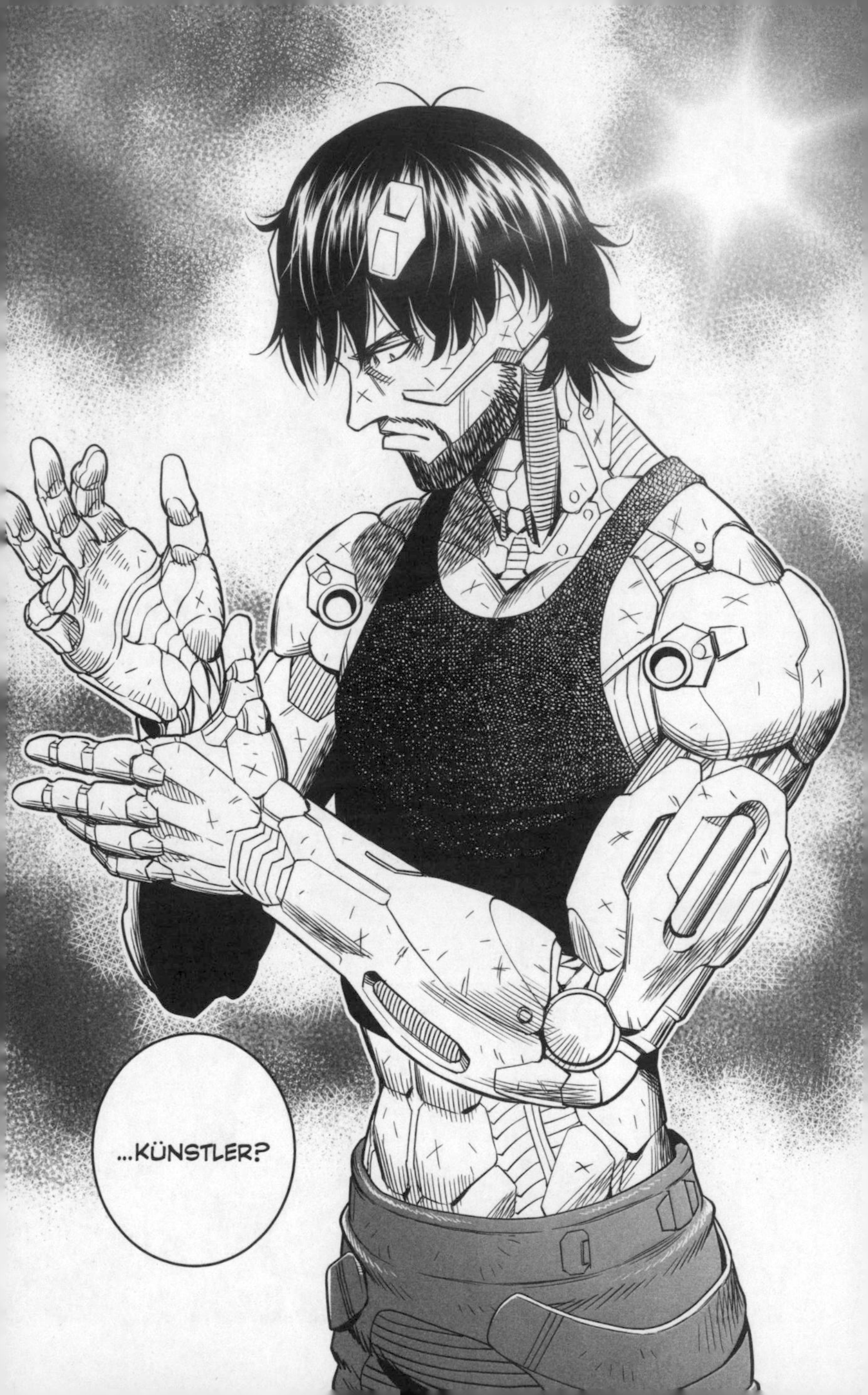
...KÜNSTLER?

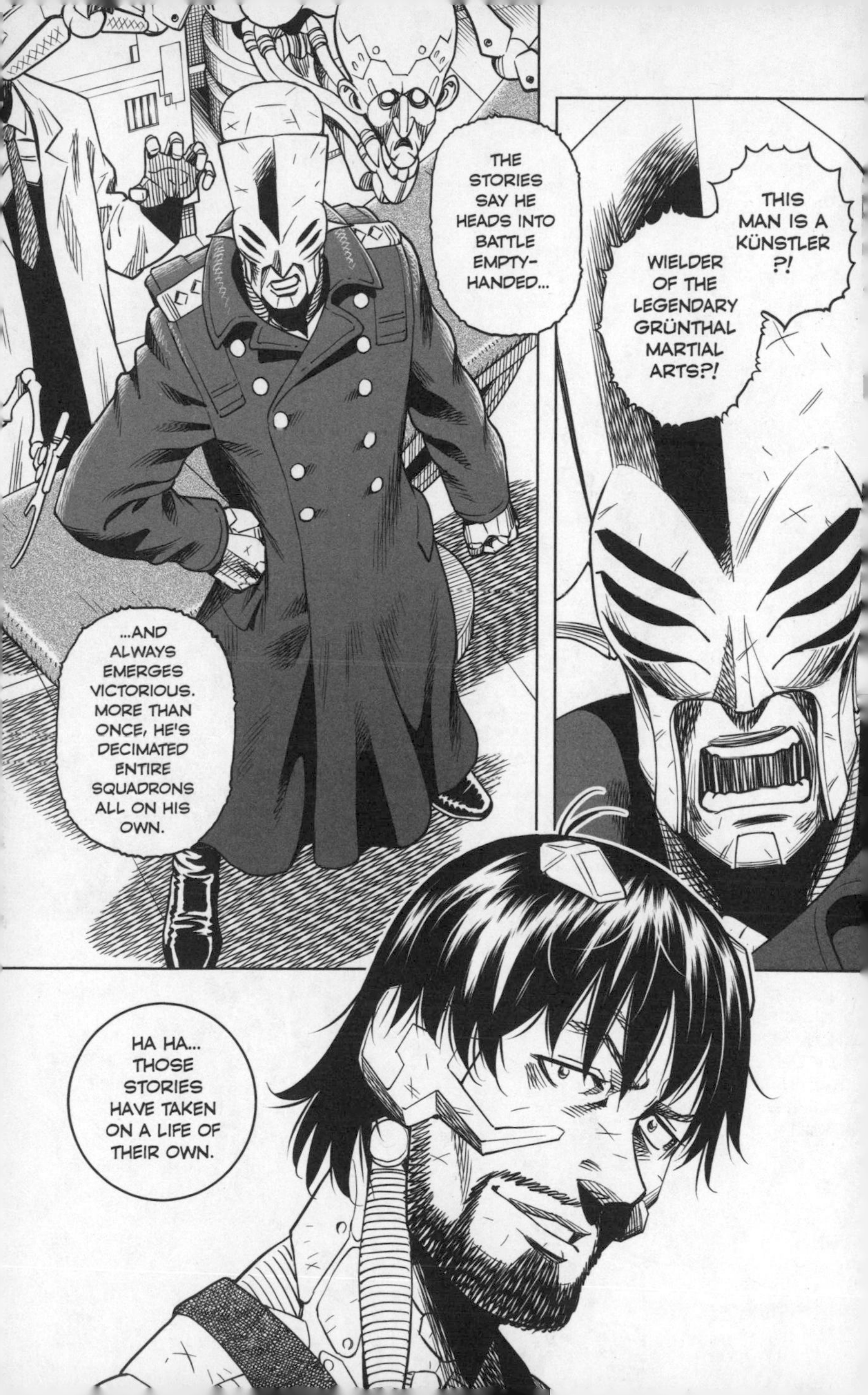
THIS MAN IS A KÜNSTLER ?!
WIELDER OF THE LEGENDARY GRÜNTHAL MARTIAL ARTS?!
THE STORIES SAY HE HEADS INTO BATTLE EMPTY-HANDED...
...AND ALWAYS EMERGES VICTORIOUS. MORE THAN ONCE, HE'S DECIMATED ENTIRE SQUADRONS ALL ON HIS OWN.
HA HA... THOSE STORIES HAVE TAKEN ON A LIFE OF THEIR OWN.

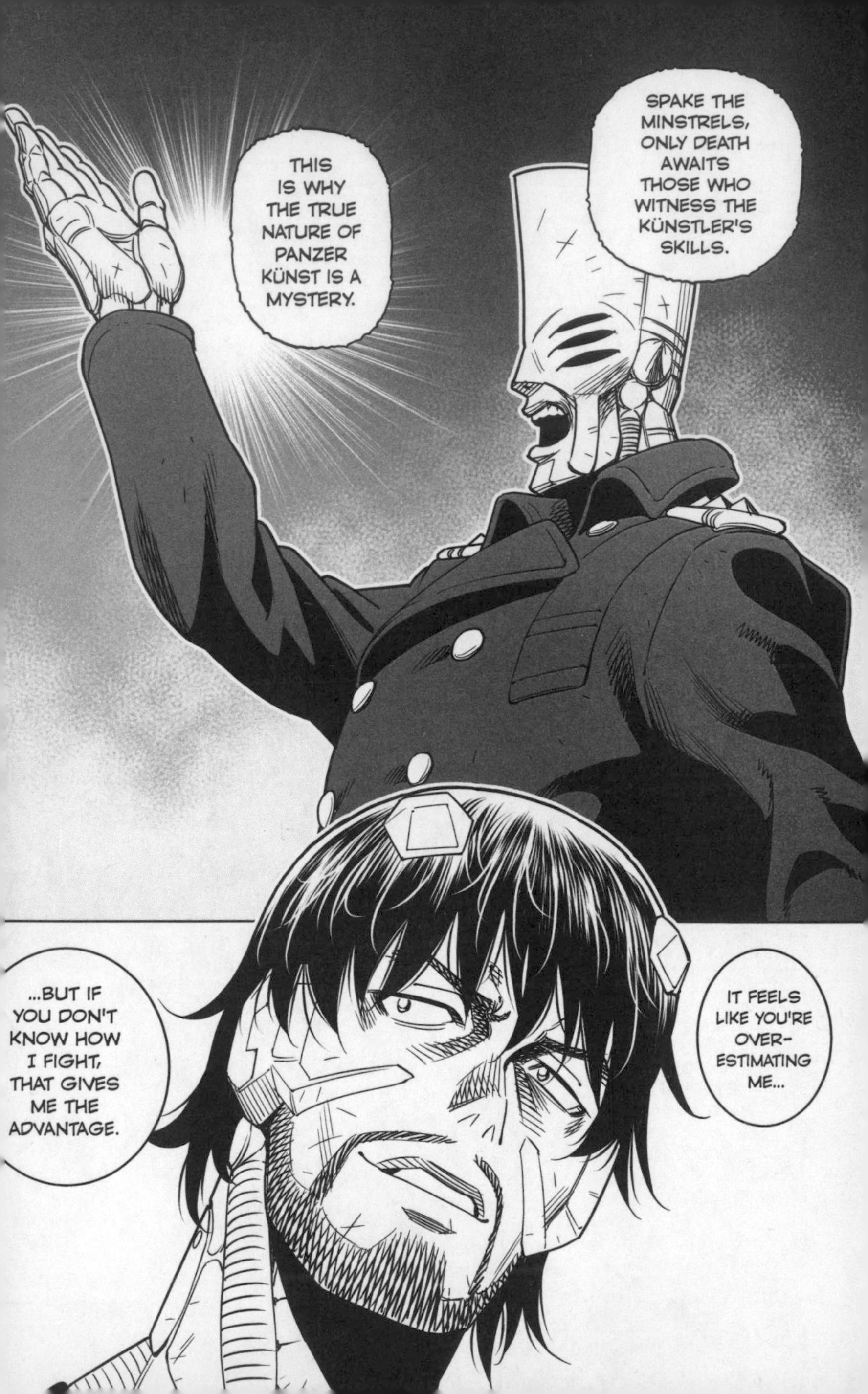
SPAKE THE MINSTRELS, ONLY DEATH AWAITS THOSE WHO WITNESS THE KÜNSTLER'S SKILLS.
THIS IS WHY THE TRUE NATURE OF PANZER KÜNST IS A MYSTERY.
IT FEELS LIKE YOU'RE OVER-ESTIMATING ME...
...BUT IF YOU DON'T KNOW HOW I FIGHT, THAT GIVES ME THE ADVANTAGE.

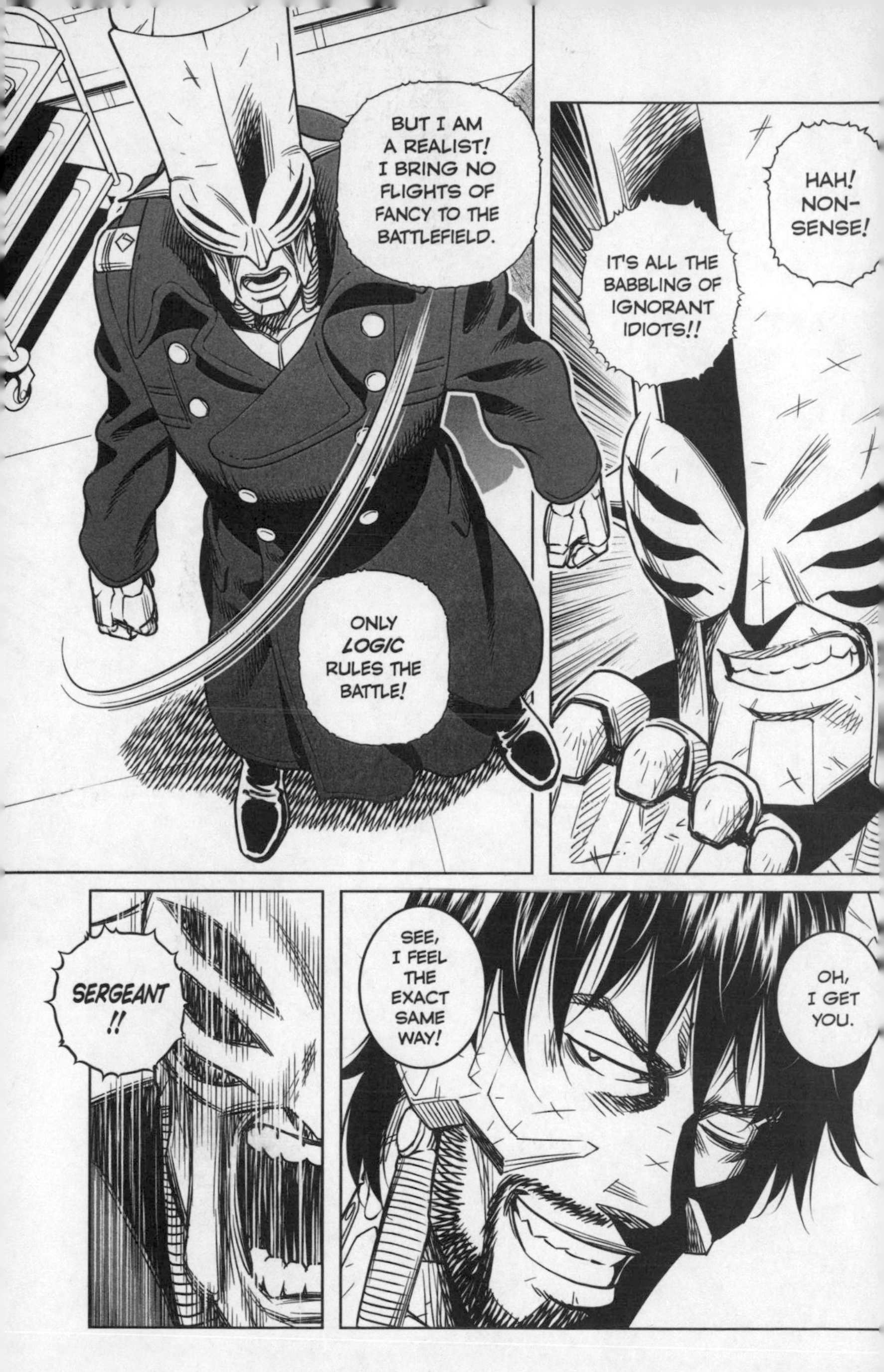
HAH! NON-SENSE!
IT'S ALL THE BABBLING OF IGNORANT IDIOTS!!
BUT I AM A REALIST! I BRING NO FLIGHTS OF FANCY TO THE BATTLEFIELD.
ONLY *LOGIC* RULES THE BATTLE!
OH, I GET YOU.
SEE, I FEEL THE EXACT SAME WAY!
SERGEANT !!

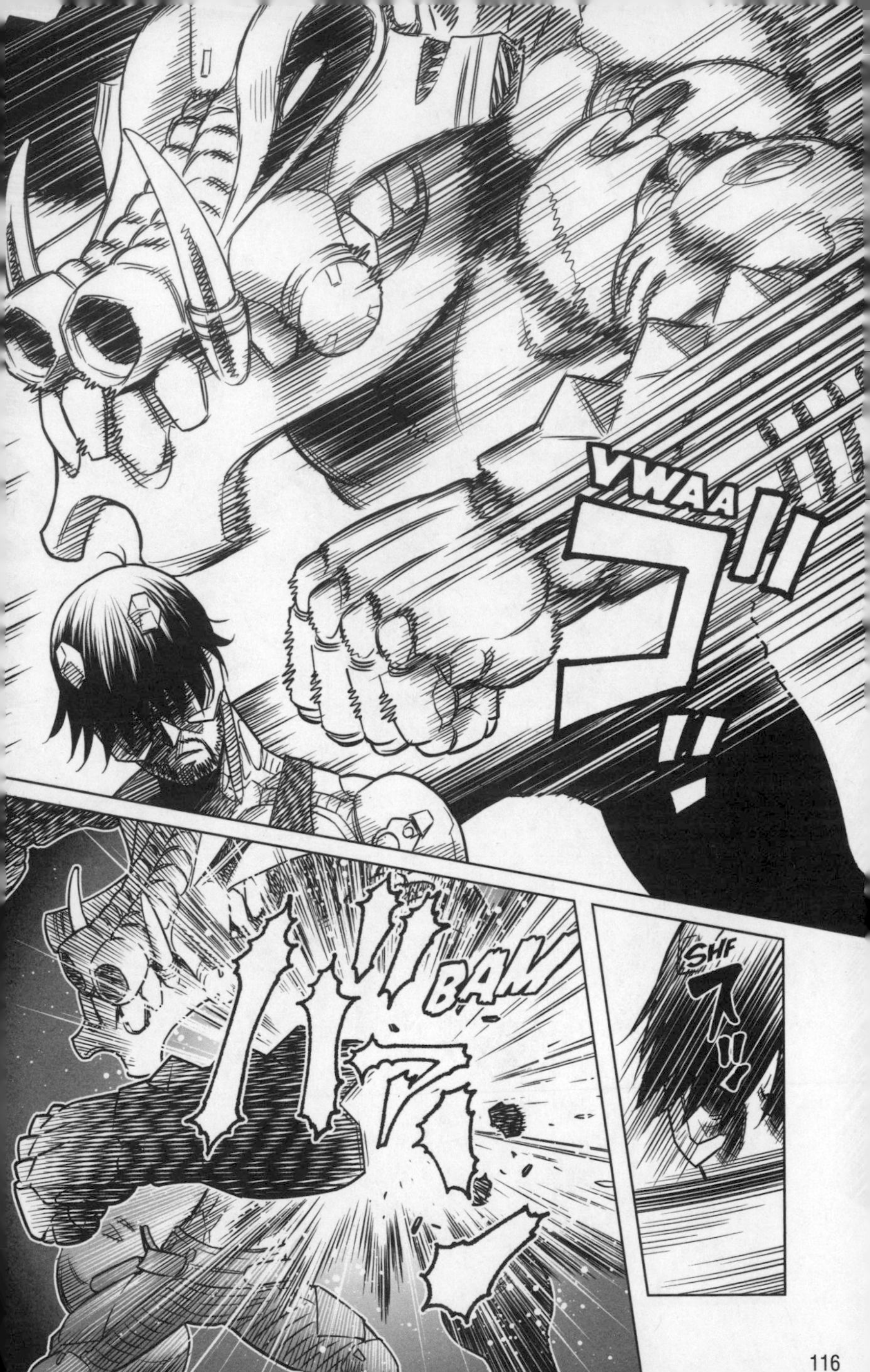
VWAA
SHF
BAM

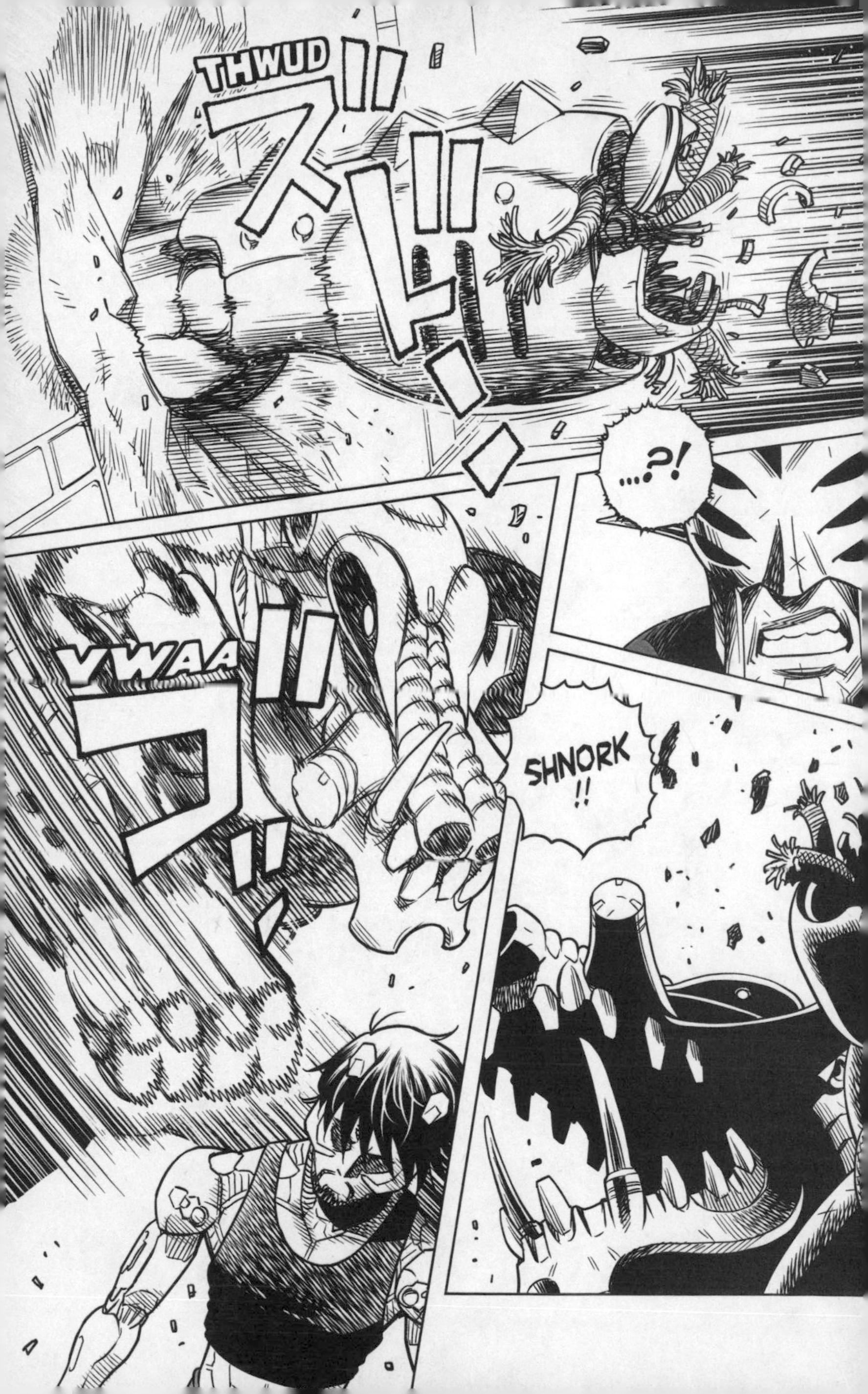
THWUD
ズドッ
....?!
SHNORK !!
YWAA
ゴッ

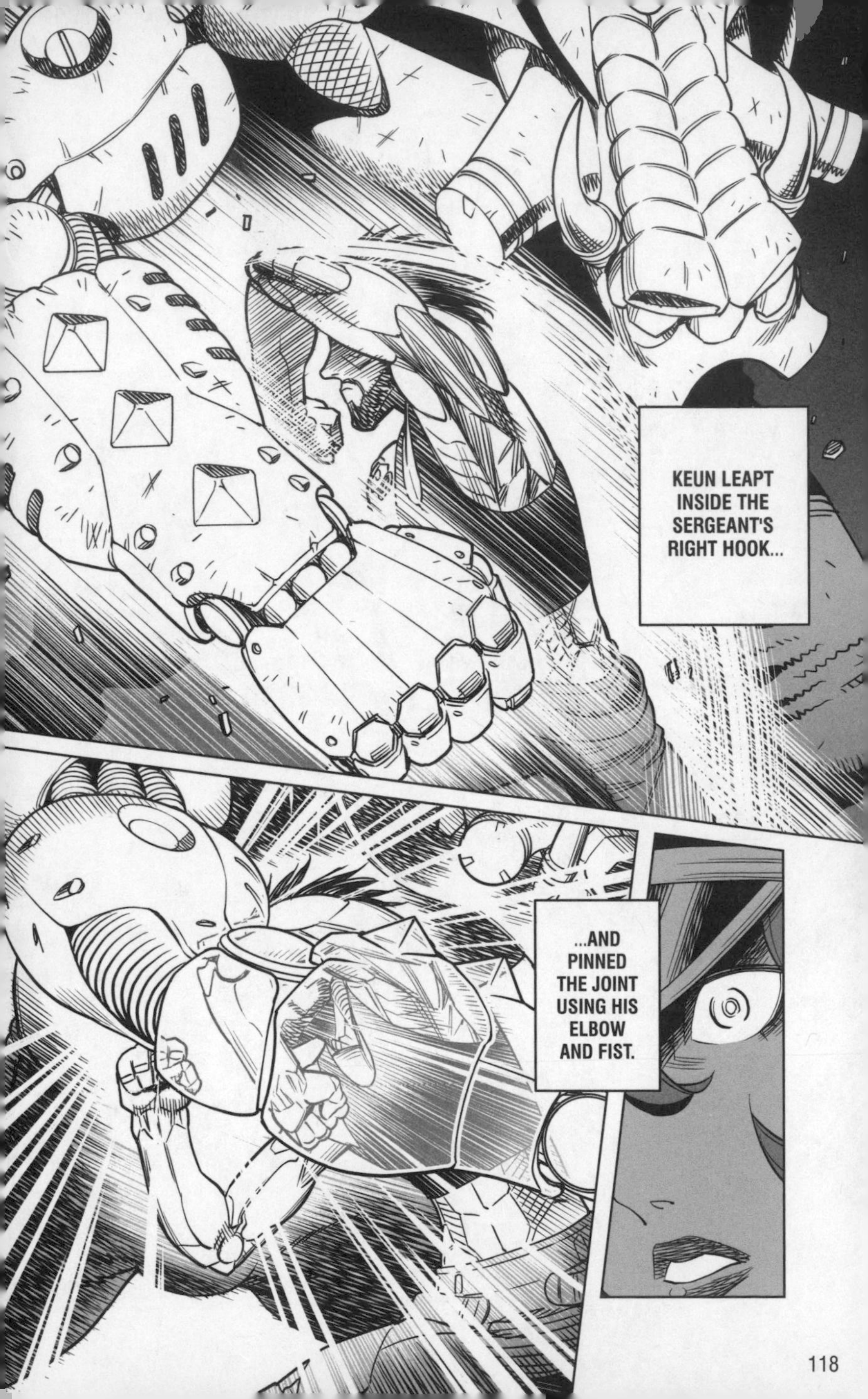
KEUN LEAPT INSIDE THE SERGEANT'S RIGHT HOOK...
...AND PINNED THE JOINT USING HIS ELBOW AND FIST.

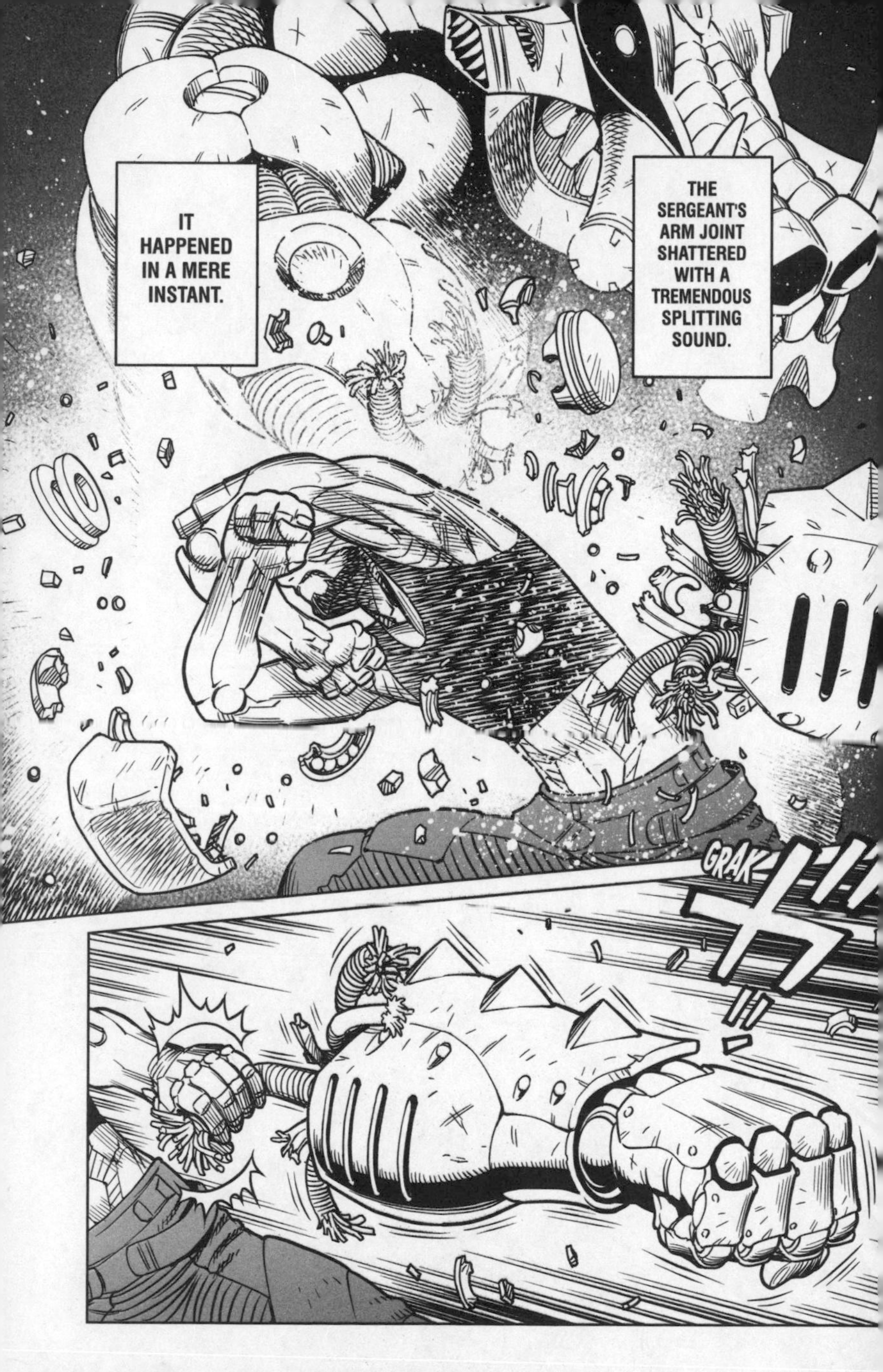
THE SERGEANT'S ARM JOINT SHATTERED WITH A TREMENDOUS SPLITTING SOUND.
IT HAPPENED IN A MERE INSTANT.
GRAK

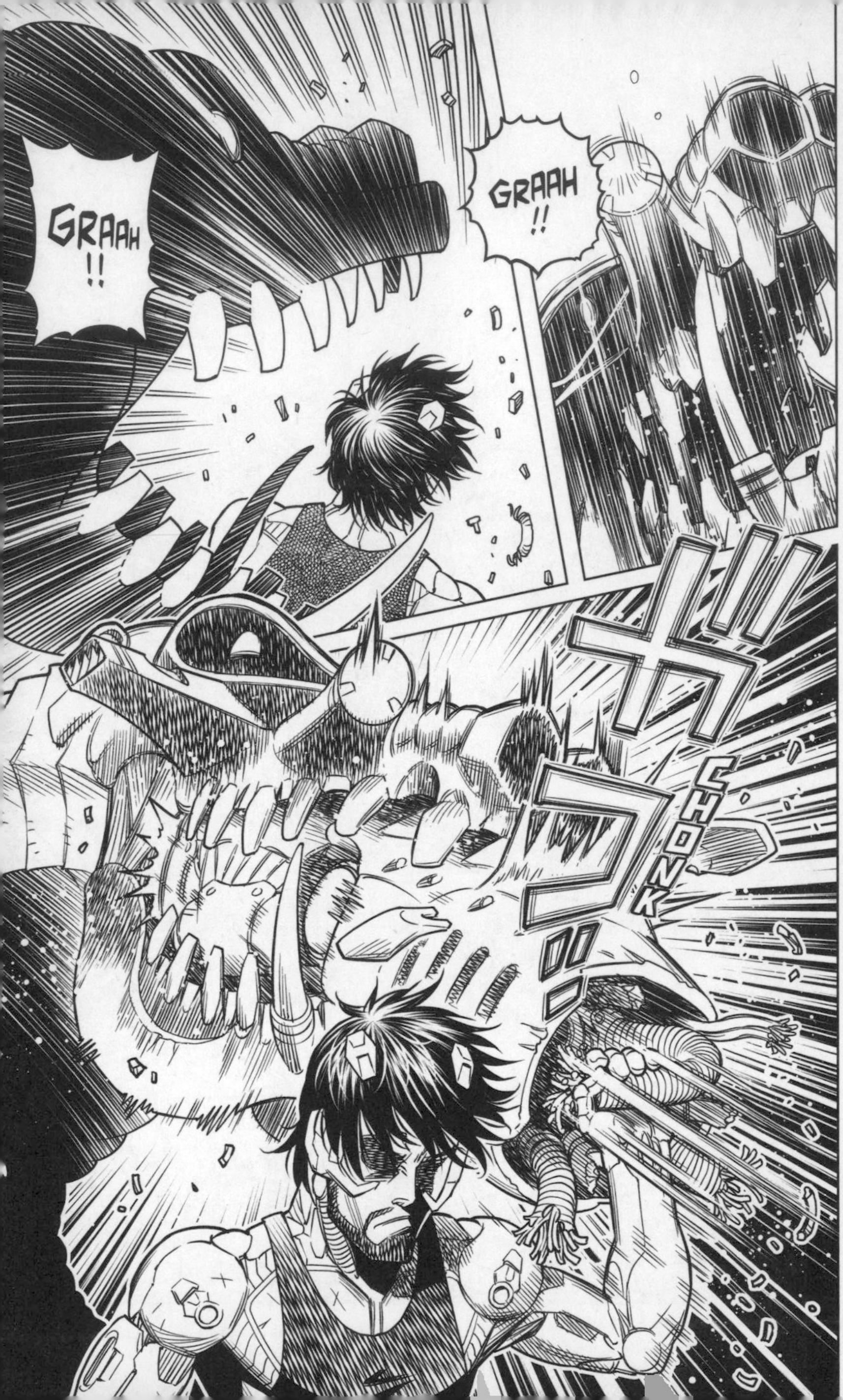
GRAAH!!
GRAAH!!
CHONK

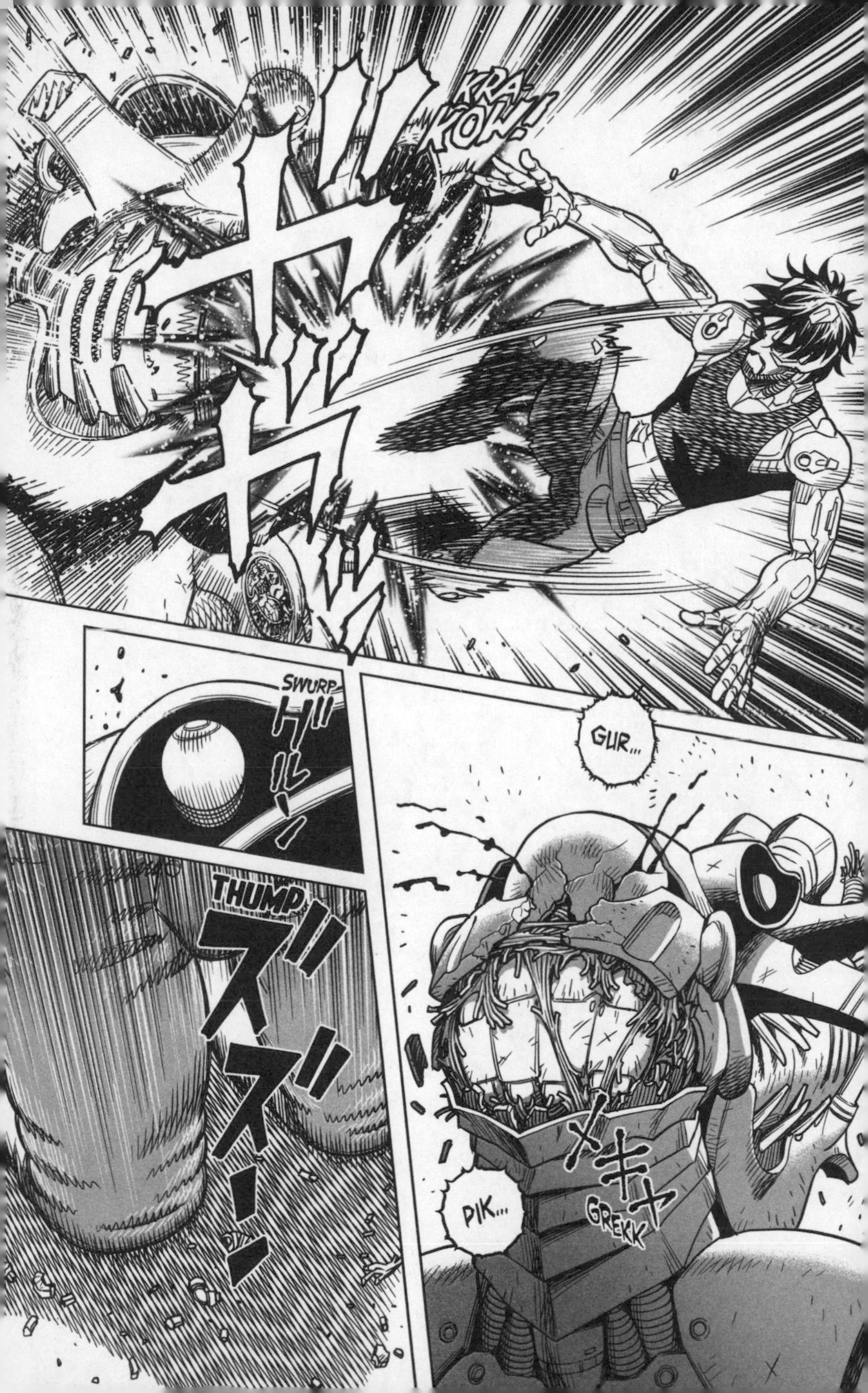
KRA-KOW!
GUR...
GREKK
PIK...
SWURP
THUMP

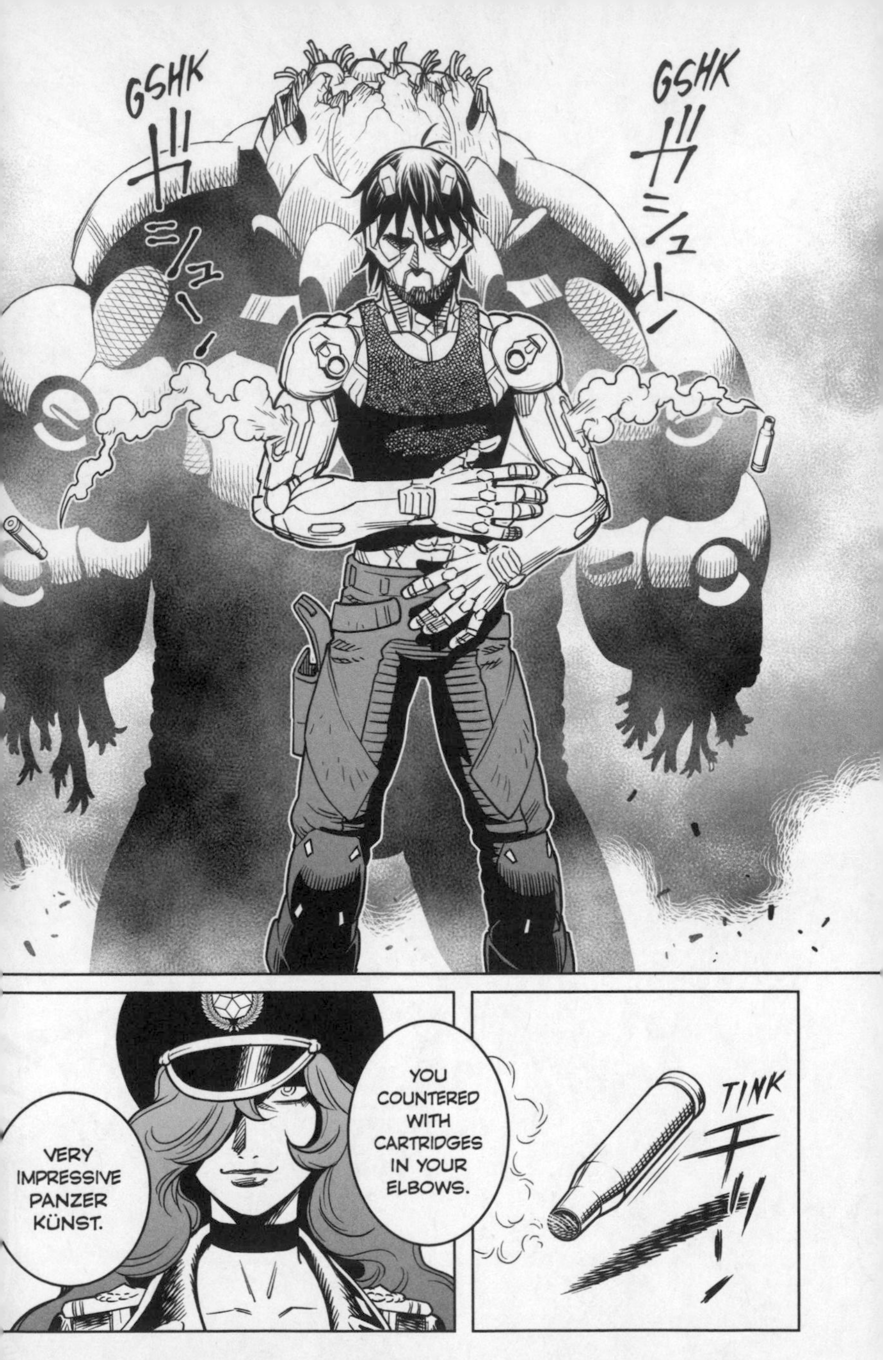
GSHK
ガシューン
GSHK
ガシューン
TINK
YOU COUNTERED WITH CARTRIDGES IN YOUR ELBOWS.
VERY IMPRESSIVE PANZER KÜNST.

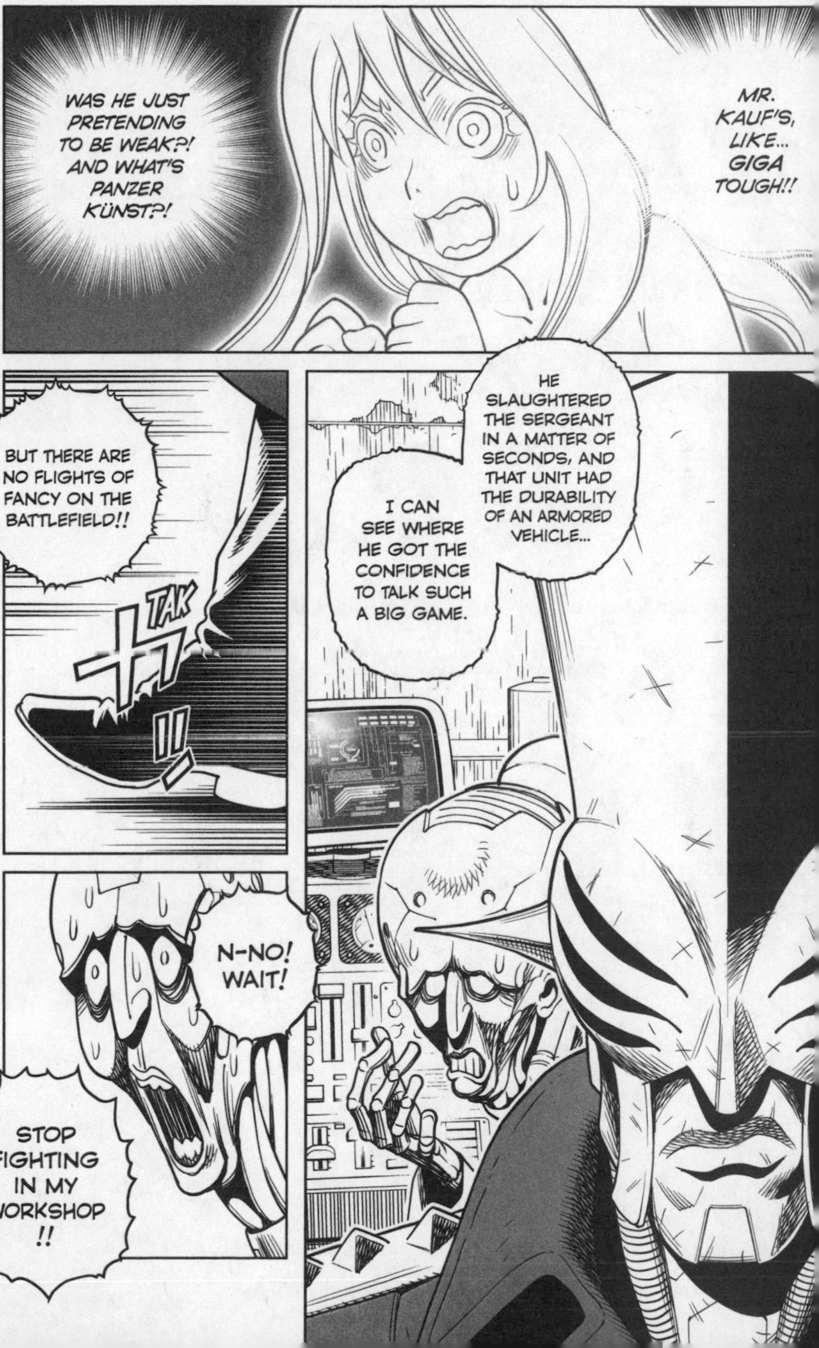
MR. KAUF'S, LIKE... GIGA TOUGH!!
WAS HE JUST PRETENDING TO BE WEAK?! AND WHAT'S PANZER KÜNST?!
HE SLAUGHTERED THE SERGEANT IN A MATTER OF SECONDS, AND THAT UNIT HAD THE DURABILITY OF AN ARMORED VEHICLE...
I CAN SEE WHERE HE GOT THE CONFIDENCE TO TALK SUCH A BIG GAME.
BUT THERE ARE NO FLIGHTS OF FANCY ON THE BATTLEFIELD!!
TAK
N-NO! WAIT!
STOP FIGHTING IN MY WORKSHOP!!

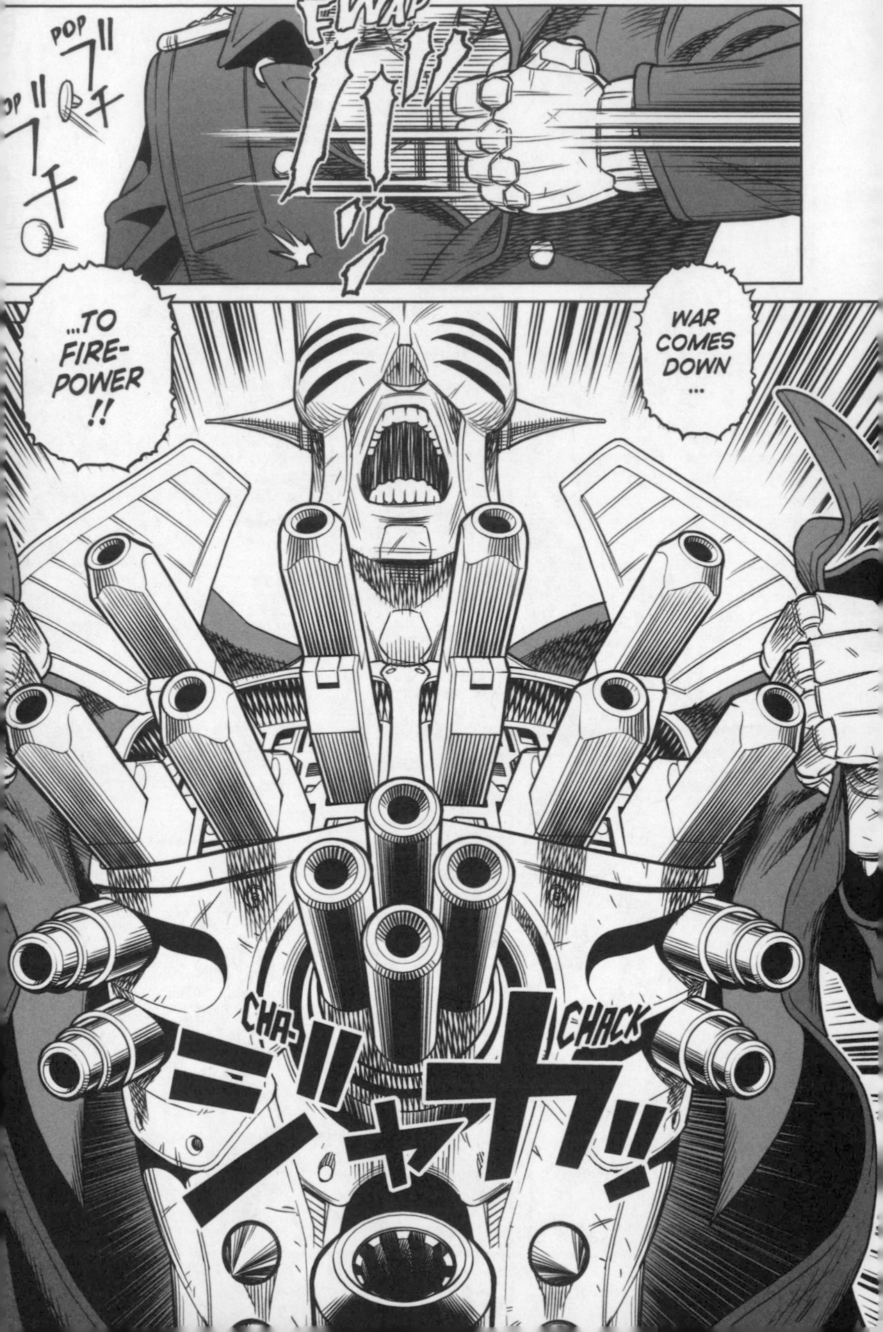
POP
OP
FWAP
WAR COMES DOWN ...
...TO FIRE-POWER !!
CHA-
CHACK

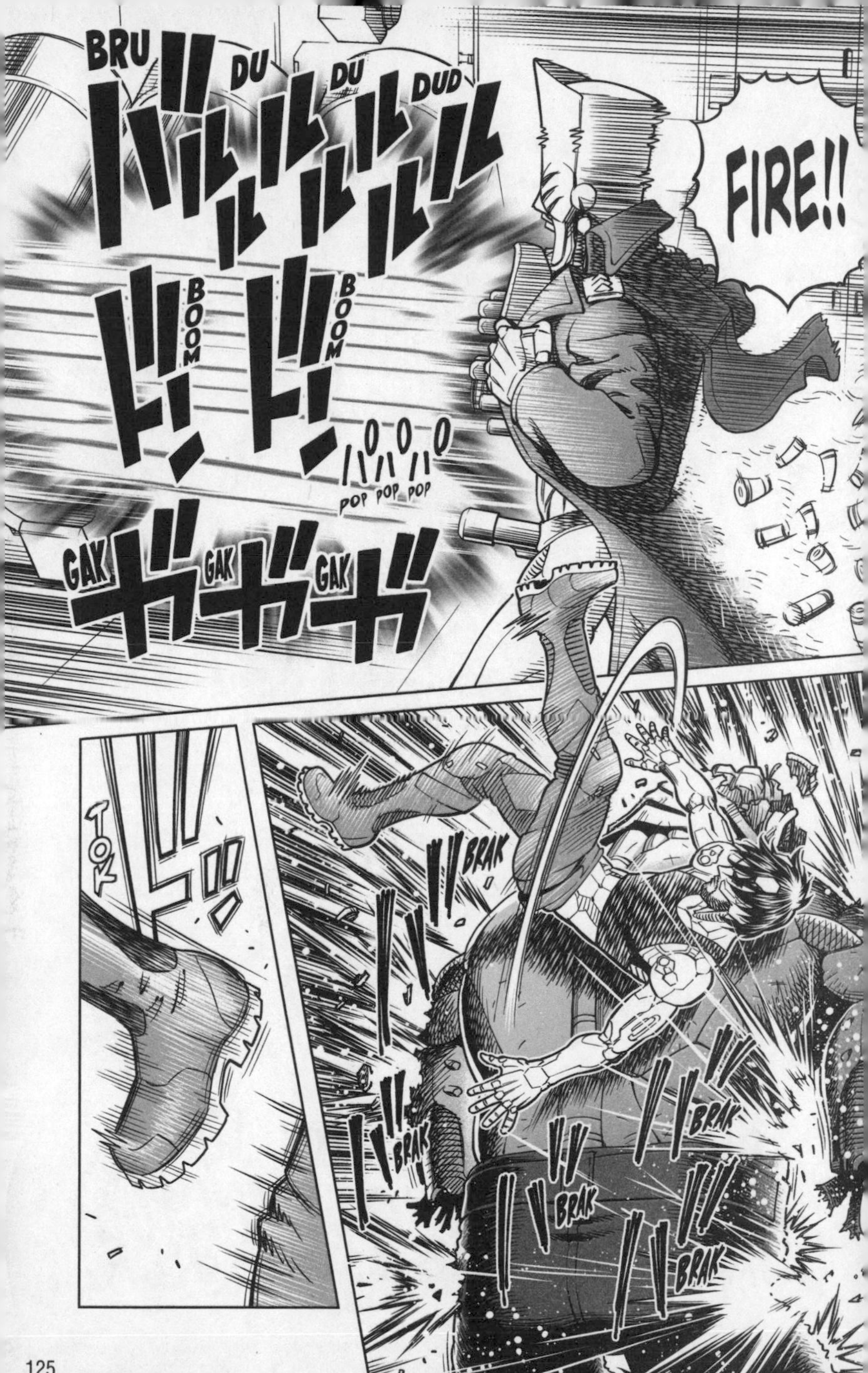
FIRE!!
BRU DU DU DUD
BOOM BOOM
POP POP POP
GAK GAK GAK
BRAK
BRAK
BRAK
BRAK
BRAK
TOK

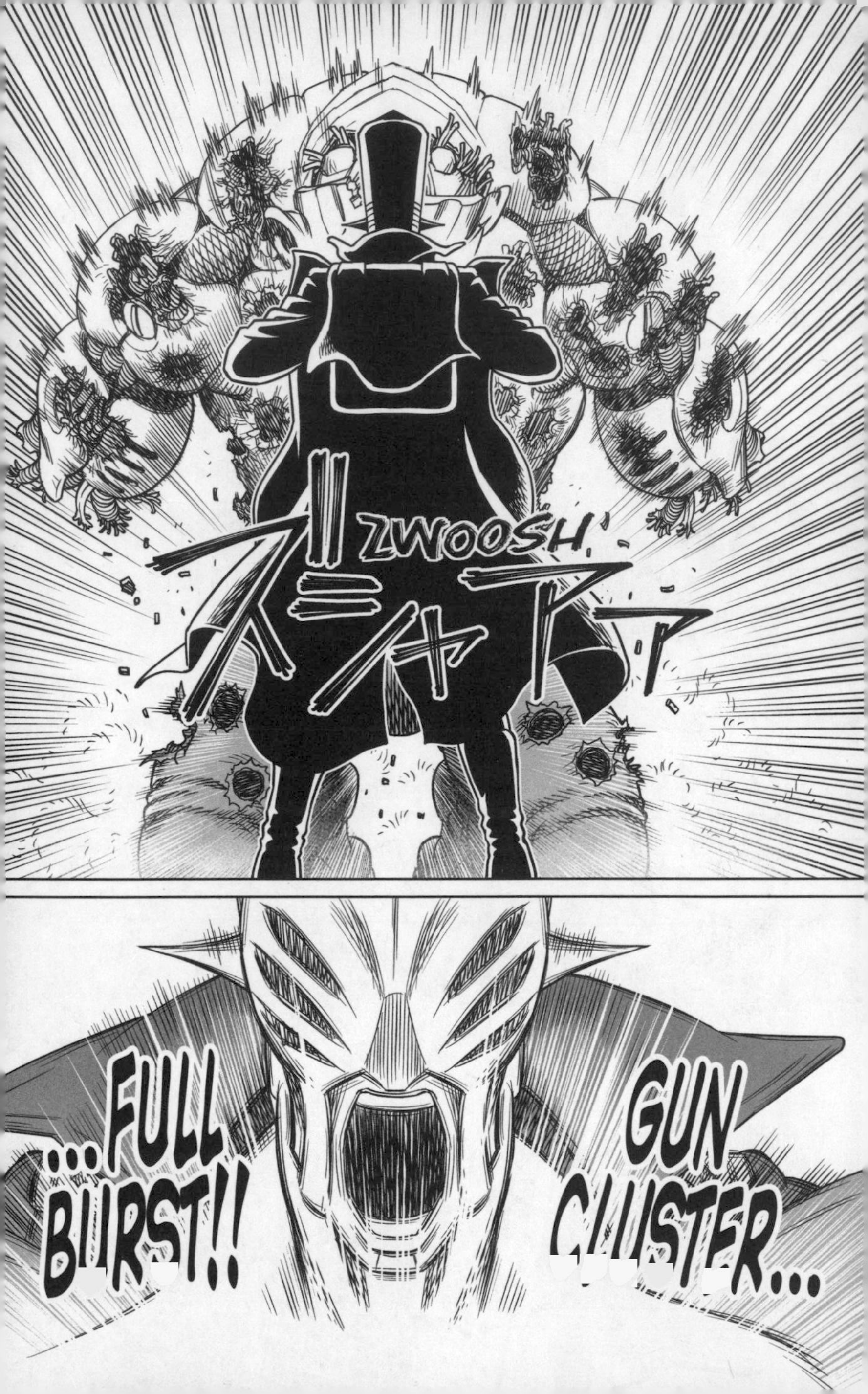
ZWOOSH
GUN CLUSTER...
...FULL BURST!!

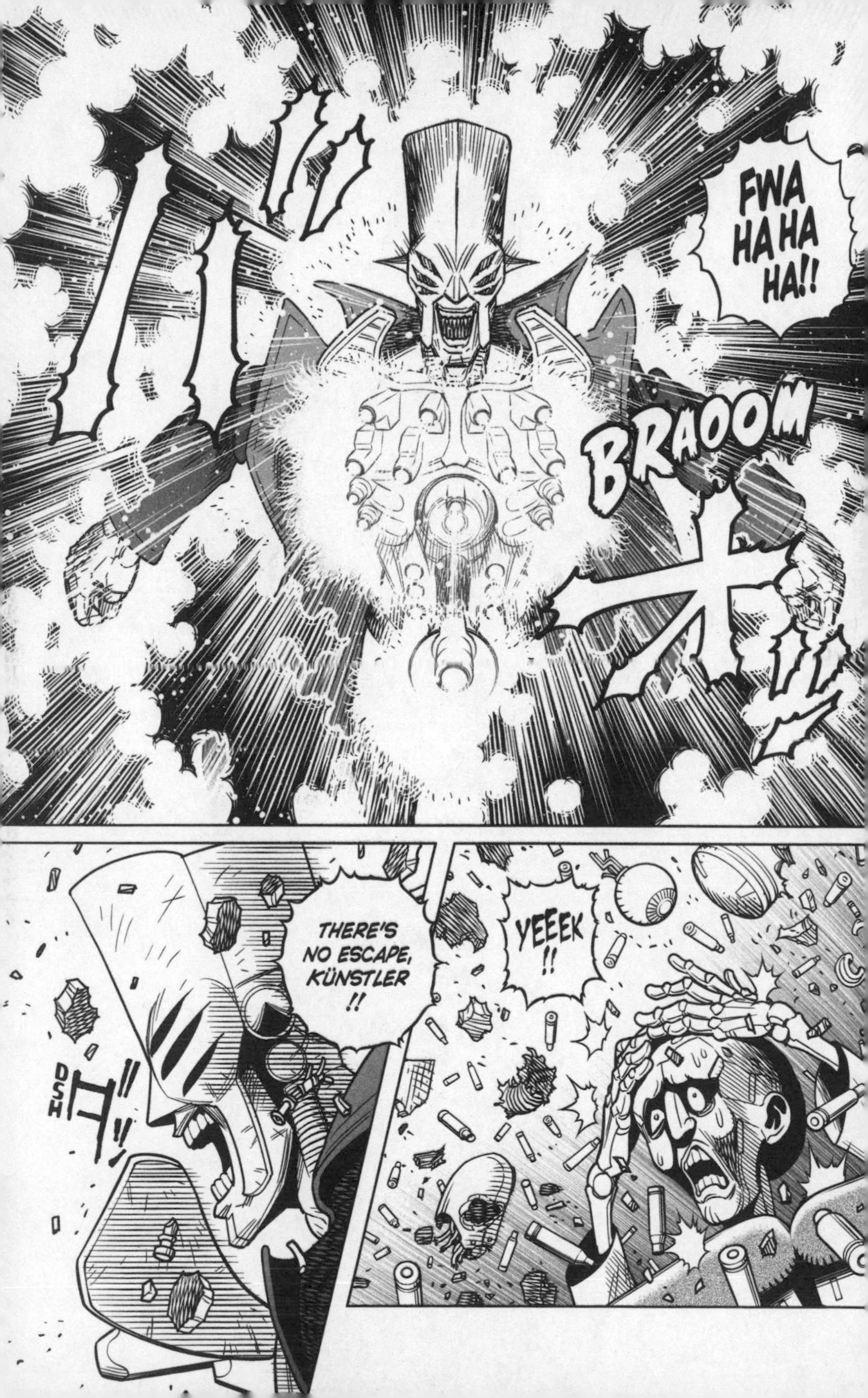
FWA HA HA HA!!
BRAOOM
YEEEK !!
THERE'S NO ESCAPE, KÜNSTLER !!
DSH

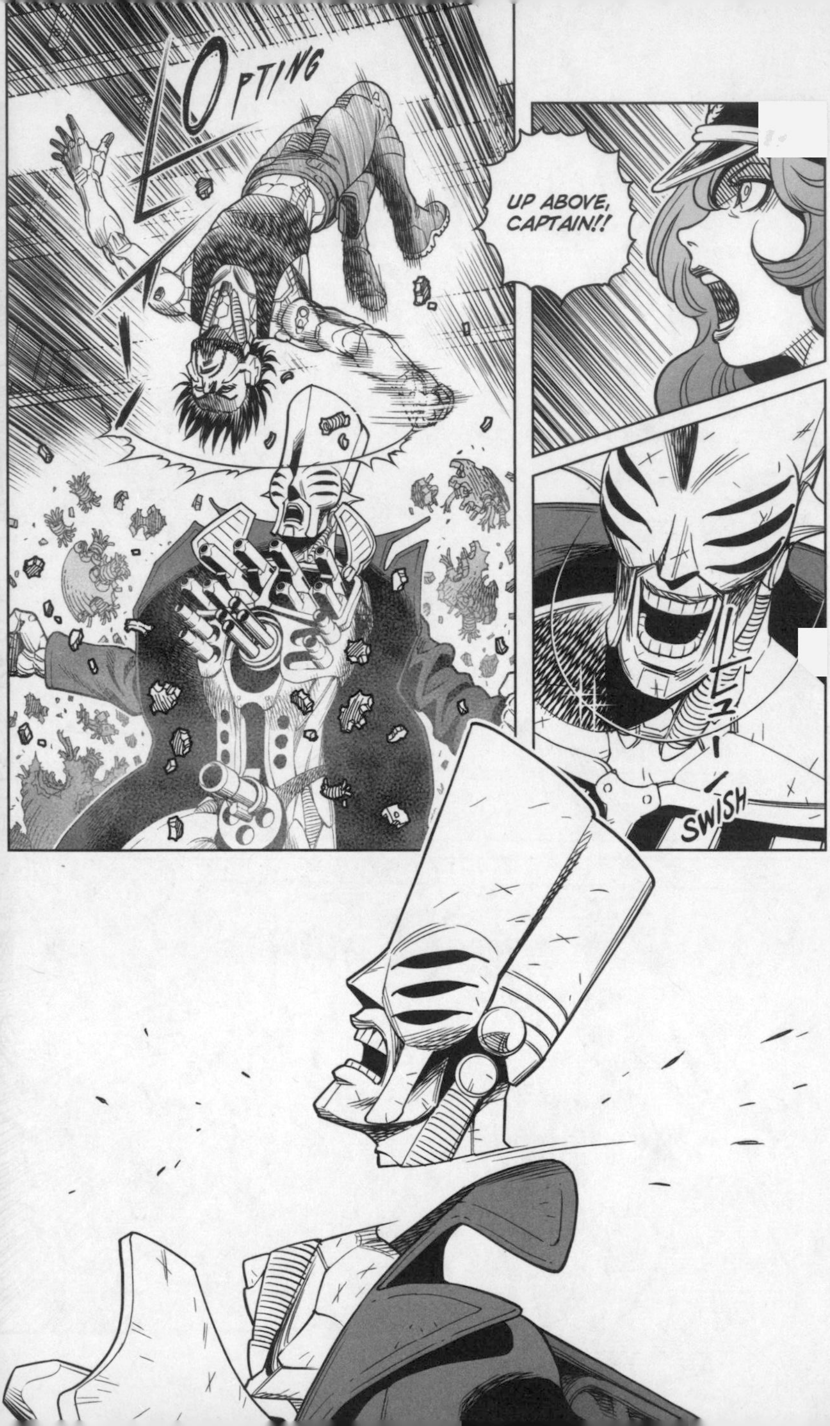
UP ABOVE, CAPTAIN!!
SWISH
ZOPTING

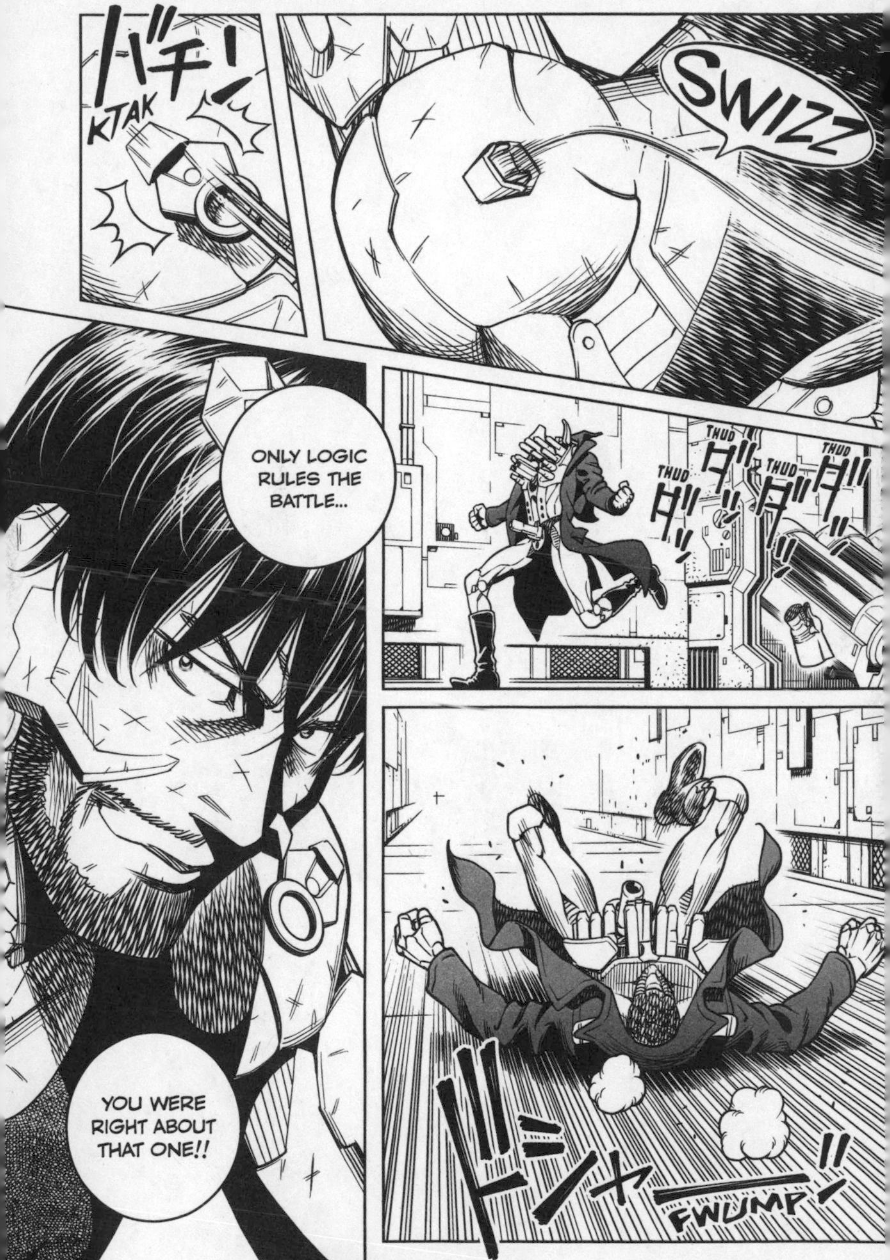
SWIZZ
バチ!
KTAK
ダッ
THUD
ダッ
THUD
ダッ
THUD
ダッ
THUD
ドシャー!!
FWUMP!
ONLY LOGIC RULES THE BATTLE...
YOU WERE RIGHT ABOUT THAT ONE!!

LOG:036

THE TERRORS

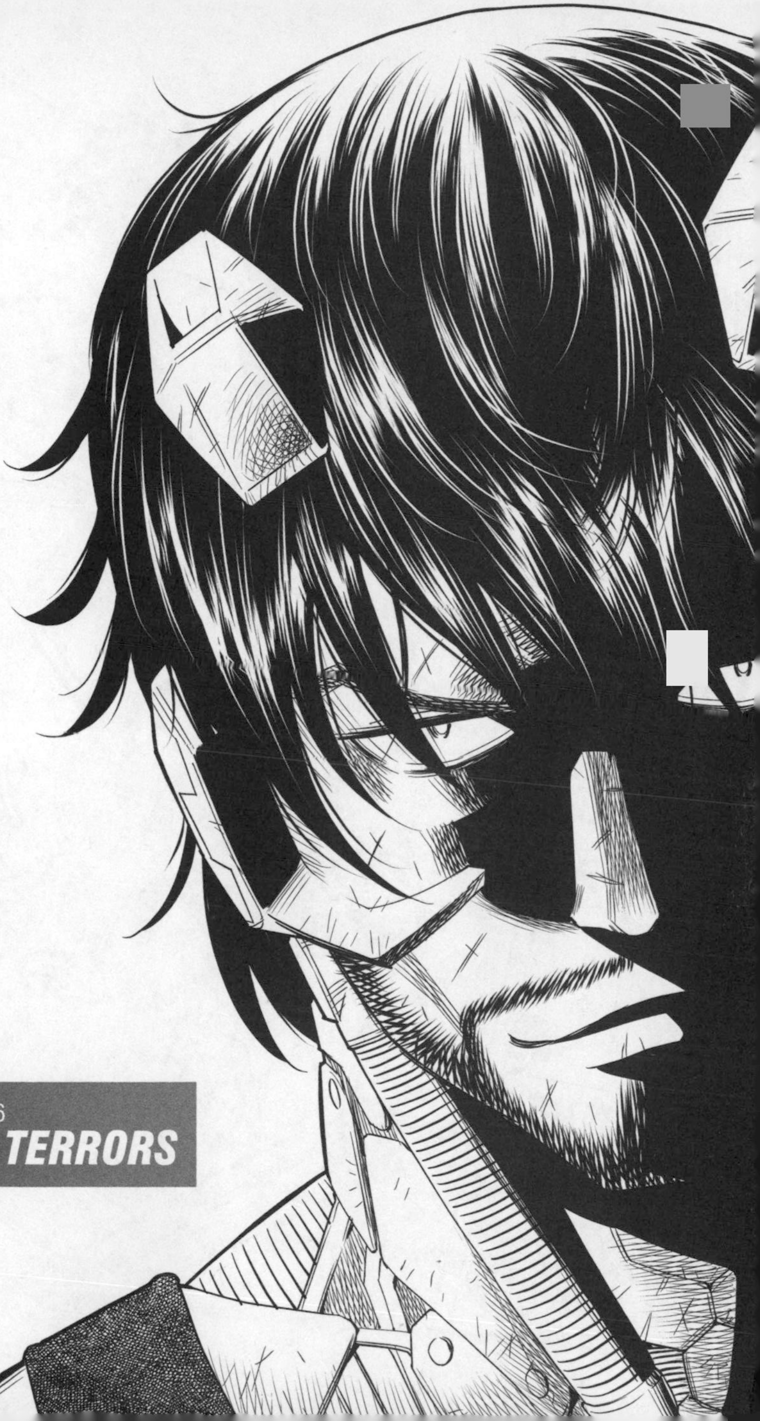

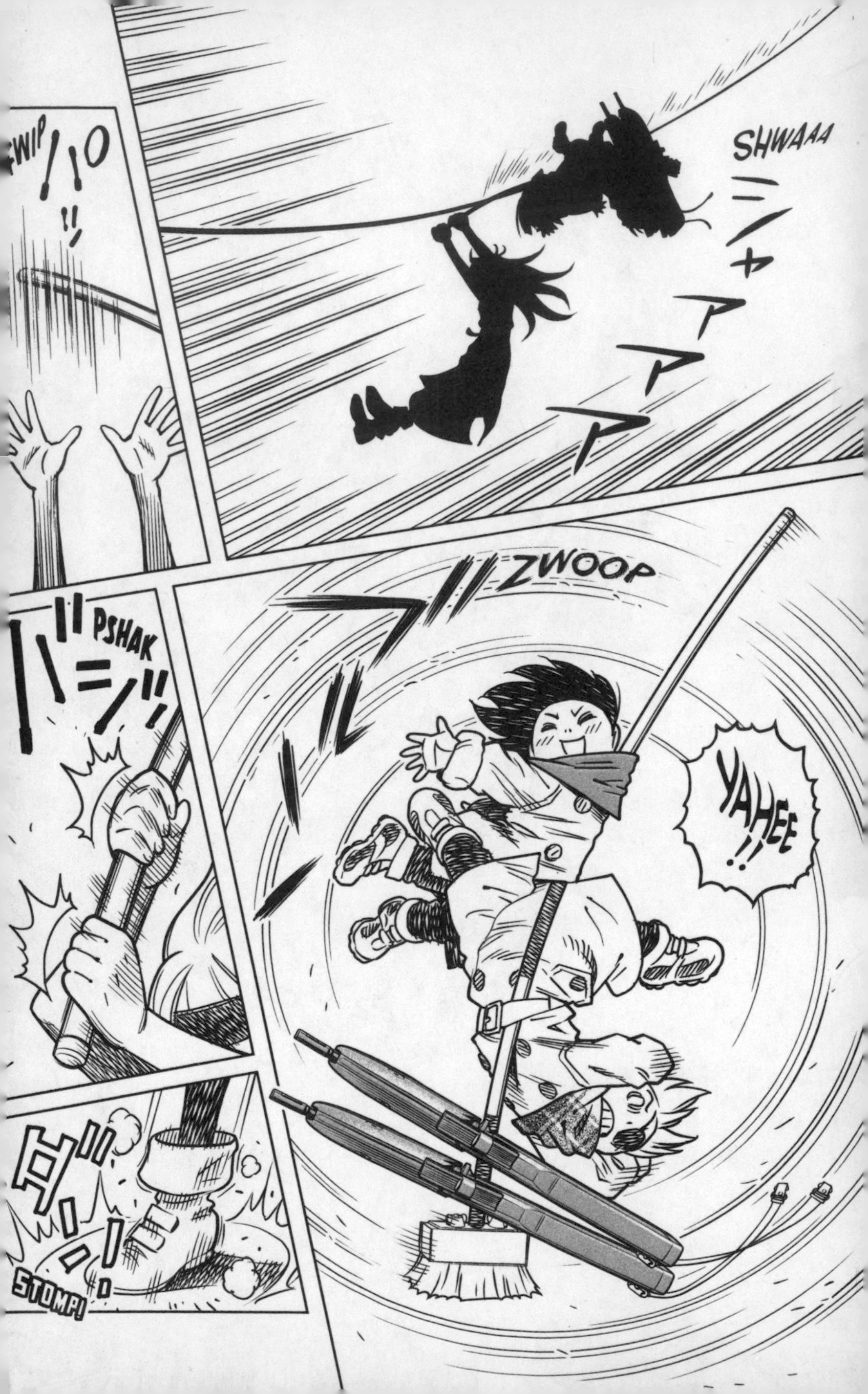
SHWAAA
FWIP
ZWOOP
YAHEE!!
PSHAK
STOMP!

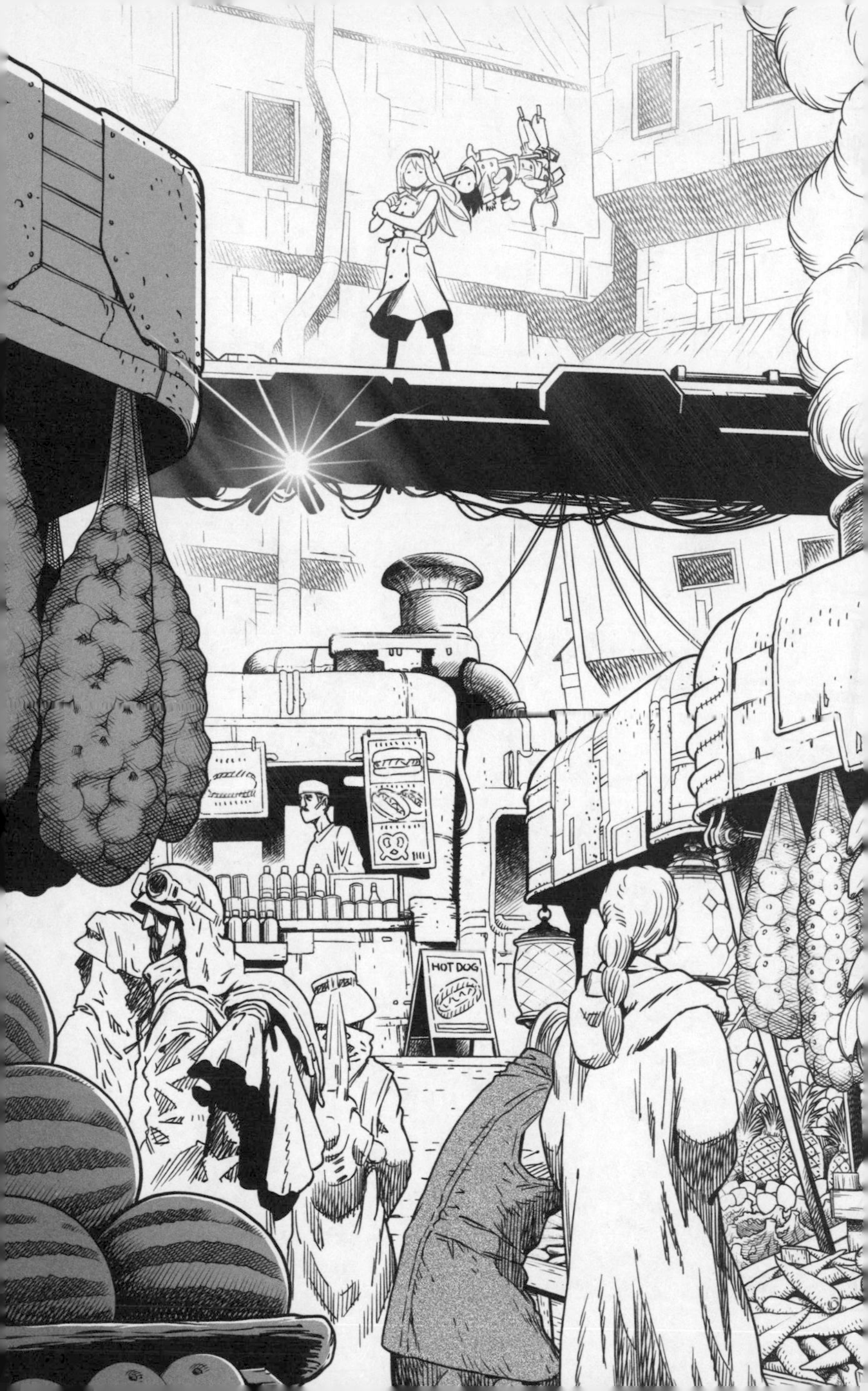
HOT DOG

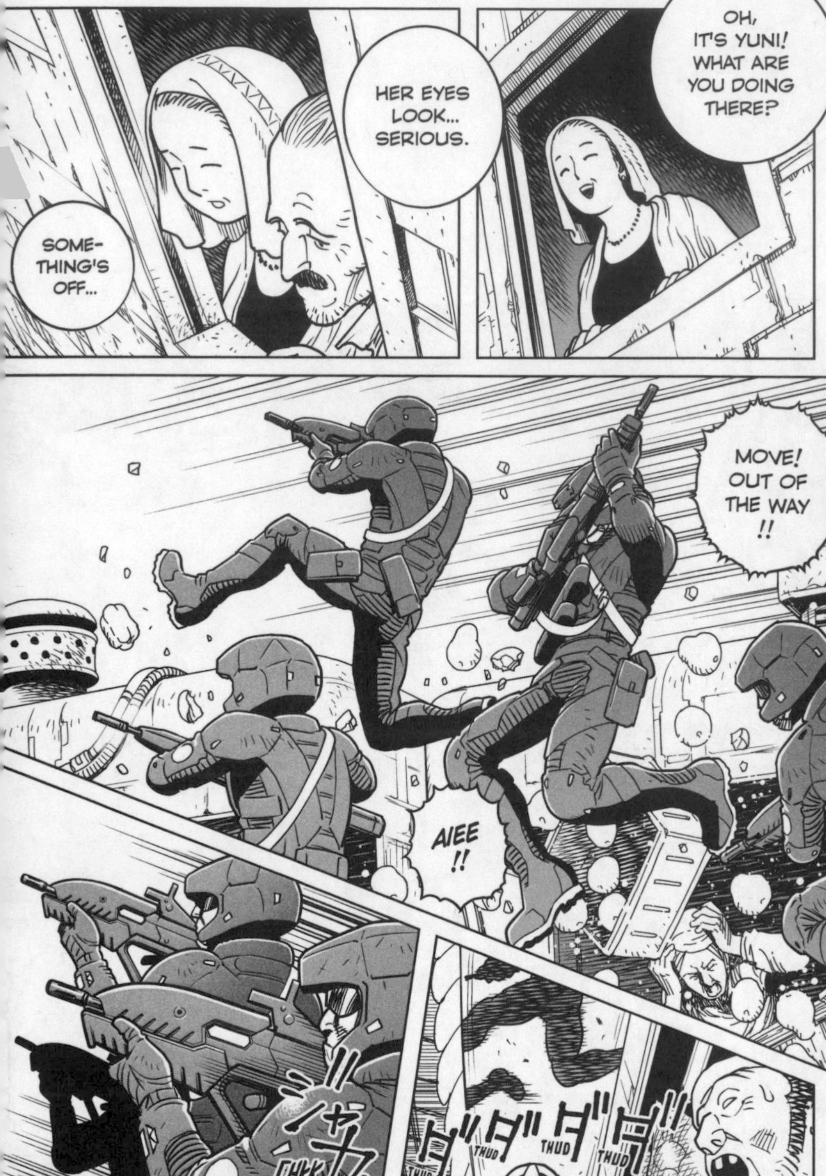
OH, IT'S YUNI! WHAT ARE YOU DOING THERE?
HER EYES LOOK... SERIOUS.
SOME-THING'S OFF...
MOVE! OUT OF THE WAY !!
AIEE !!
THUD
THUD
THUD
THUD
CHKK

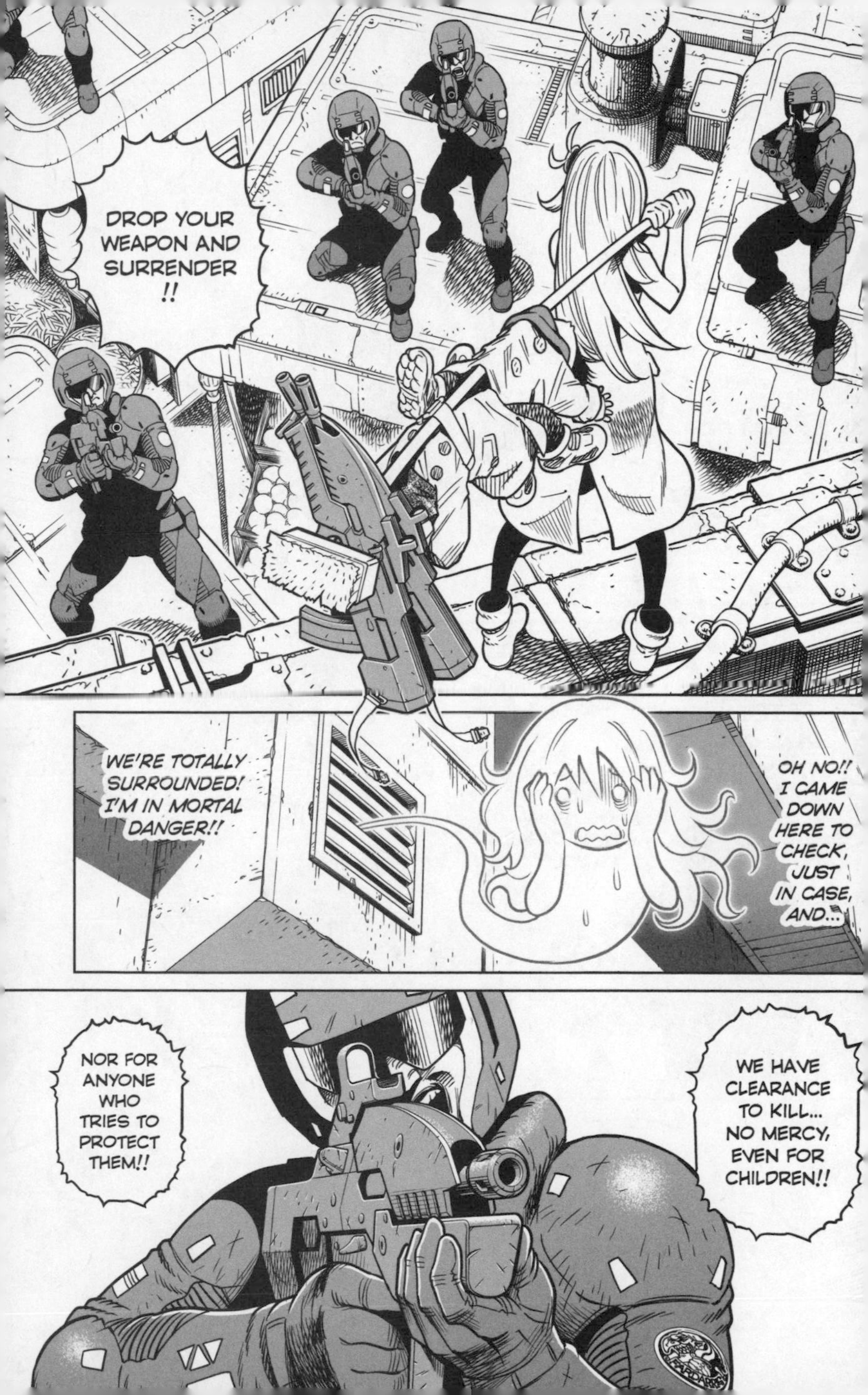
DROP YOUR WEAPON AND SURRENDER !!
OH NO!! I CAME DOWN HERE TO CHECK, JUST IN CASE, AND...
WE'RE TOTALLY SURROUNDED! I'M IN MORTAL DANGER!!
WE HAVE CLEARANCE TO KILL... NO MERCY, EVEN FOR CHILDREN!!
NOR FOR ANYONE WHO TRIES TO PROTECT THEM!!

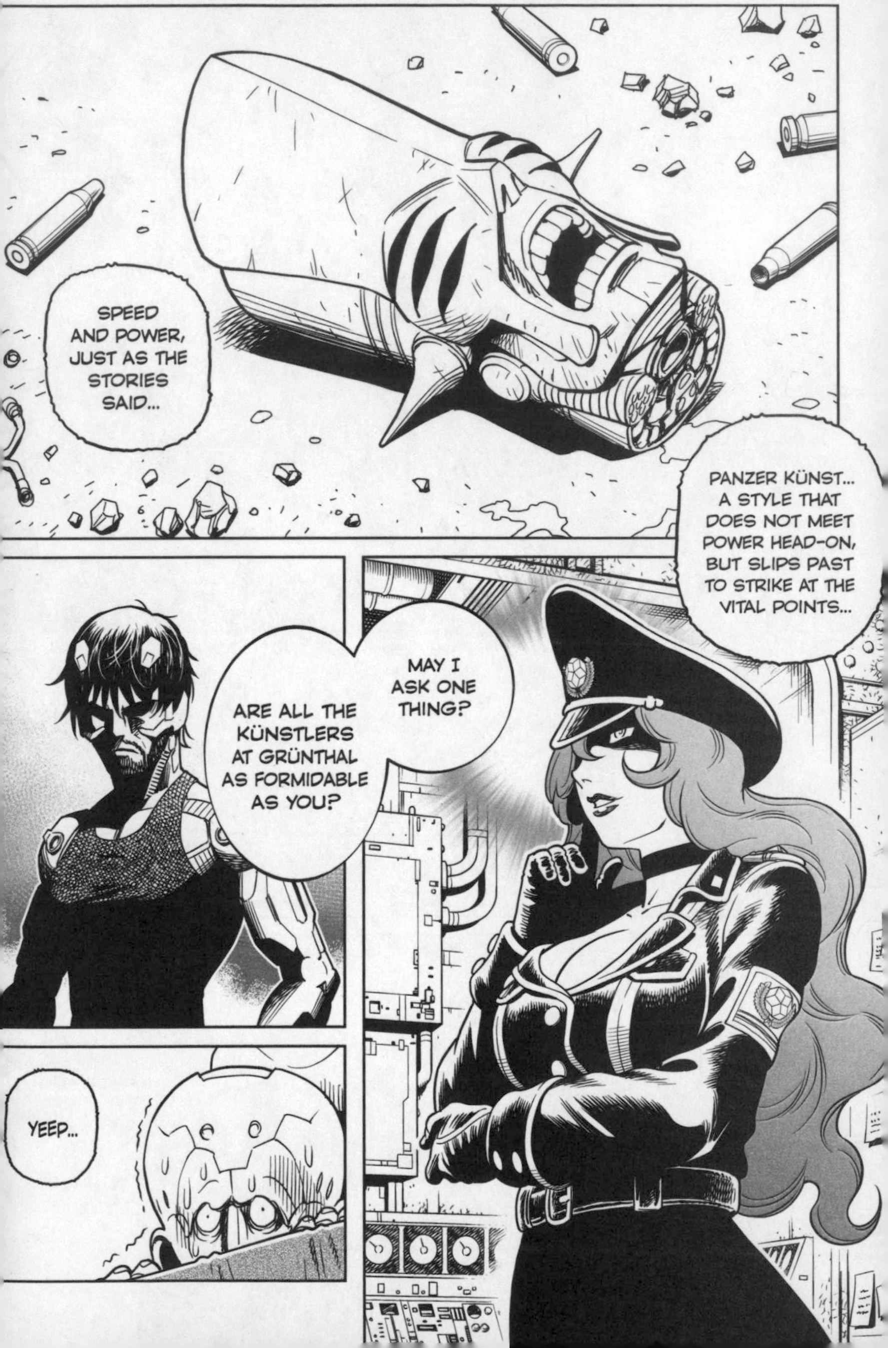
SPEED AND POWER, JUST AS THE STORIES SAID...
PANZER KÜNST... A STYLE THAT DOES NOT MEET POWER HEAD-ON, BUT SLIPS PAST TO STRIKE AT THE VITAL POINTS...
MAY I ASK ONE THING?
ARE ALL THE KÜNSTLERS AT GRÜNTHAL AS FORMIDABLE AS YOU?
YEEP...

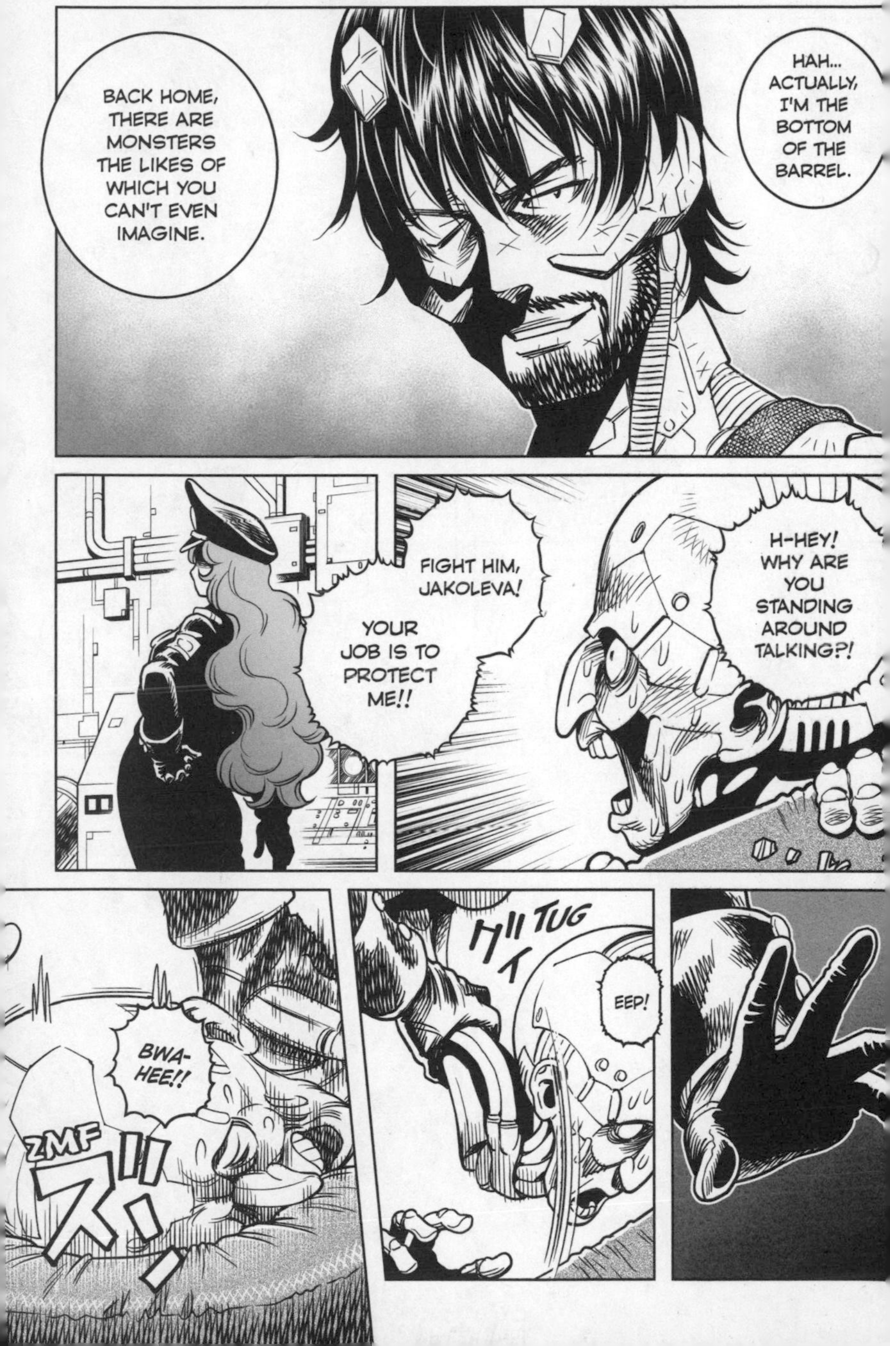
HAH... ACTUALLY, I'M THE BOTTOM OF THE BARREL.
BACK HOME, THERE ARE MONSTERS THE LIKES OF WHICH YOU CAN'T EVEN IMAGINE.
H-HEY! WHY ARE YOU STANDING AROUND TALKING?!
FIGHT HIM, JAKOLEVA!
YOUR JOB IS TO PROTECT ME!!
TUG
EEP!
BWA-HEE!!
ZMF

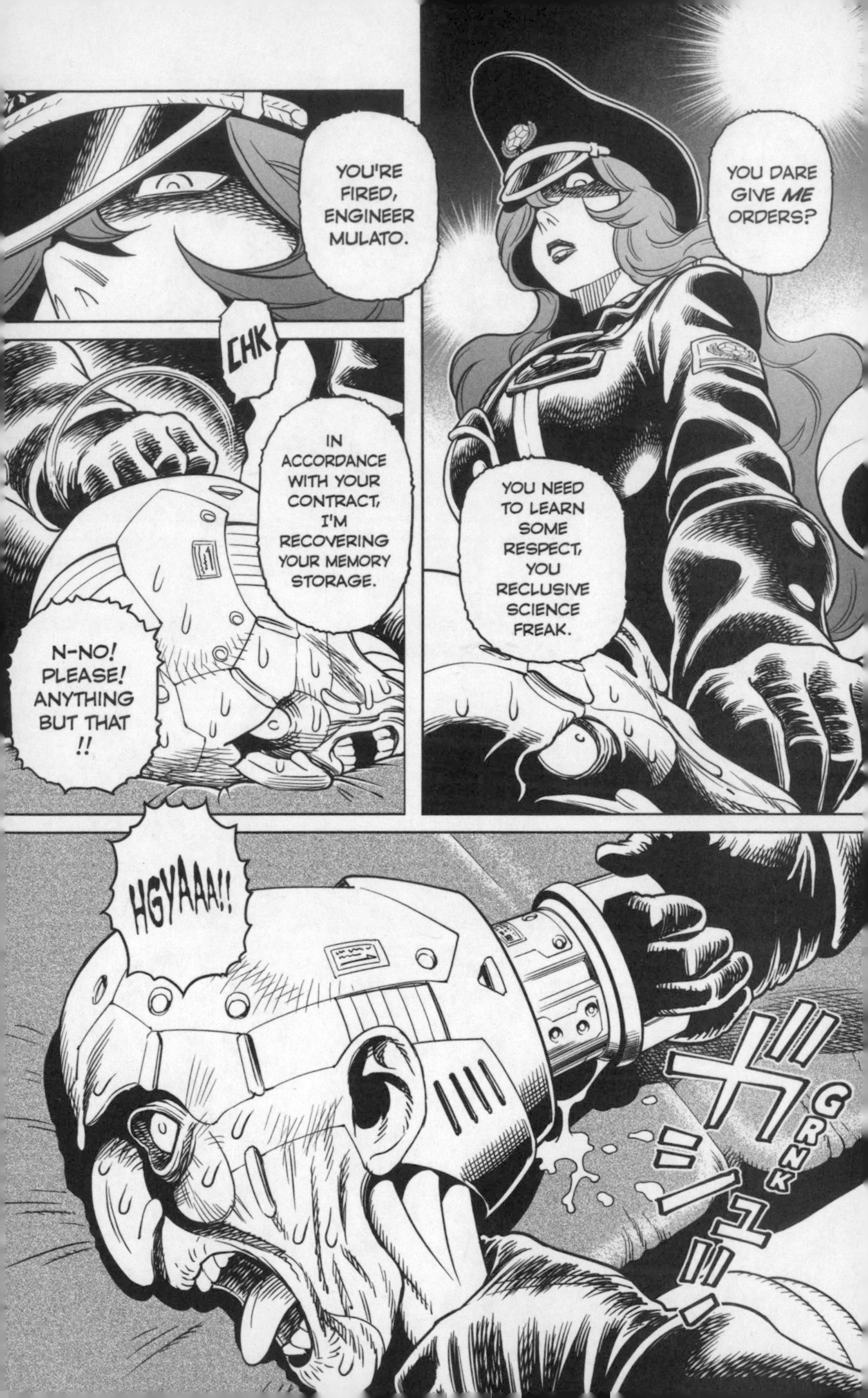
YOU DARE GIVE *ME* ORDERS?
YOU NEED TO LEARN SOME RESPECT, YOU RECLUSIVE SCIENCE FREAK.
YOU'RE FIRED, ENGINEER MULATO.
CHK
IN ACCORDANCE WITH YOUR CONTRACT, I'M RECOVERING YOUR MEMORY STORAGE.
N-NO! PLEASE! ANYTHING BUT THAT !!
HGYAAA!!
GRNK

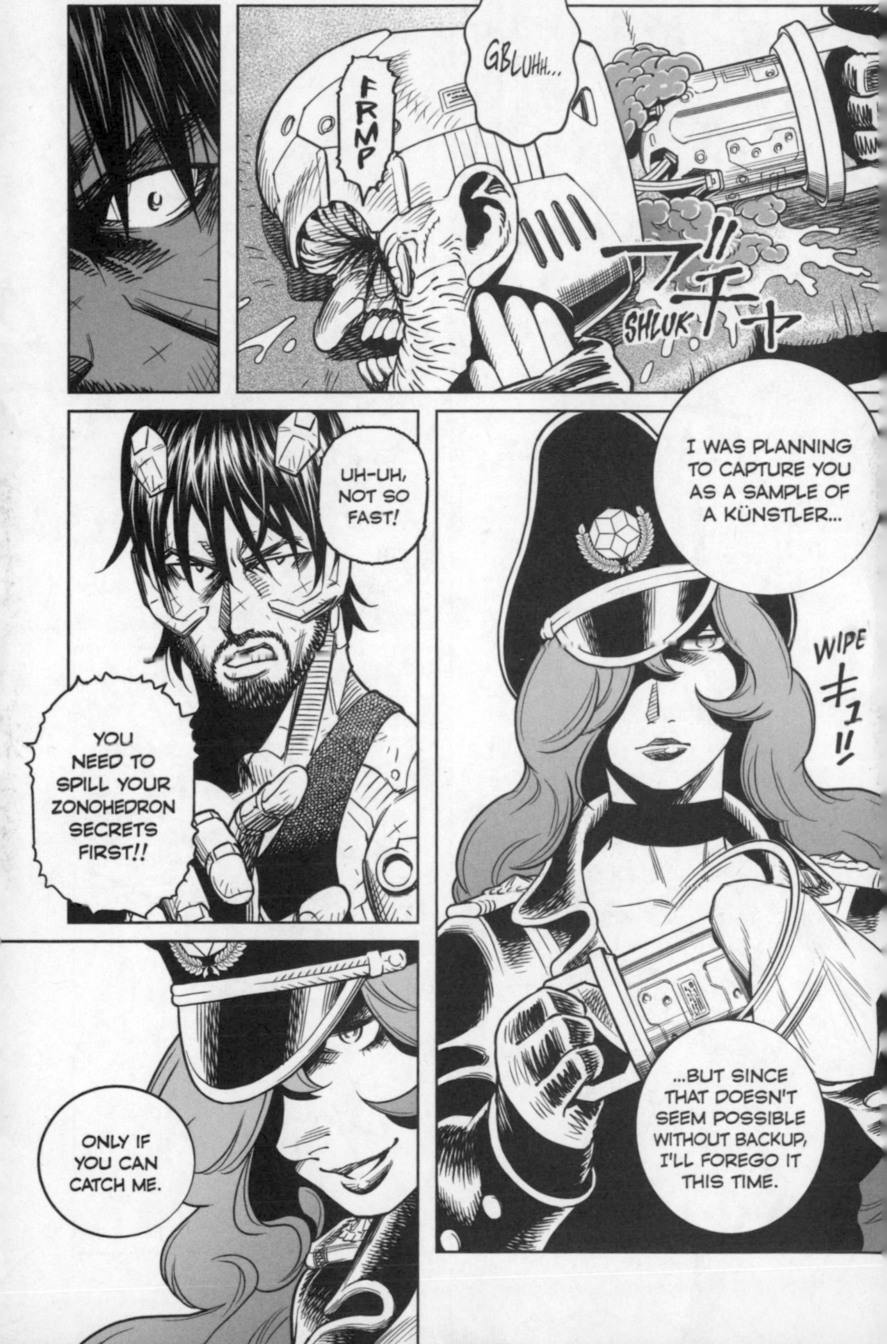
GBLUHH...
FRMP
SHLUK
I WAS PLANNING TO CAPTURE YOU AS A SAMPLE OF A KÜNSTLER...
WIPE
...BUT SINCE THAT DOESN'T SEEM POSSIBLE WITHOUT BACKUP, I'LL FOREGO IT THIS TIME.
UH-UH, NOT SO FAST!
YOU NEED TO SPILL YOUR ZONOHEDRON SECRETS FIRST!!
ONLY IF YOU CAN CATCH ME.

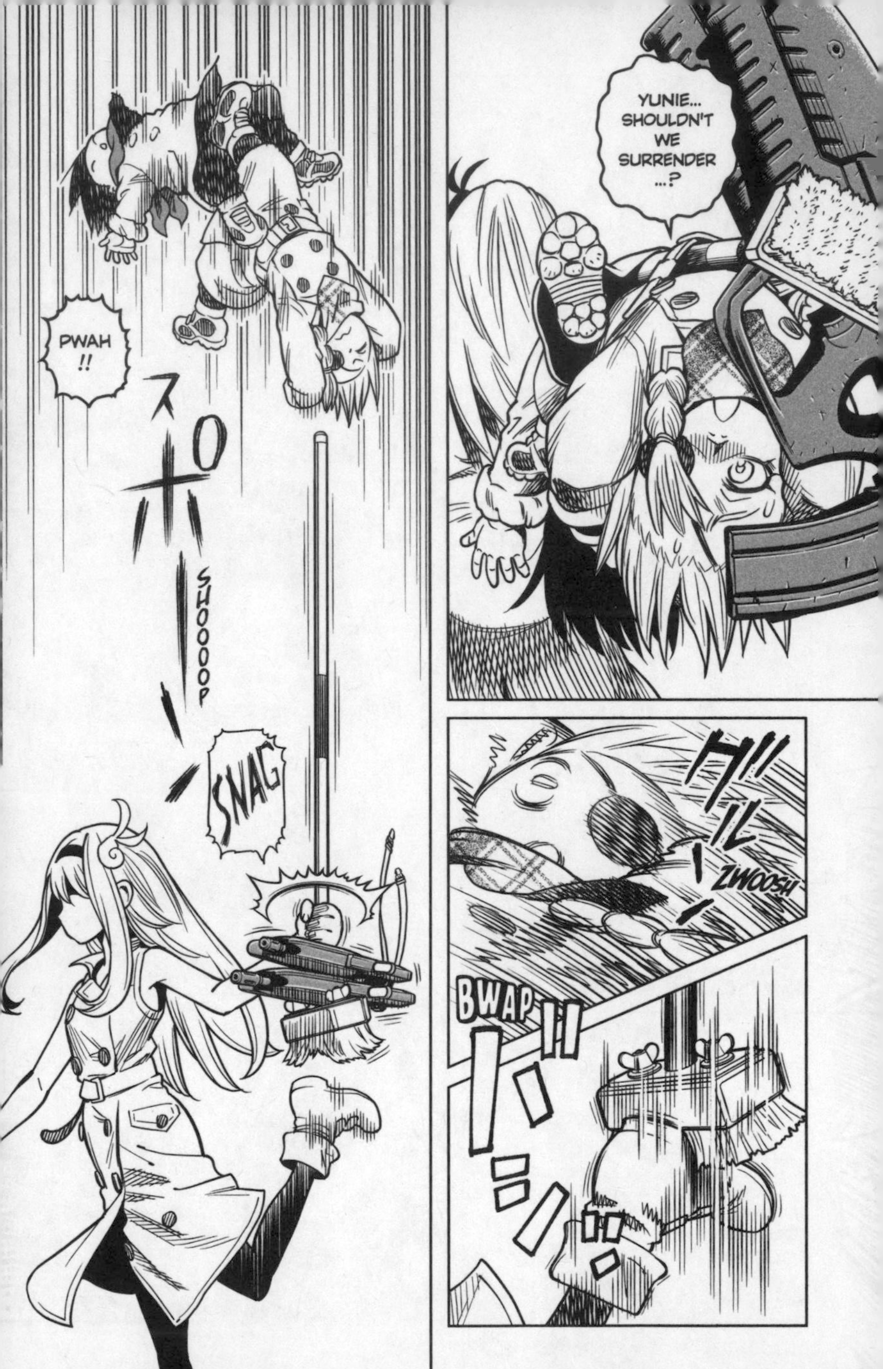
YUNIE... SHOULDN'T WE SURRENDER ...?
ZWOOSH
BWAP!!
PWAH!!
SHOOOOOP
SNAG

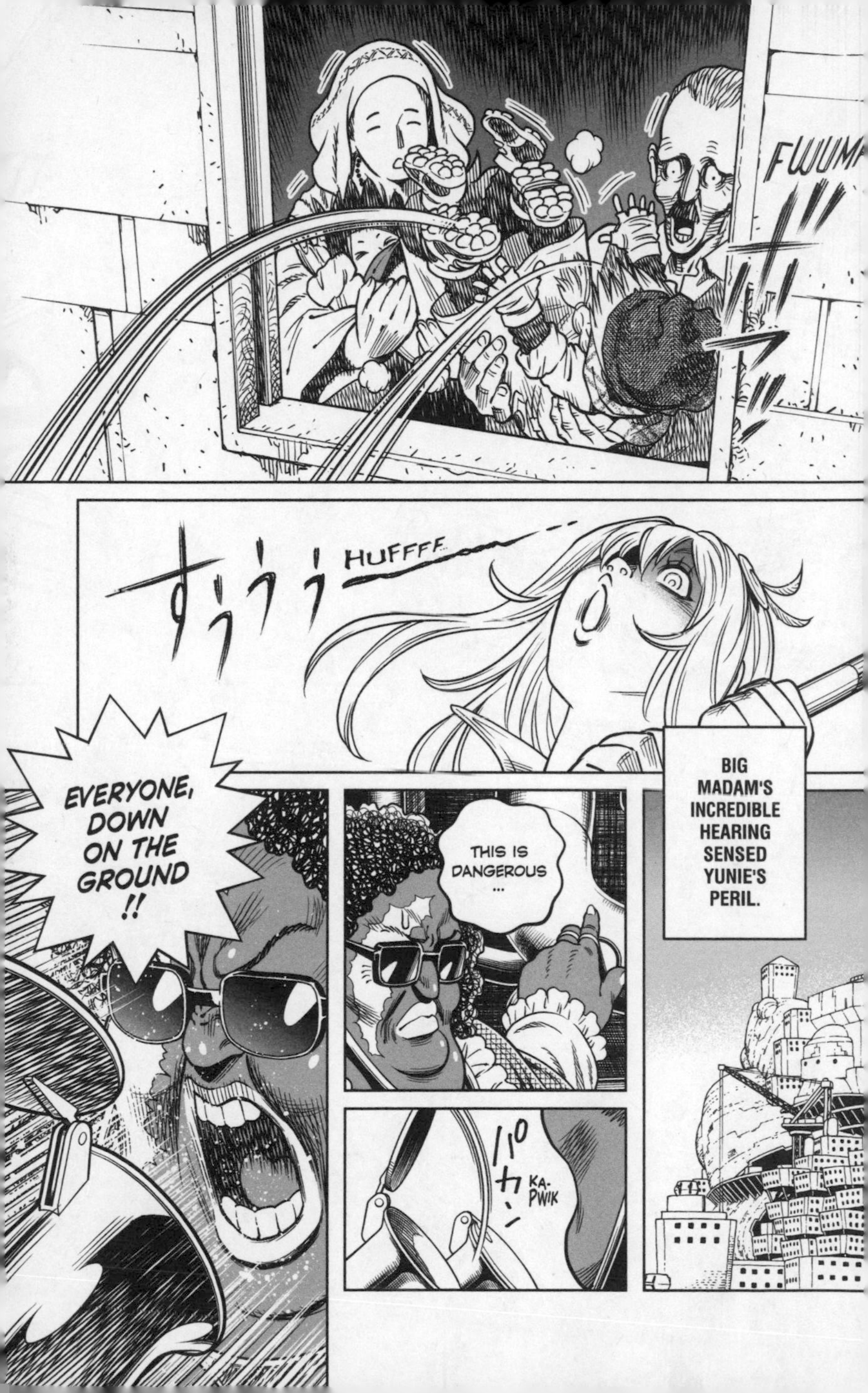
FWUUM!!
すううう
HUFFFF...
BIG MADAM'S INCREDIBLE HEARING SENSED YUNIE'S PERIL.
THIS IS DANGEROUS...
パカッ
KA-PWIK
EVERYONE, DOWN ON THE GROUND!!

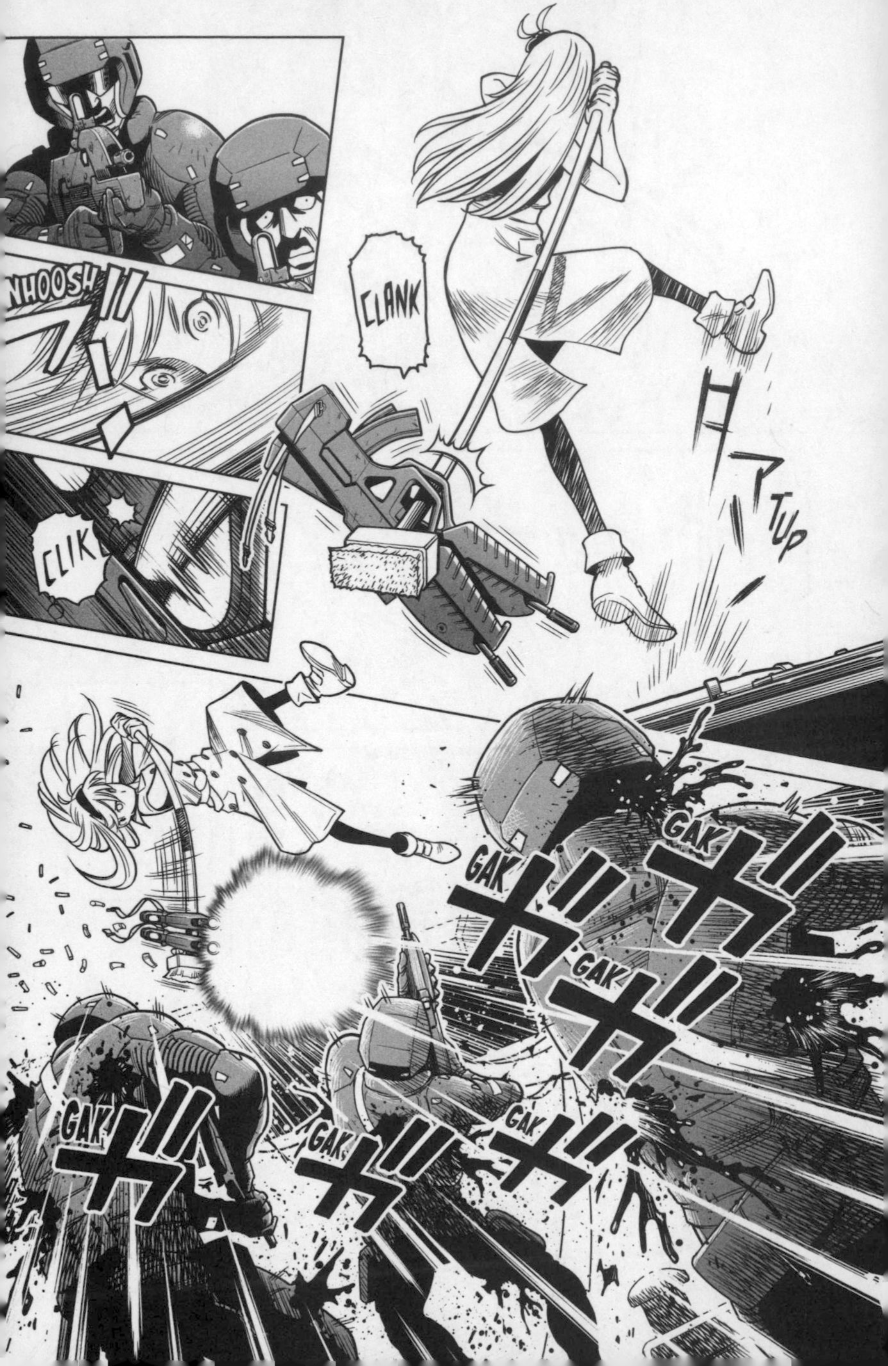
CLANK
TUP
WHOOSH
CLIK
GAK
GAK
GAK
GAK
GAK
GAK

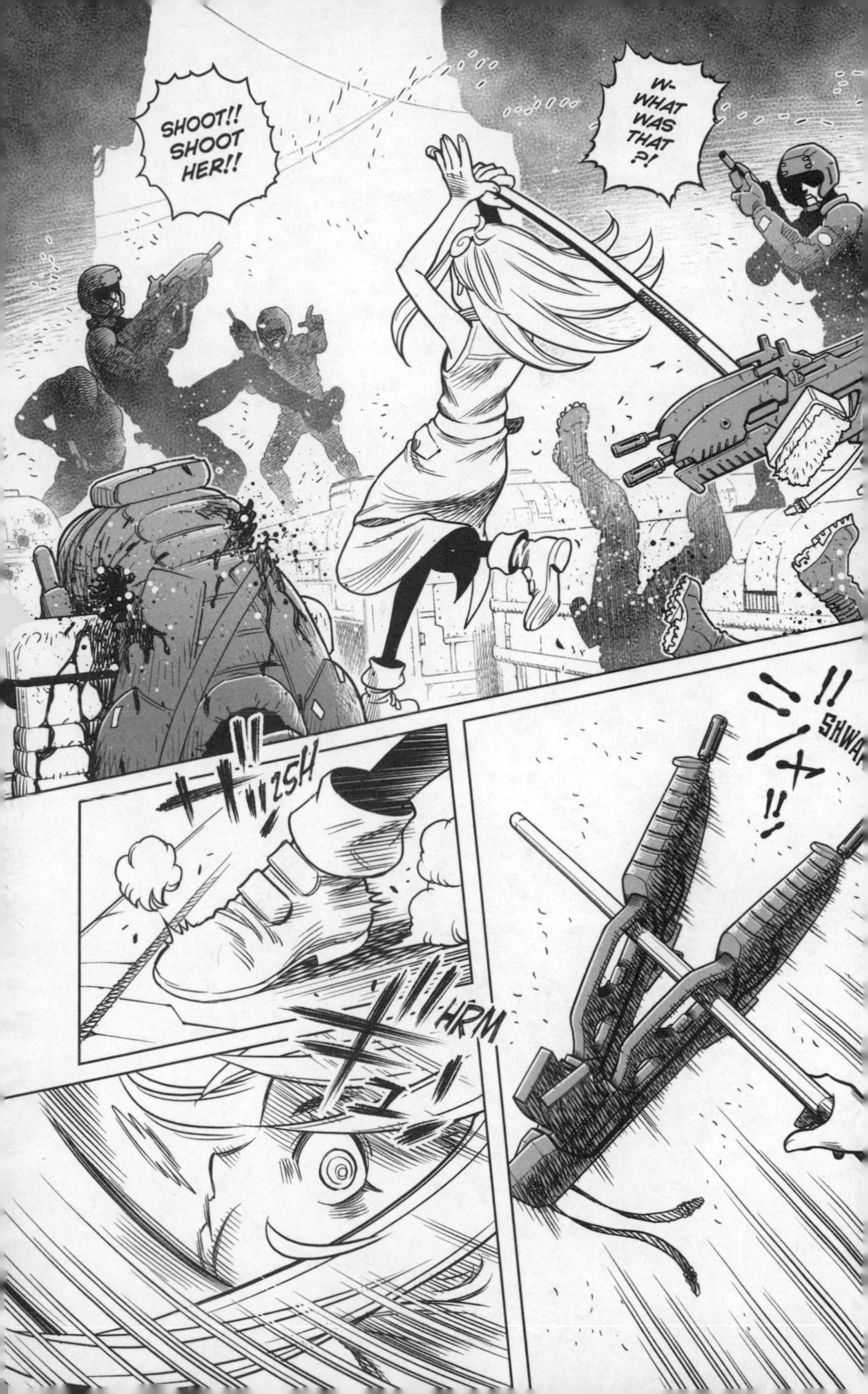
W-WHAT WAS THAT?!
SHOOT!! SHOOT HER!!
!! SHWA !!
ZSH
HRM

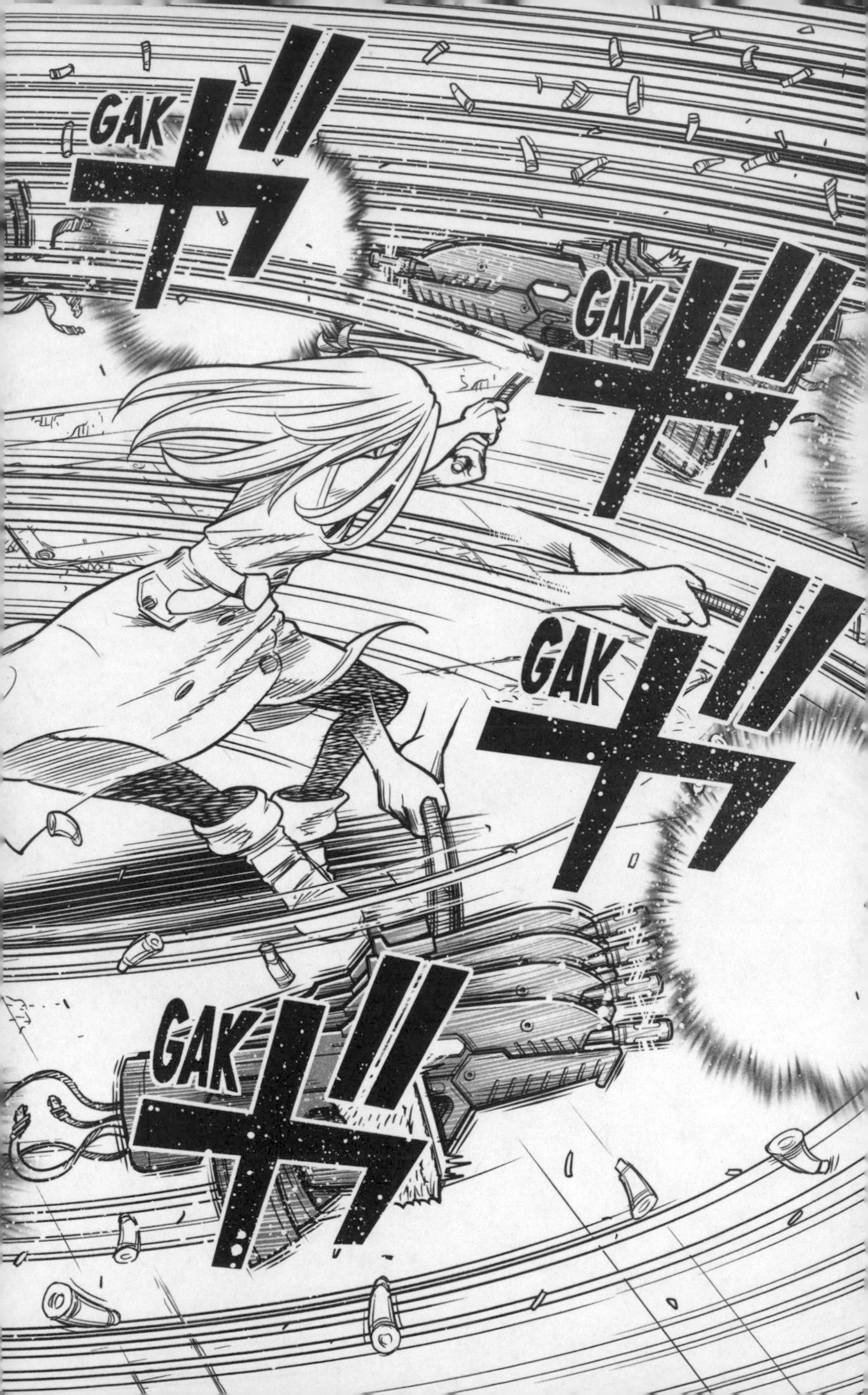
GAK
GAK
GAK
GAK

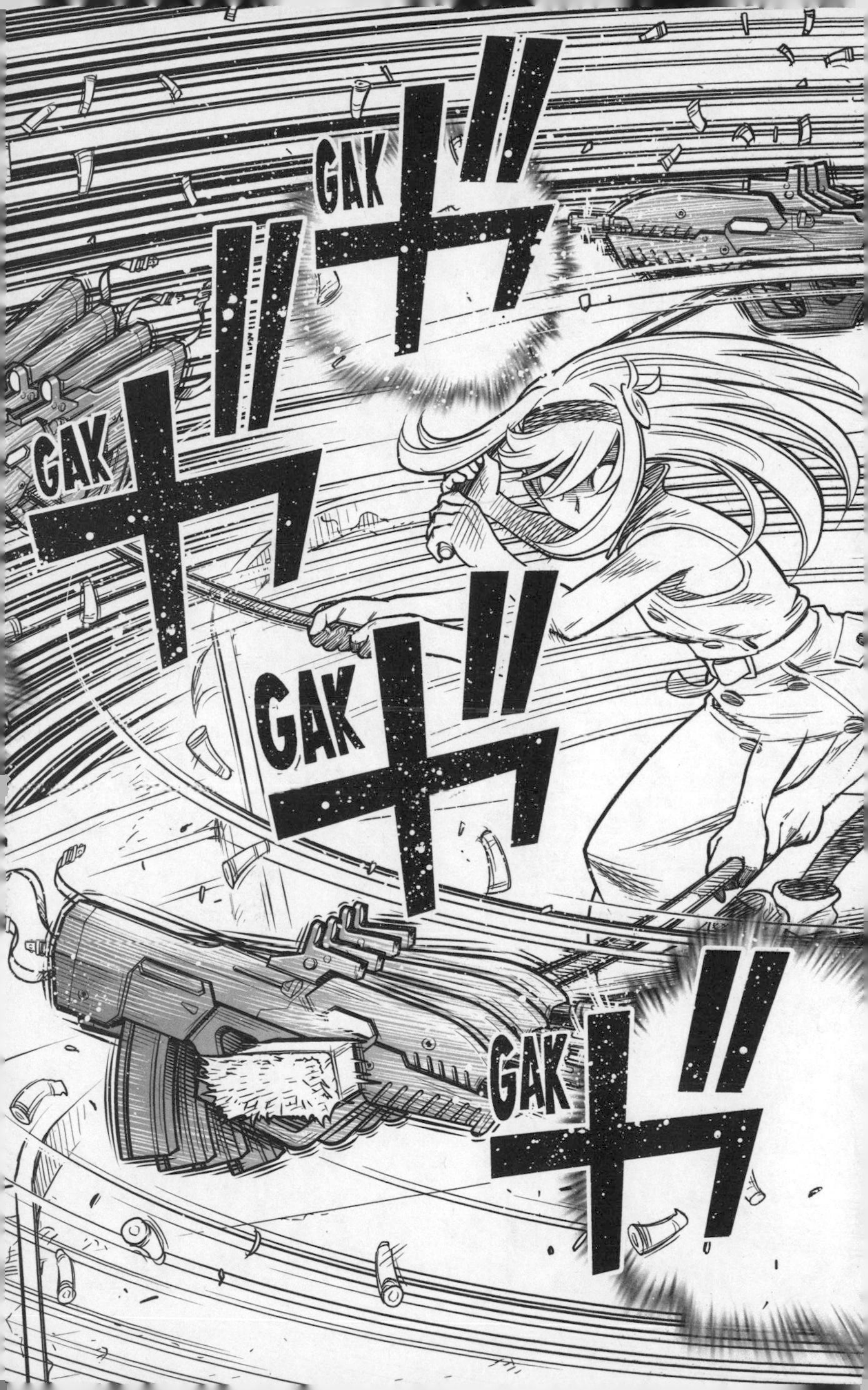
GAK
GAK
GAK
GAK

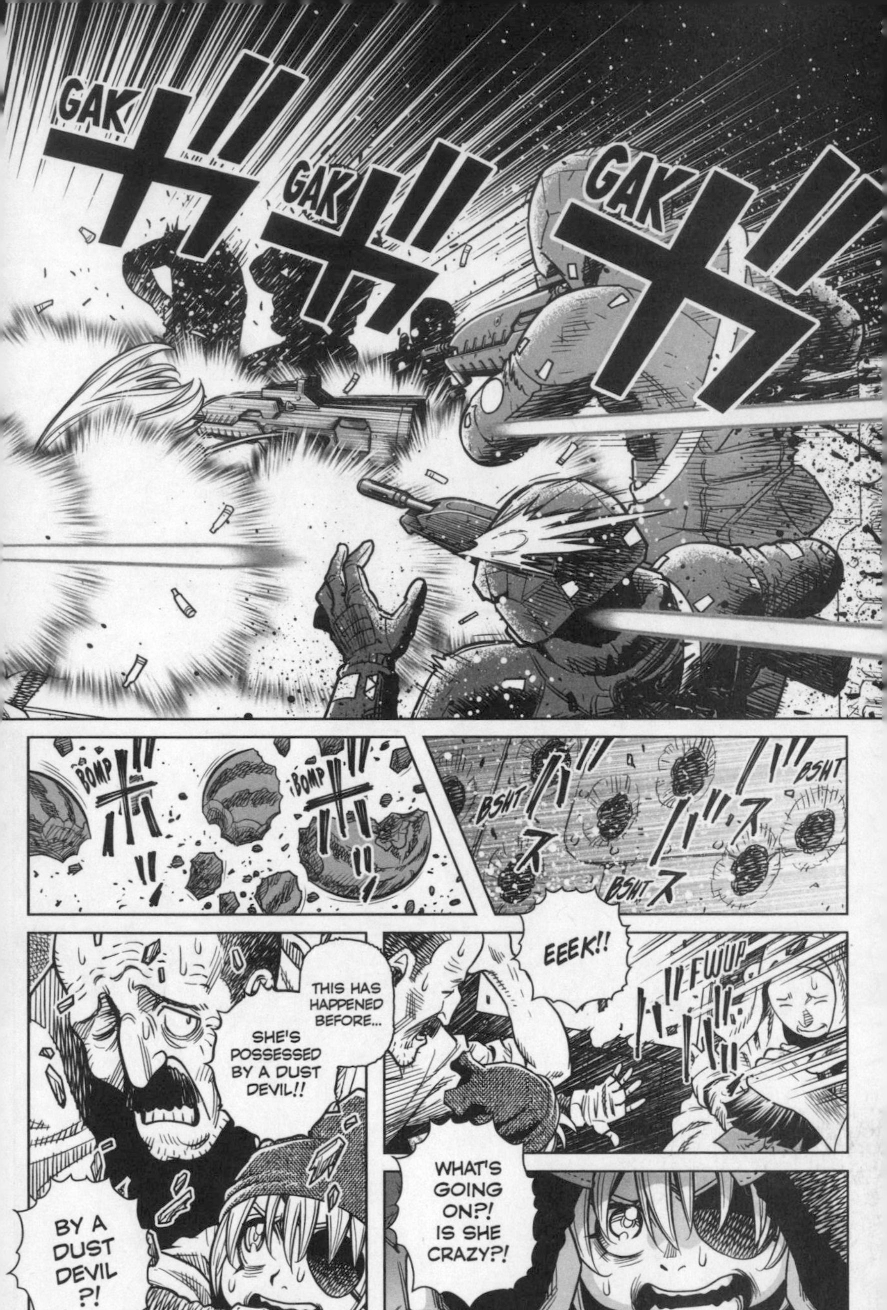
GAK
GAK
GAK
BSHT
BSHT
BSHT
BOMP
BOMP
EEEK!!
FWUP
WHAT'S GOING ON?! IS SHE CRAZY?!
THIS HAS HAPPENED BEFORE...
SHE'S POSSESSED BY A DUST DEVIL!!
BY A DUST DEVIL ?!

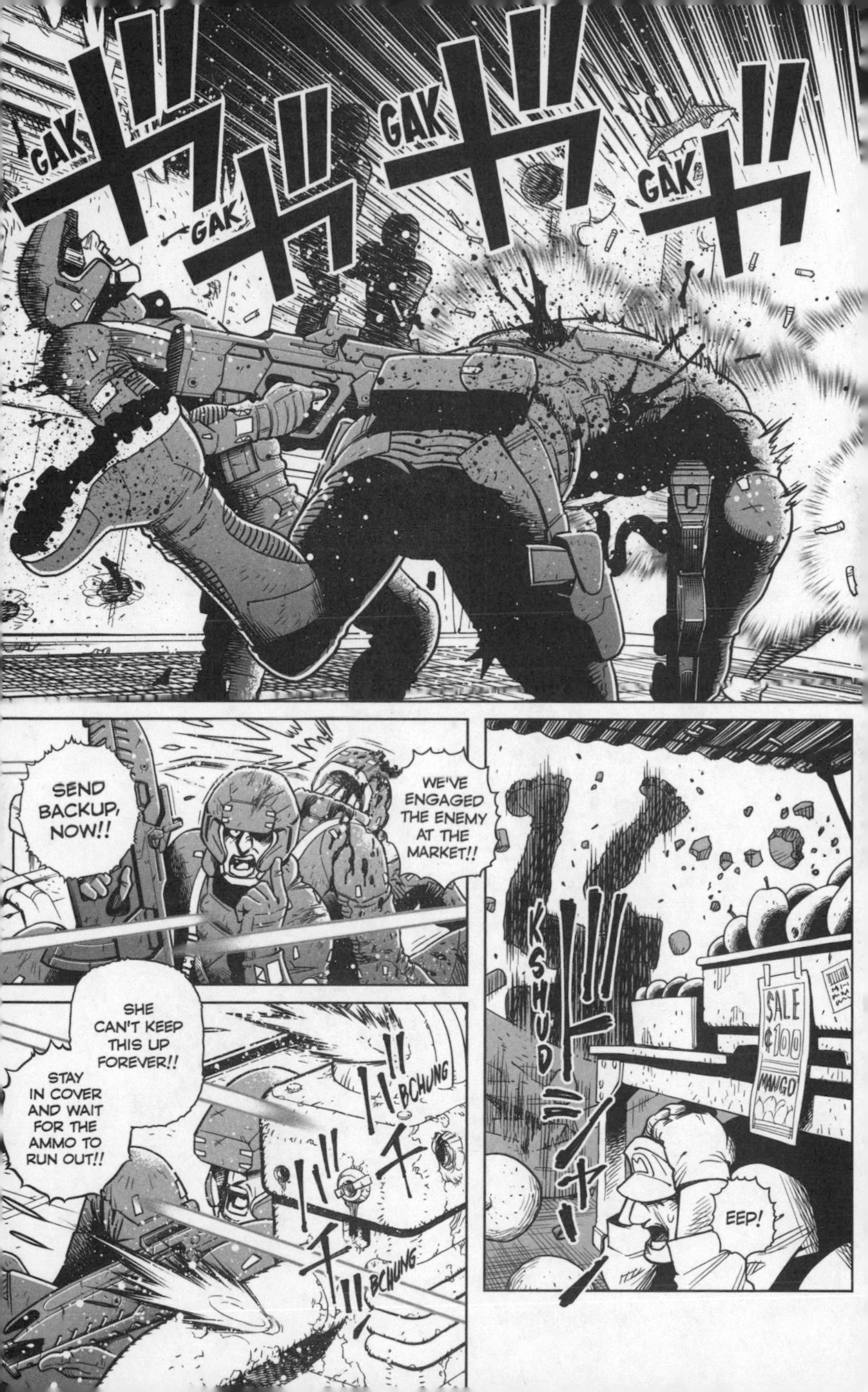

GAK
GAK
GAK
GAK
KSHUD
SALE
¢100
MANGO
EEP!
WE'VE ENGAGED THE ENEMY AT THE MARKET!!
SEND BACKUP, NOW!!
SHE CAN'T KEEP THIS UP FOREVER!!
STAY IN COVER AND WAIT FOR THE AMMO TO RUN OUT!!
BCHUNG
BCHUNG

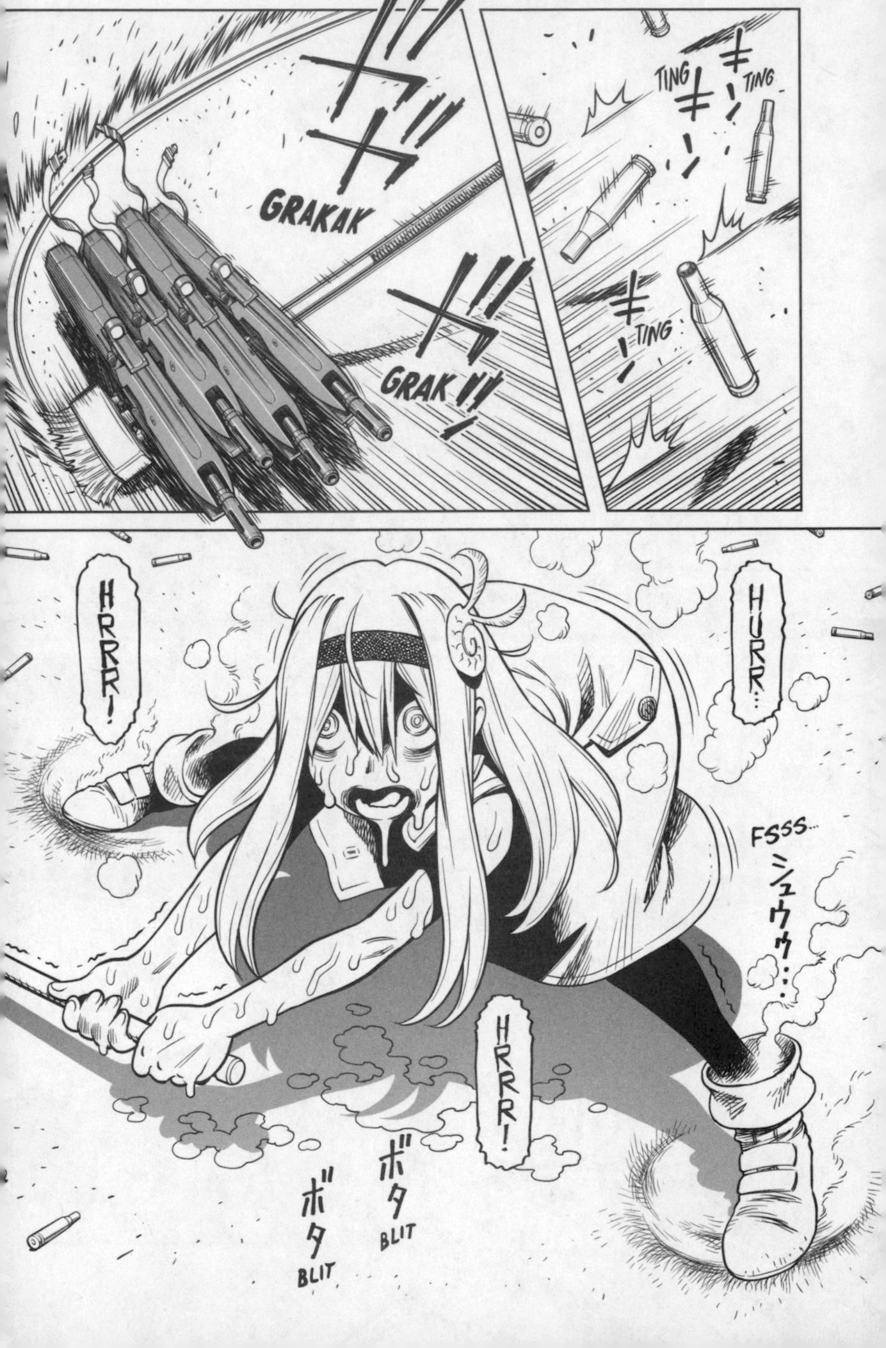

TING
TING
TING
GRAKAK
GRAK!!
HURRR...
FSSS...
シュウウ…
HRRRR!
ボタ
BLIT
ボタ
BLIT
HRRRR!

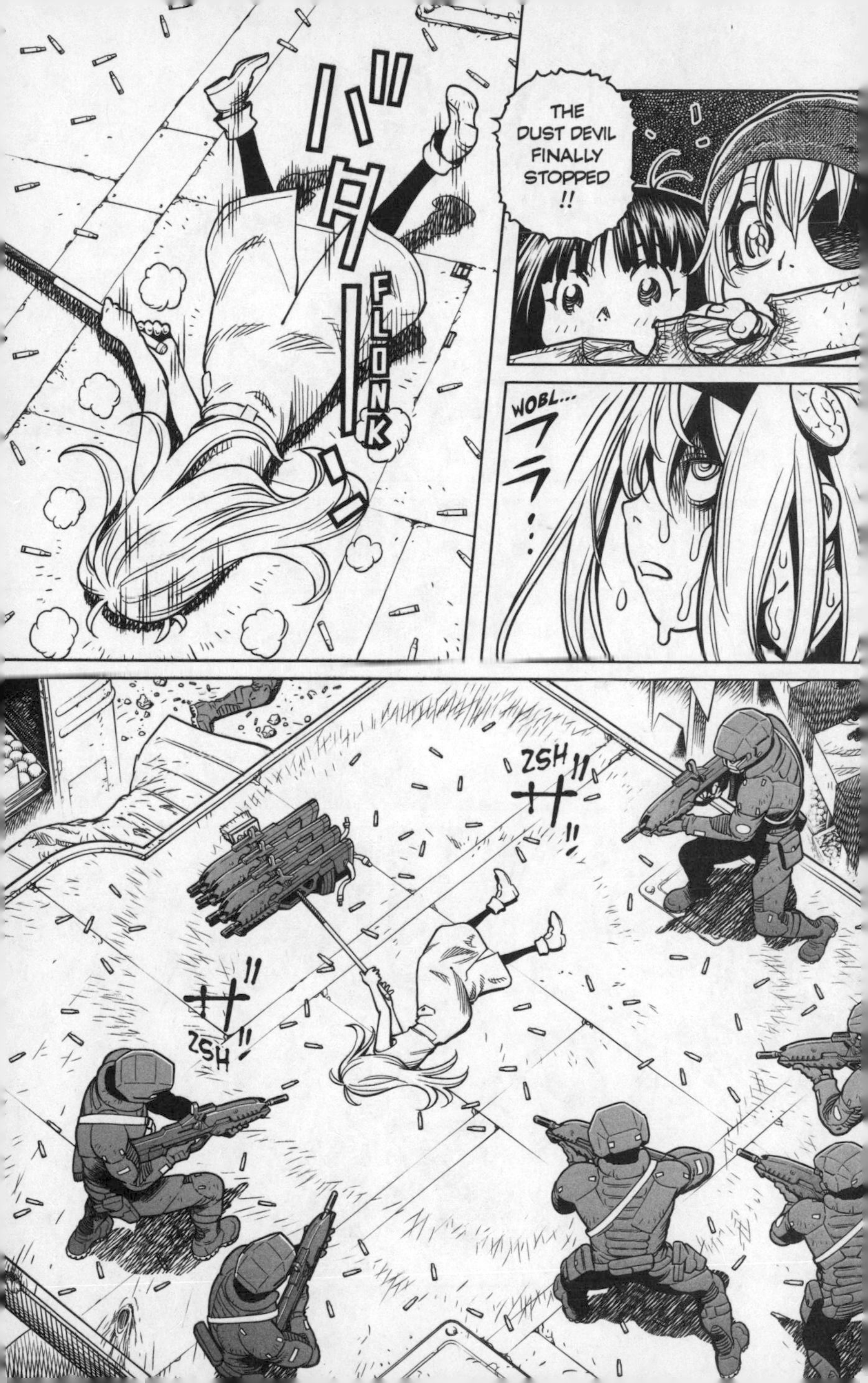
THE DUST DEVIL FINALLY STOPPED !!
WOBL...
フラ…
FLONK
ZSH!!
ZSH!!

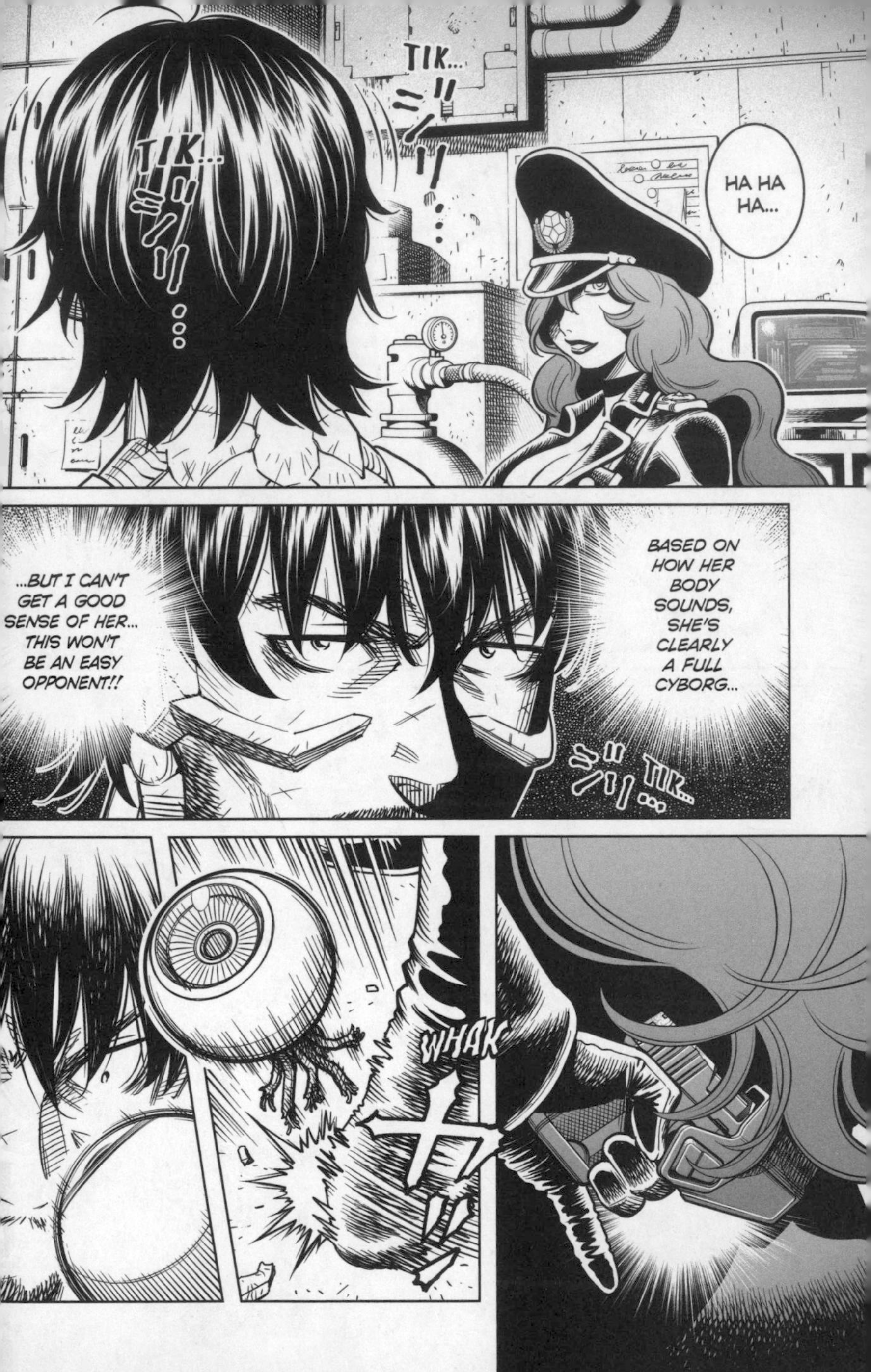
HA HA HA...
TIK...
TIK...
BASED ON HOW HER BODY SOUNDS, SHE'S CLEARLY A FULL CYBORG...
...BUT I CAN'T GET A GOOD SENSE OF HER... THIS WON'T BE AN EASY OPPONENT!!
TIK...
WHAK

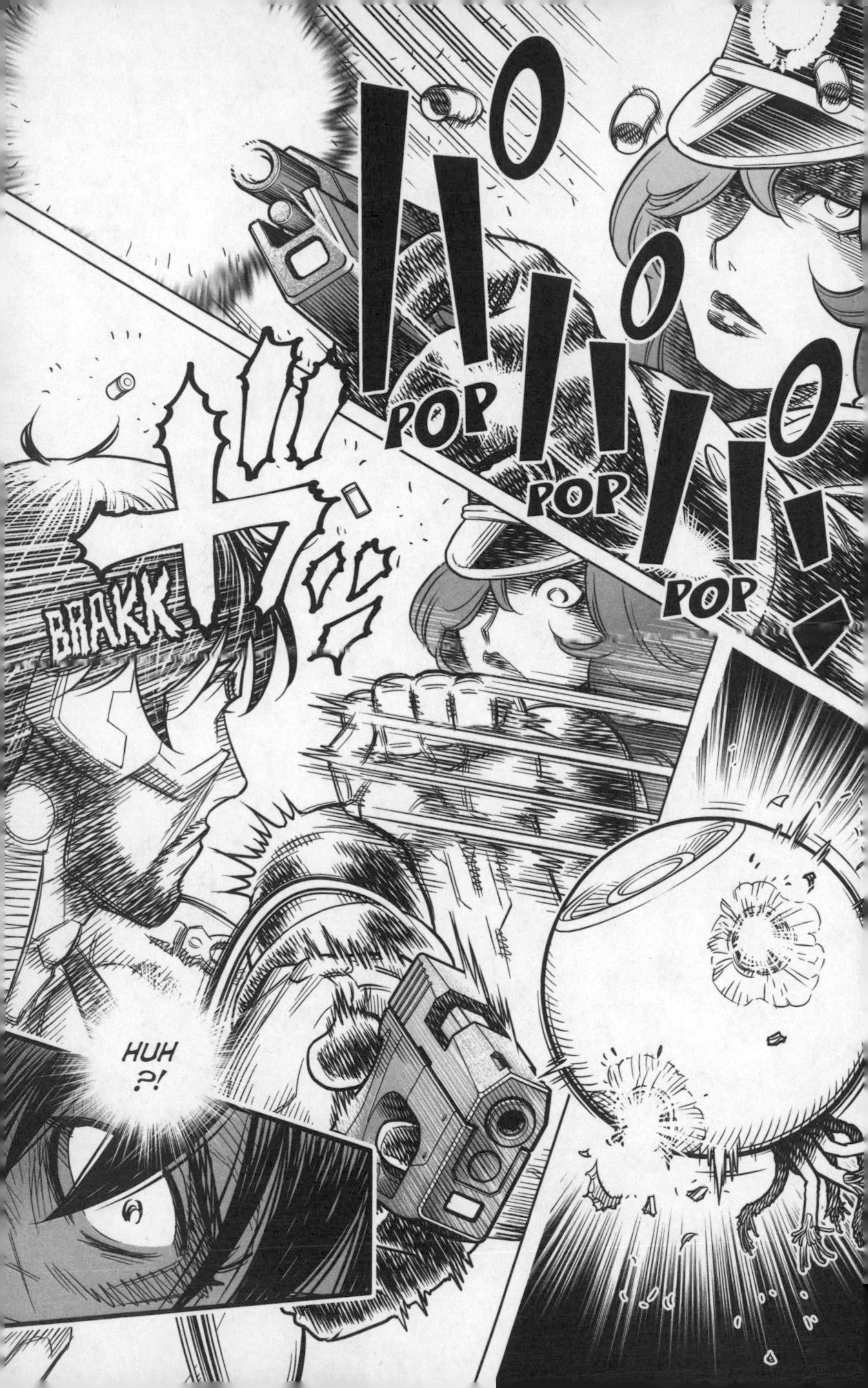
POP
POP
POP
BRAKK
HUH ?!

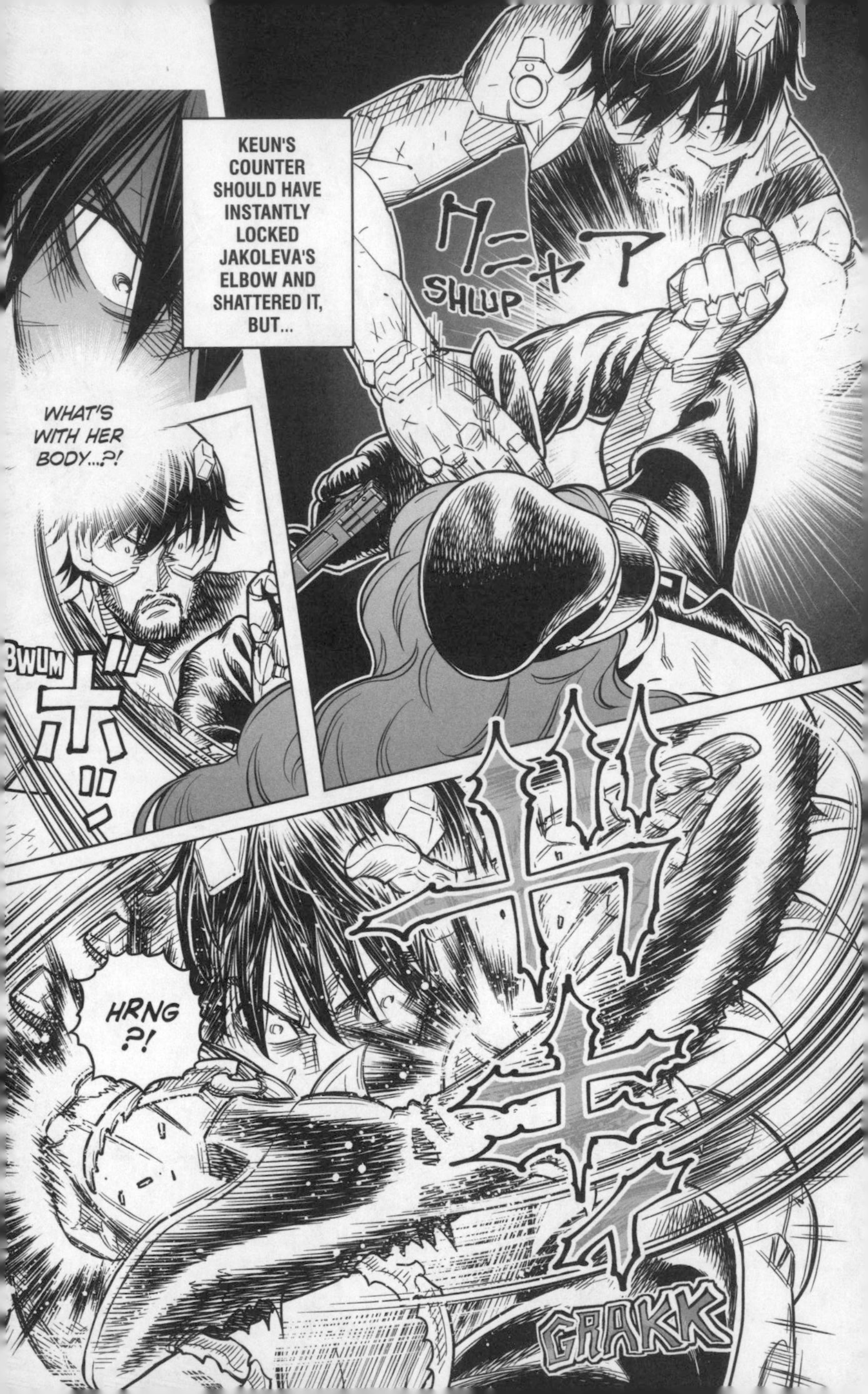
KEUN'S COUNTER SHOULD HAVE INSTANTLY LOCKED JAKOLEVA'S ELBOW AND SHATTERED IT, BUT...
SHLUP
WHAT'S WITH HER BODY...?!
BWUM
HRNG ?!
GRAKK

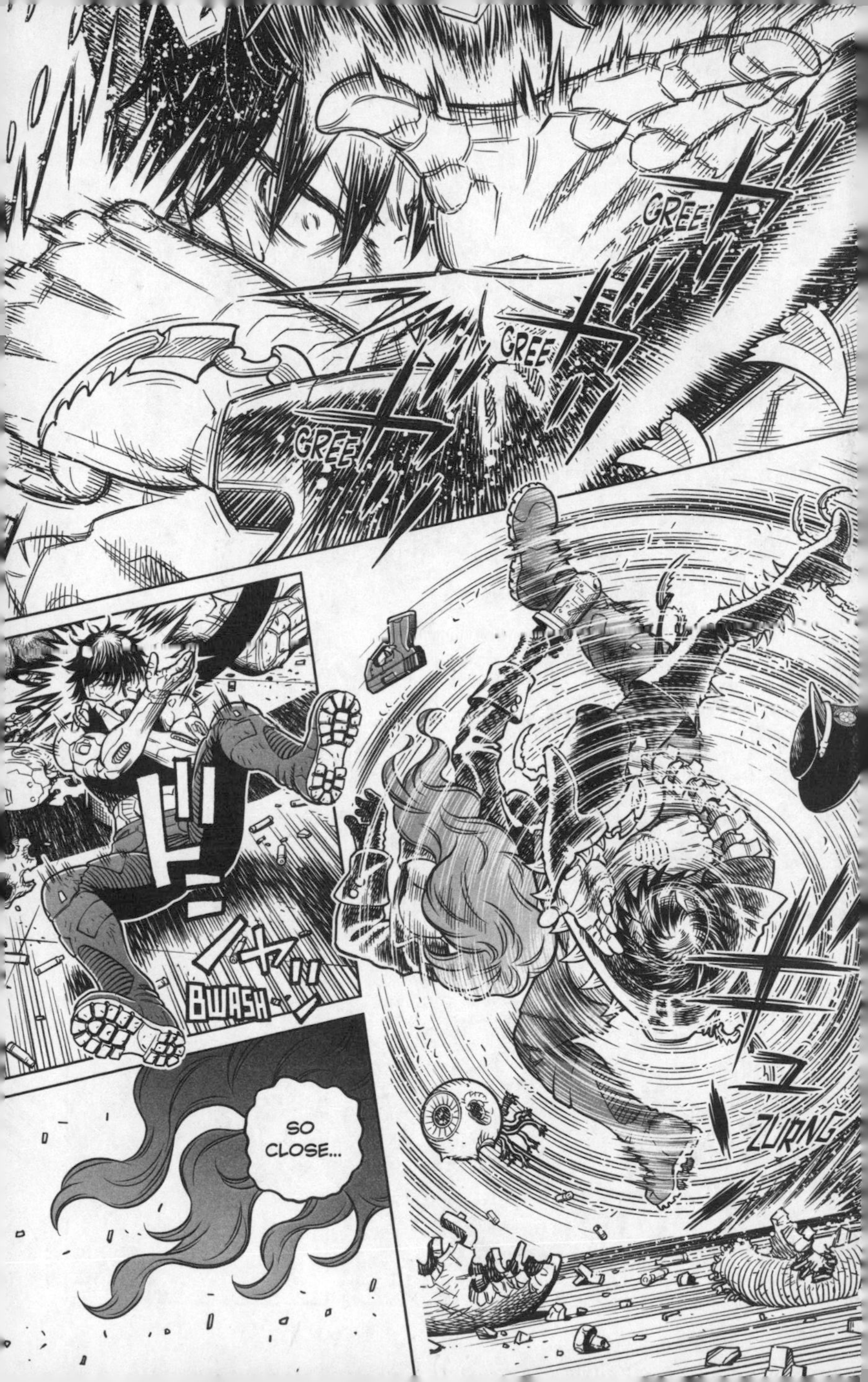
GREE
GREE
GREE
ZURNG
BWASH
SO CLOSE...

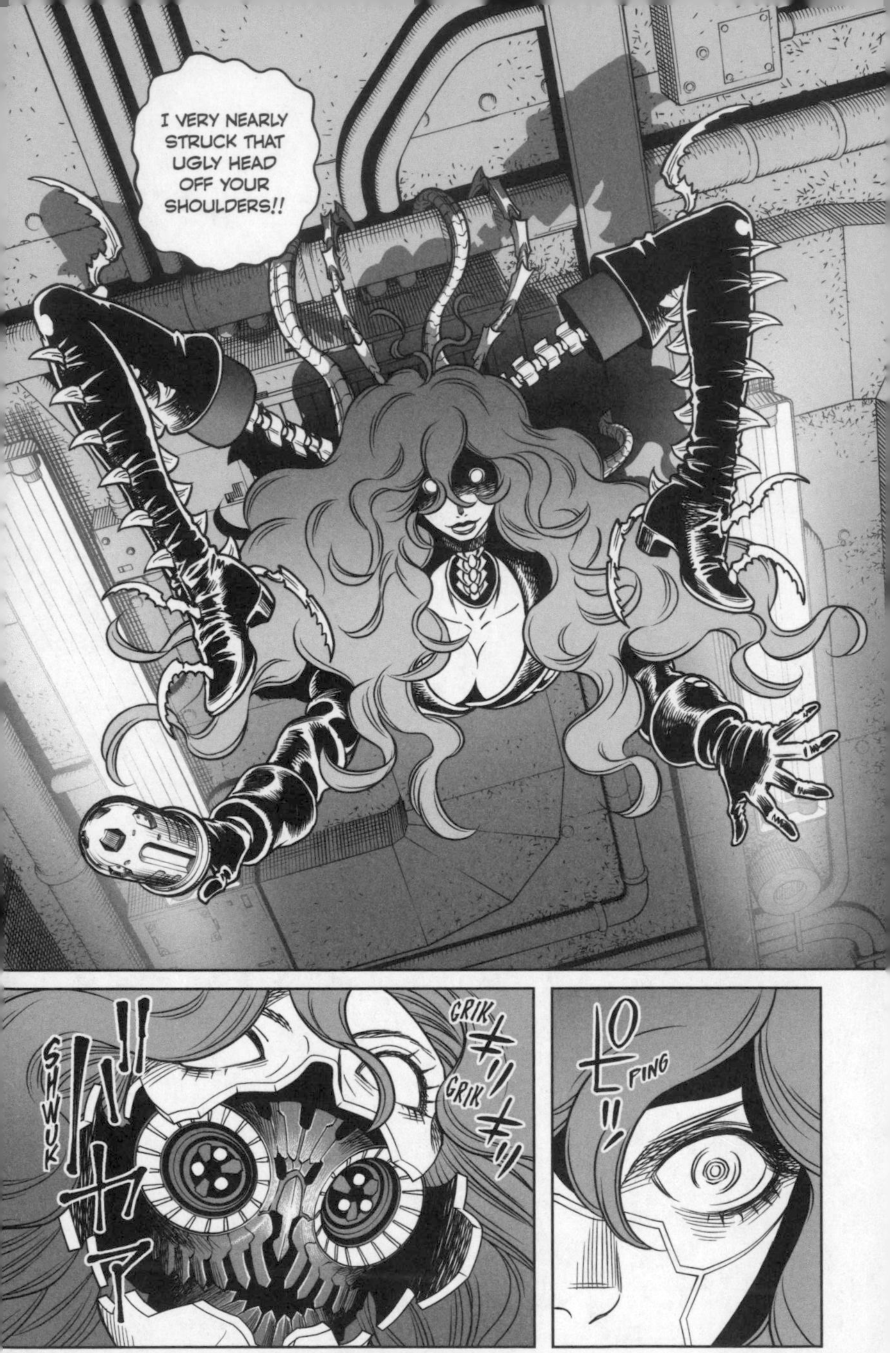
I VERY NEARLY STRUCK THAT UGLY HEAD OFF YOUR SHOULDERS!!
PING
GRIK
GRIK
SHWUK

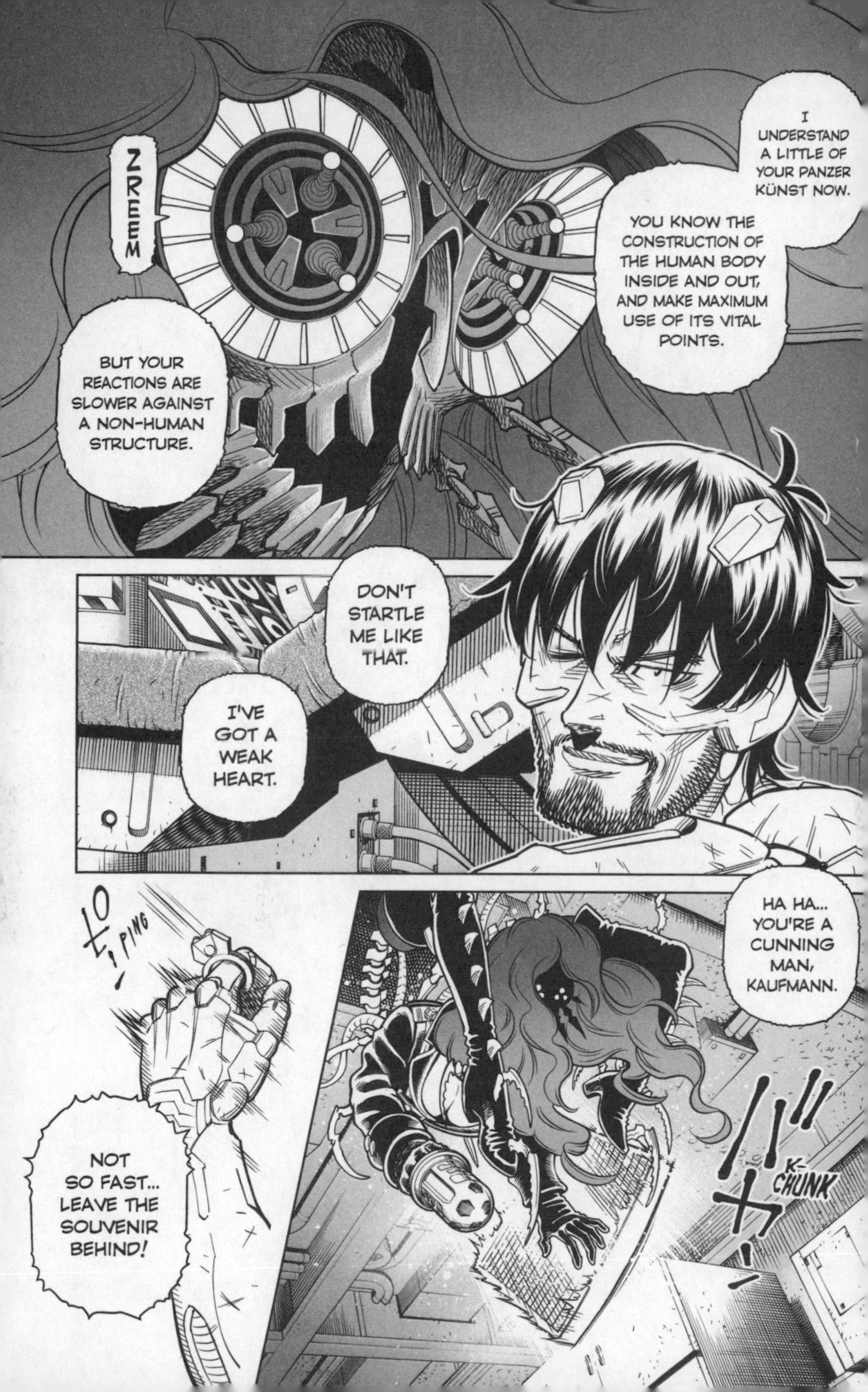
I UNDERSTAND A LITTLE OF YOUR PANZER KÜNST NOW.
YOU KNOW THE CONSTRUCTION OF THE HUMAN BODY INSIDE AND OUT, AND MAKE MAXIMUM USE OF ITS VITAL POINTS.
ZREEM
BUT YOUR REACTIONS ARE SLOWER AGAINST A NON-HUMAN STRUCTURE.
DON'T STARTLE ME LIKE THAT.
I'VE GOT A WEAK HEART.
HA HA... YOU'RE A CUNNING MAN, KAUFMANN.
K-CHUNK
PING
NOT SO FAST... LEAVE THE SOUVENIR BEHIND!

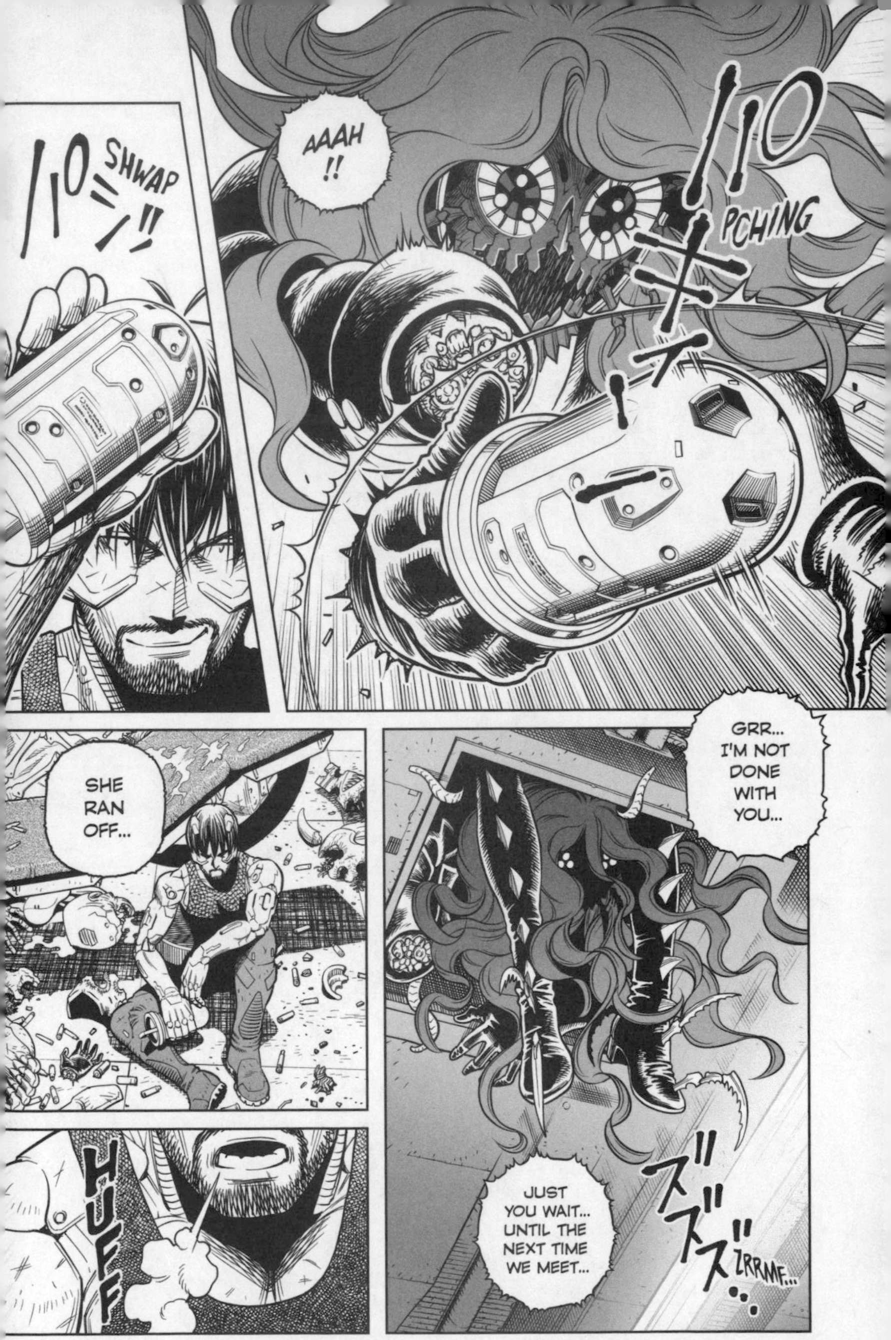
AAAH!!
PCHING
SHWAP
GRR... I'M NOT DONE WITH YOU...
JUST YOU WAIT... UNTIL THE NEXT TIME WE MEET...
ZRRMF...
SHE RAN OFF...
HUFF

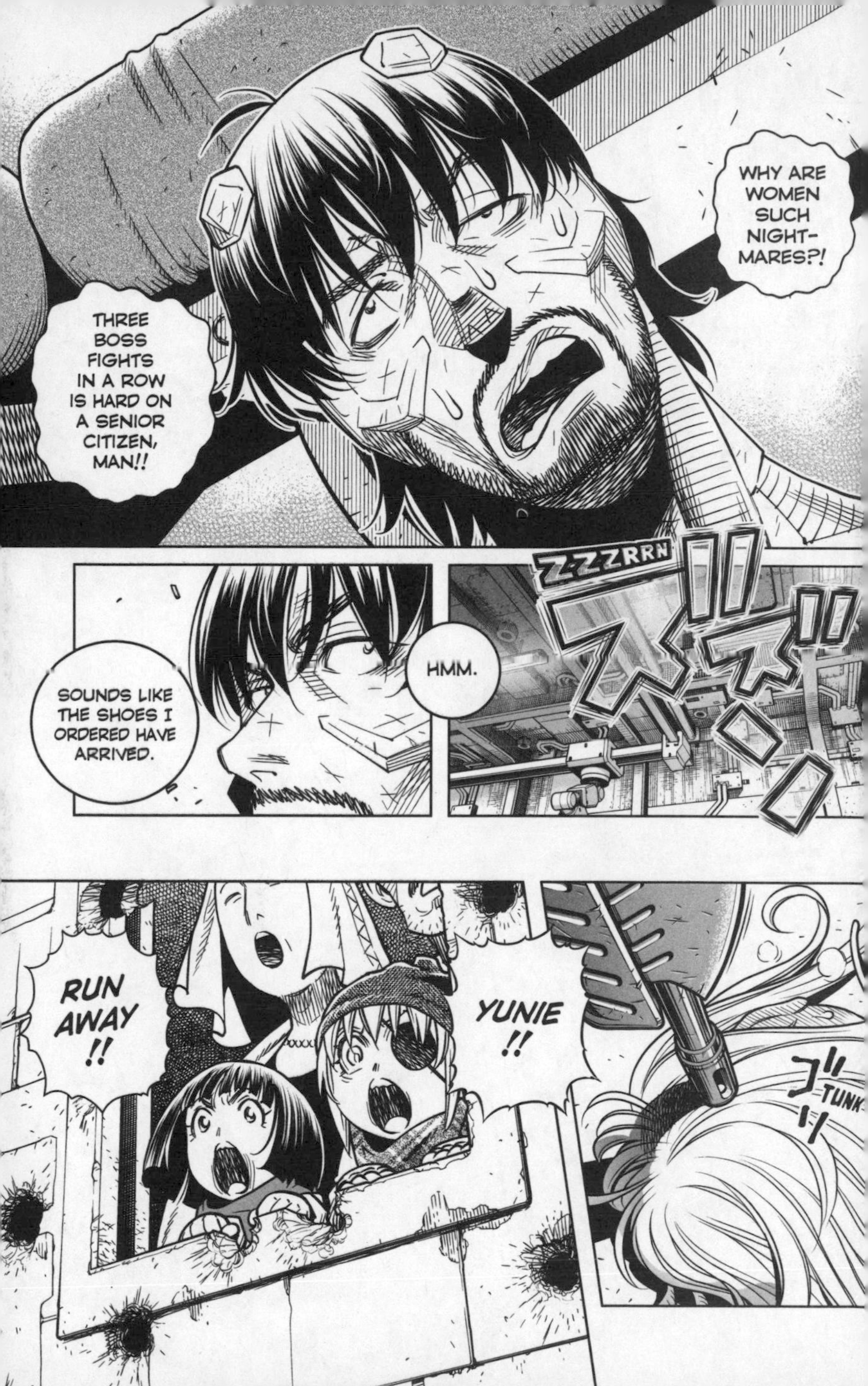
WHY ARE WOMEN SUCH NIGHT-MARES?!
THREE BOSS FIGHTS IN A ROW IS HARD ON A SENIOR CITIZEN, MAN!!
Z-Z-ZRRN
HMM.
SOUNDS LIKE THE SHOES I ORDERED HAVE ARRIVED.
TUNK
YUNIE!!
RUN AWAY!!

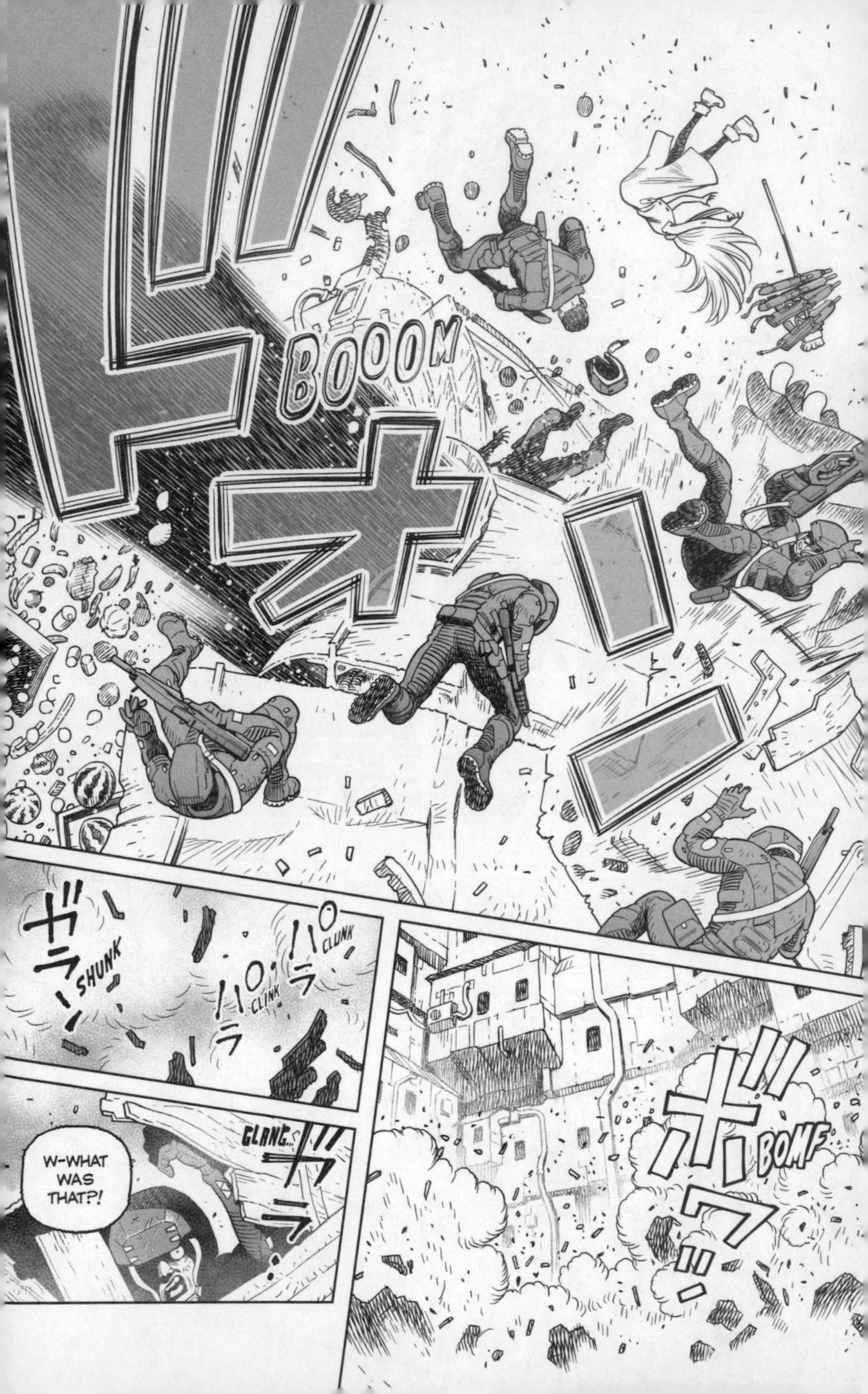
BOOOM
BOMF
CLINK
CLINK
SHUNK
CLANG...
W-WHAT WAS THAT?!

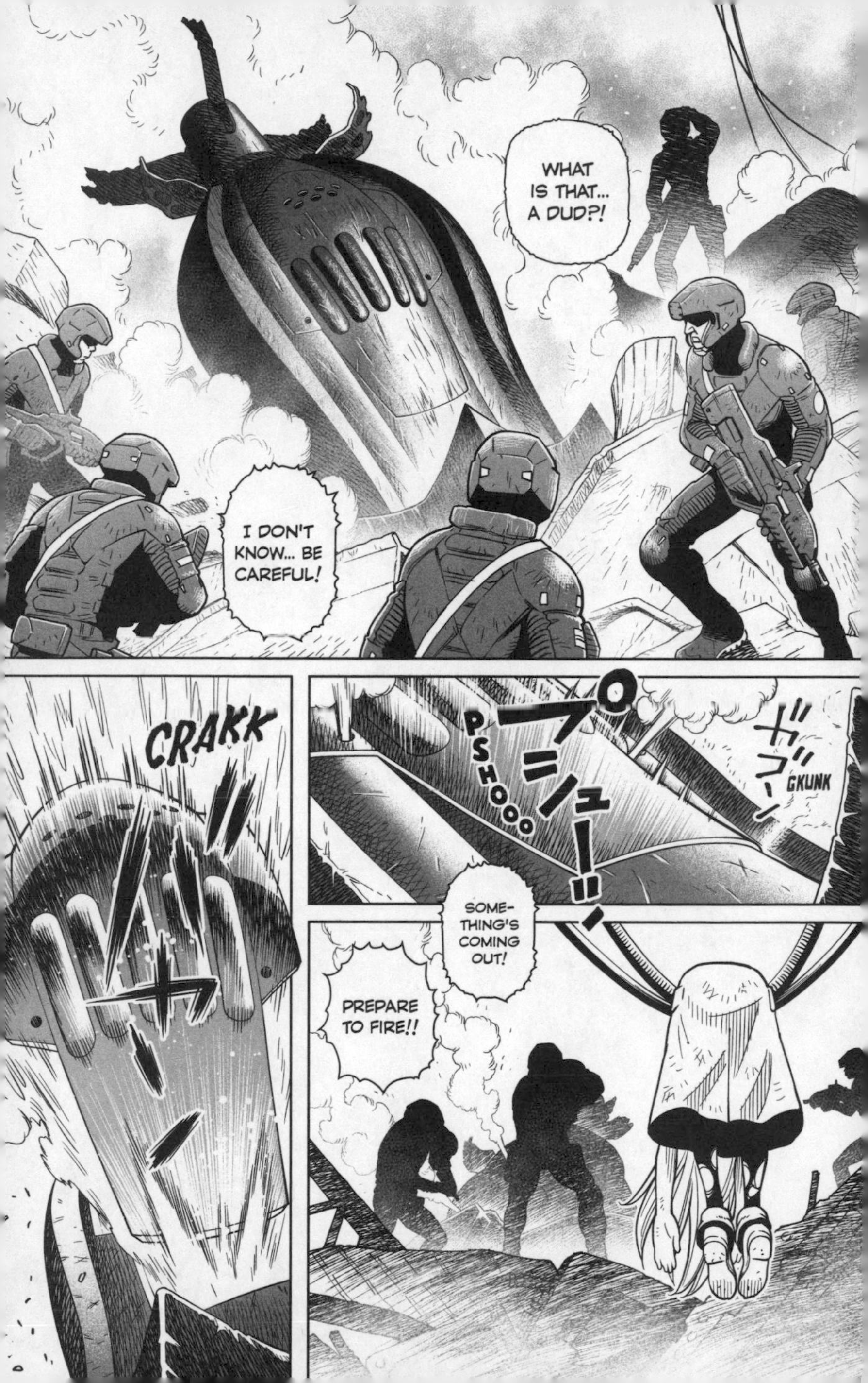
WHAT IS THAT... A DUD?!
I DON'T KNOW... BE CAREFUL!
GKUNK
プシュー!!
PSHOOO
SOME-THING'S COMING OUT!
PREPARE TO FIRE!!
CRAKK

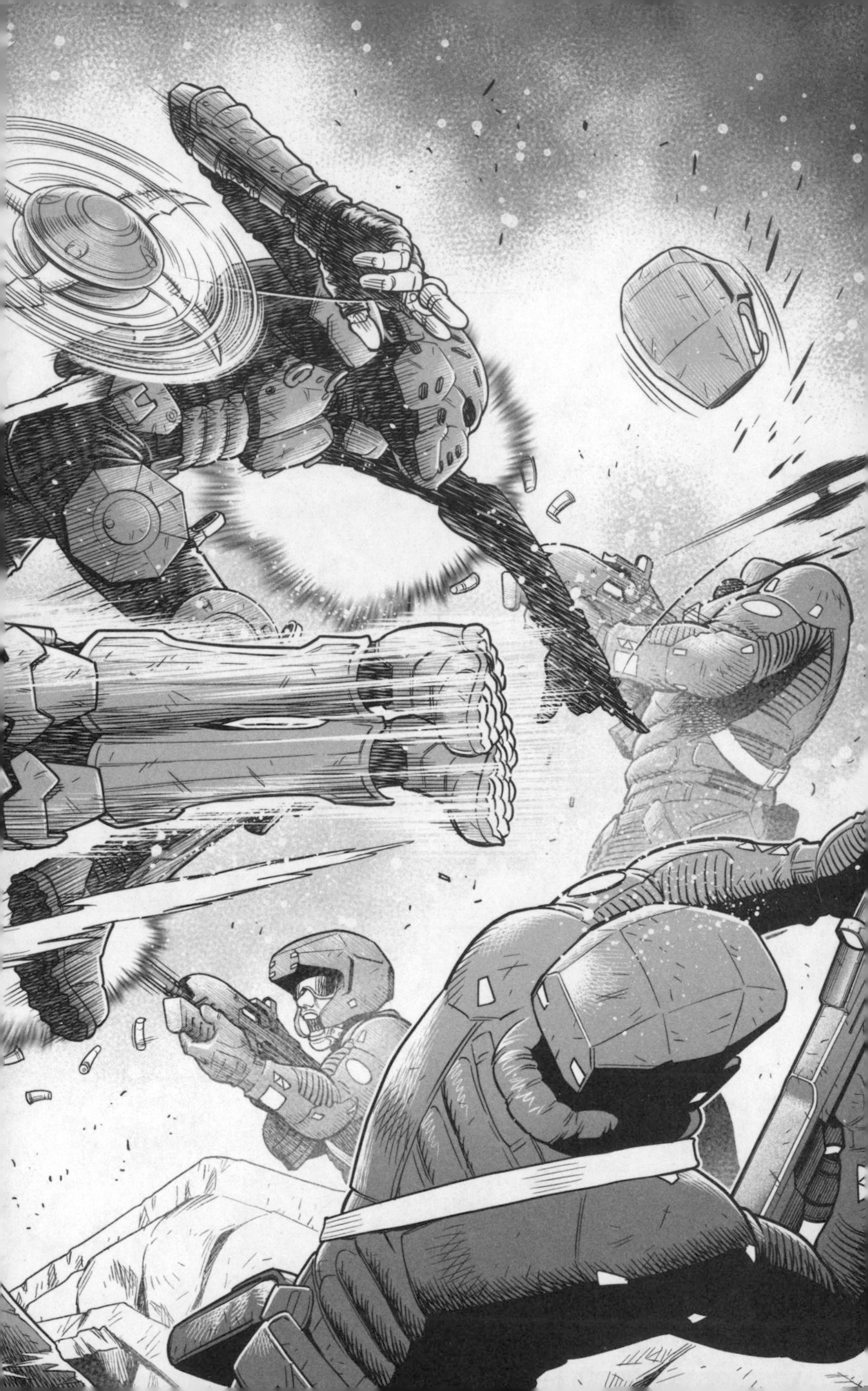

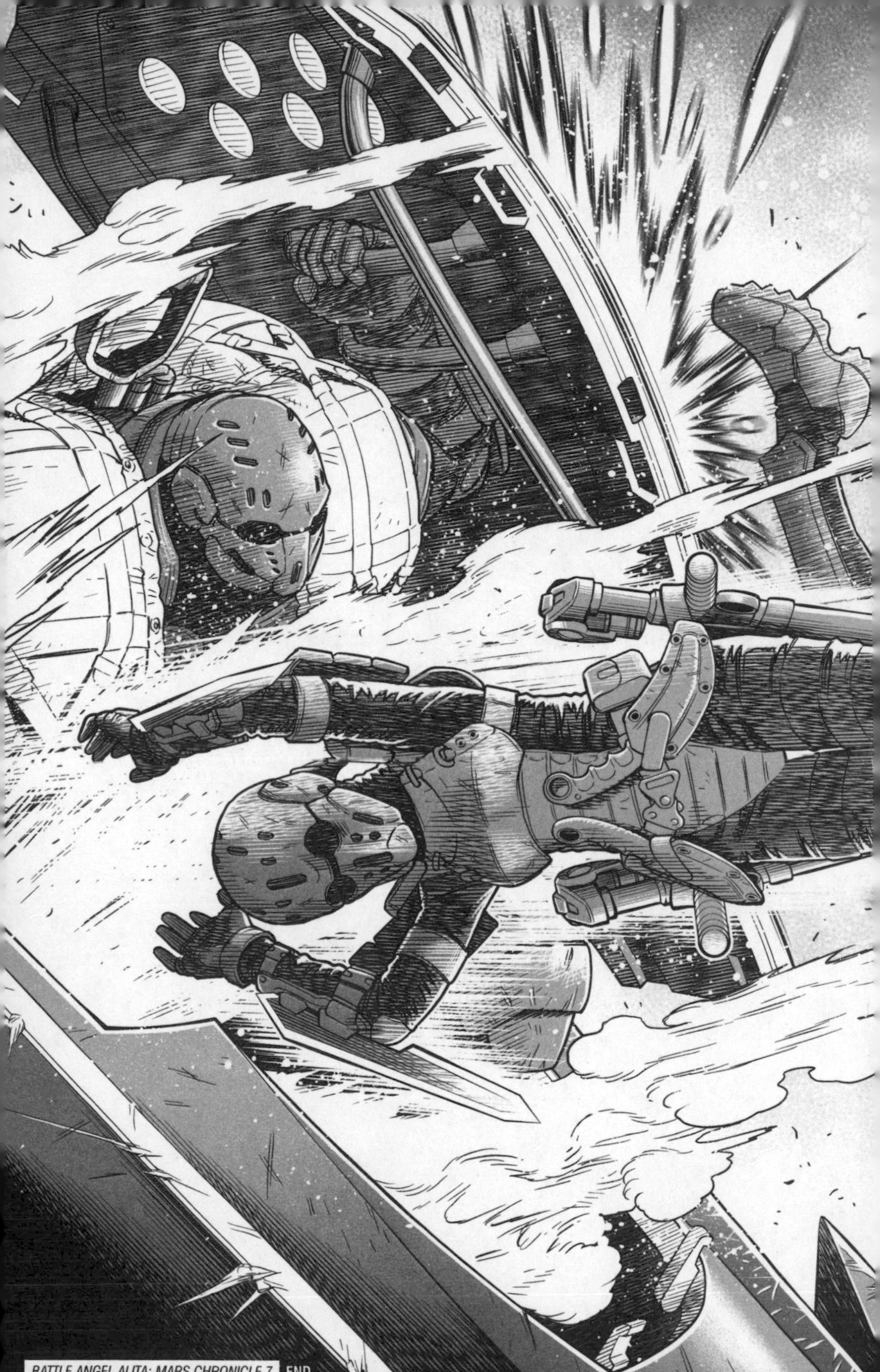

BATTLE ANGEL ALITA: MARS CHRONICLE 7 END

BATTLE ANGEL ALITA

MARS CHRONICLE

PRESENTED by YUKITO KISHIRO

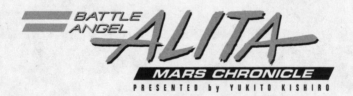

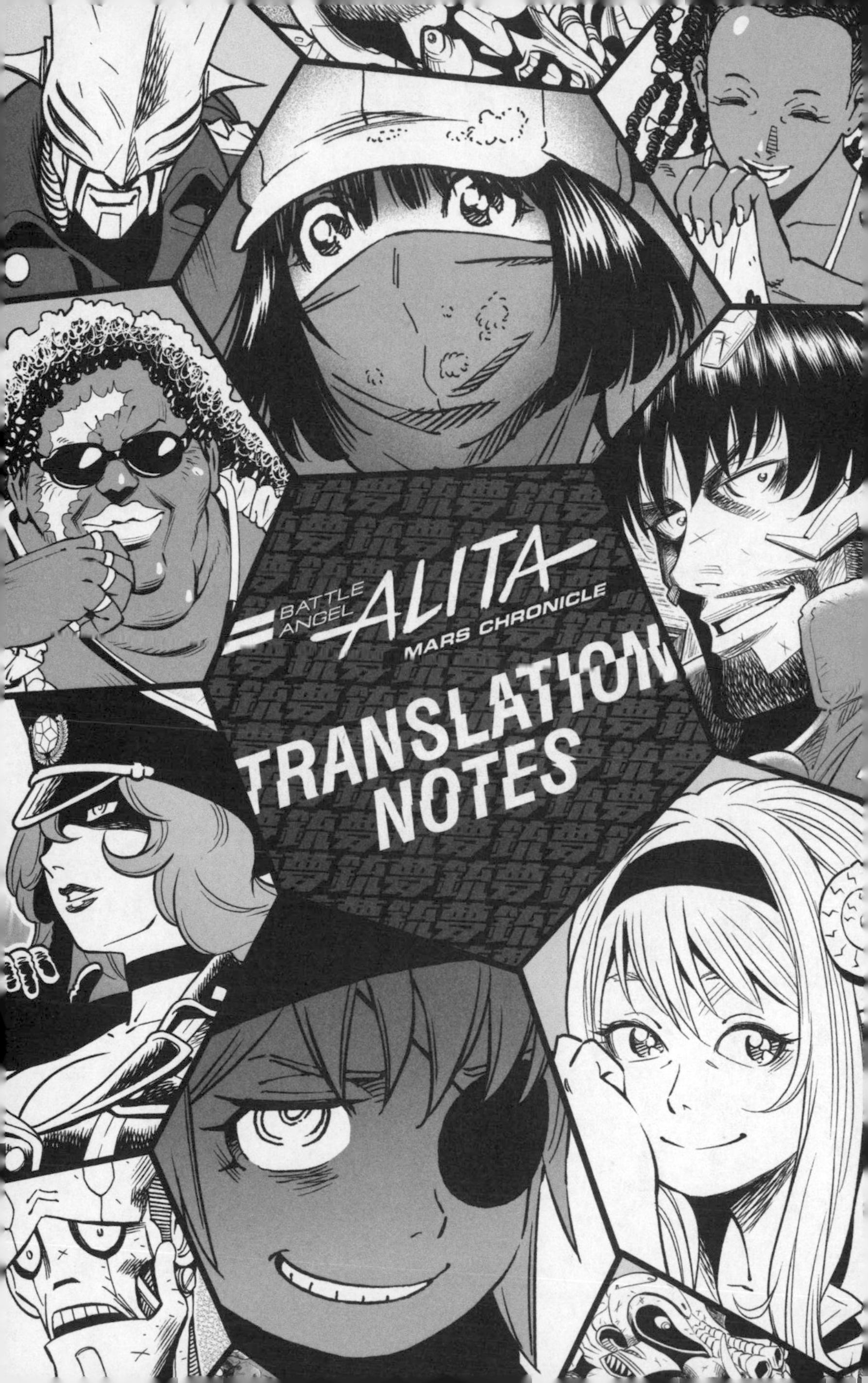
BATTLE ANGEL ALITA
MARS CHRONICLE
TRANSLATION NOTES

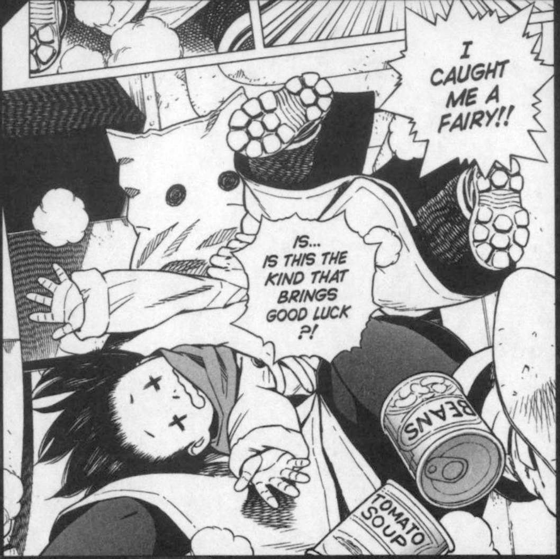
I CAUGHT ME A FAIRY!!
IS... IS THIS THE KIND THAT BRINGS GOOD LUCK ?!
BEANS
TOMATO SOUP

FAIRY

pg. 23

The precise type of fairy Yunie is talking about here is a *zashiki-warashi,* a kind of traditional Japanese spirit that means "parlor child." They are mischievous, and play many pranks, but are said to bring great fortune to whoever succeeds in spotting them.

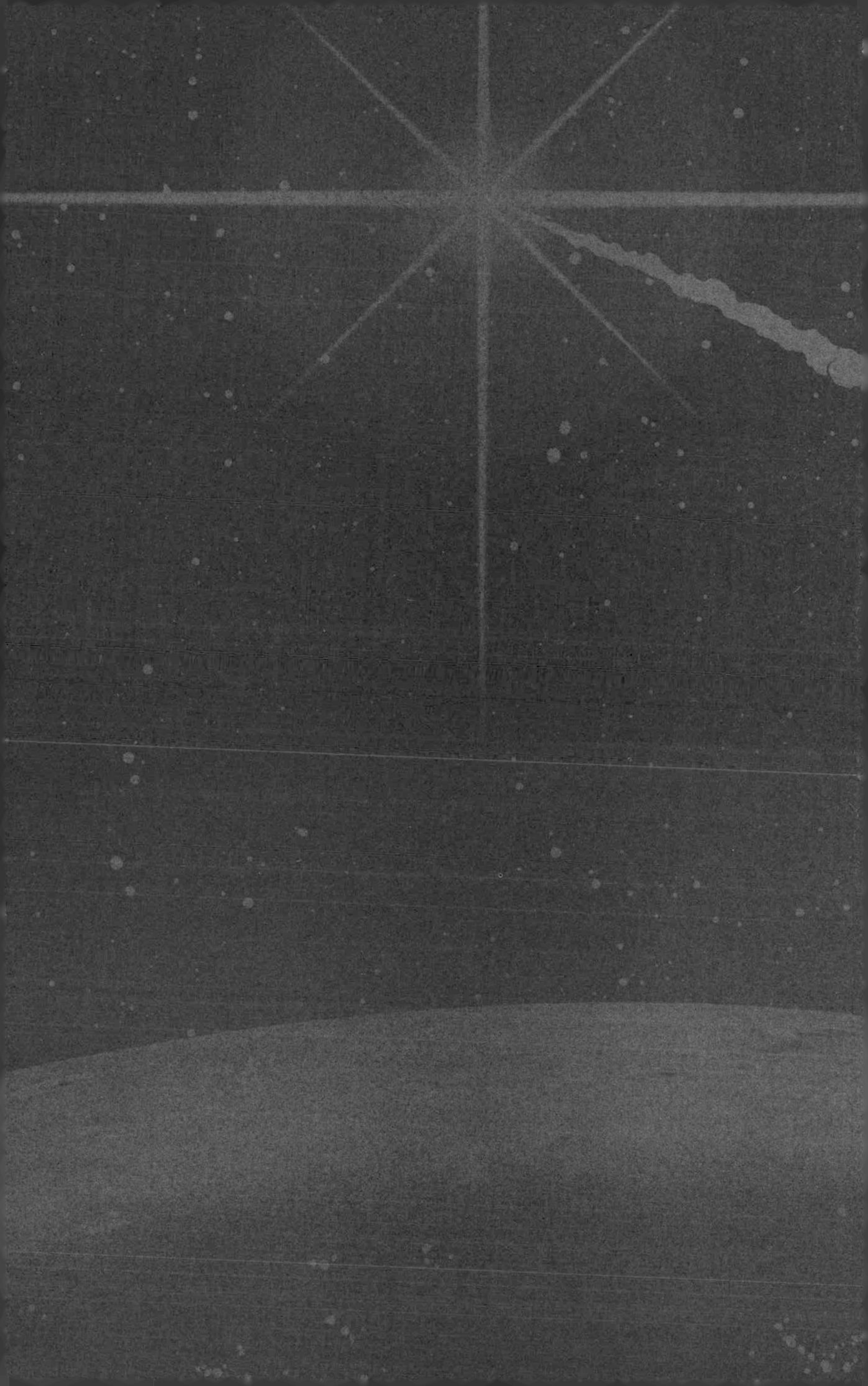

The boys are back, in 400-page hardcovers that are as pretty and badass as they are!

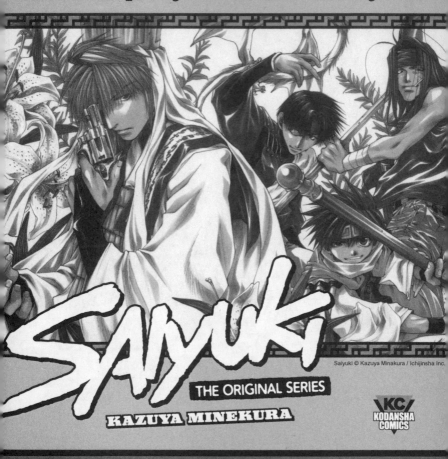

Saiyuki © Kazuya Minakura / Ichijinsha Inc.

SAIYUKI

THE ORIGINAL SERIES

KAZUYA MINEKURA

'AN EDGY COMIC LOOK AT AN ANCIENT CHINESE TALE." —YALSA

Genjo Sanzo is a Buddhist priest in the city of Togenkyo, which is being ravaged by yokai spirits that have fallen out of balance with the natural order. His superiors send him on a journey far to the west to discover why this is happening and how to stop it. His companions are three yokai with human souls. But this is no day trip — the four will encounter many discoveries and horrors on the way.

FEATURES NEW TRANSLATION, COLOR PAGES, AND BEAUTIFUL WRAPAROUND COVER ART!

Young characters and steampunk setting, like *Howl's Moving Castle* and *Battle Angel Alita*

Beyond the Clouds © 2018 Nicke / Ki-oon

A boy with a talent for machines and a mysterious girl whose wings he's fixed will take you beyond the clouds! In the tradition of the high-flying, resonant adventure stories of Studio Ghibli comes a gorgeous tale about the longing of young hearts for adventure and friendship!

PERFECT WORLD

Rie Aruga

A TOUCHING NEW SERIES ABOUT LOVE AND COPING WITH DISABILITY

An office party reunites Tsugumi with her high school crush Itsuki. He's realized his dream of becoming an architect, but along the way, he experienced a spinal injury that put him in a wheelchair. Now Tsugumi's rekindled feelings will butt up against prejudices she never considered — and Itsuki will have to decide if he's ready to let someone into his heart...

"Depicts with great delicacy and courage the difficulties some with disabilities experience getting involved in romantic relationships... Rie Aruga refuses to romanticize, pushing her heroine to face the reality of disability. She invites her readers to the same tasks of empathy, knowledge and recognition."
—Slate.fr

"An important entry [in manga romance]... The emotional core of both plot and characters indicates thoughtfulness... [Aruga's] research is readily apparent in the text and artwork, making this feel like a real story."
—Anime News Network

A SMART, NEW ROMANTIC COMEDY FOR FANS OF *SHORTCAKE CAKE* AND *TERRACE HOUSE!*

A romance manga starring high school girl Meeko, who learns to live on her own in a boarding house whose living room is home to the odd (but handsome) Matsunaga-san. She begins to adjust to her new life away from her parents, but Meeko soon learns that no matter how far away from home she is, she's still a young girl at heart — especially when she finds herself falling for Matsunaga-san.

The adorable new odd-couple cat comedy manga from the creator of the beloved *Chi's Sweet Home*, in full color!

Praise for *Chi's Sweet Home*

"Nearly impossible to turn away... a true all-ages title that anyone, young or old, cat lover or not, will enjoy. The stories will bring a smile to your face and warm your heart."

—School Library Journal

Sue & Tai-chan

Konami Kanata

Sue is an aging housecat who's looking forward to living out her life in peace... but her plans change when the mischievous black tomcat Tai-chan enters the picture! Hey! Sue never signed up to be a catsitter! *Sue & Tai-chan* is the latest from the reigning meow-narch of cute kitty comics, Konami Kanata.

CUTE ANIMALS AND LIFE LESSONS, PERFECT FOR ASPIRING PET VETS OF ALL AGES!

YUZU THE PET VET

1

BY **MINGO ITO**

In collaboration with
NIPPON COLUMBIA CO., LTD.

Yuzu the Pet Vet © Mingo Ito / NIPPON COLUMBIA CO., LTD./Kodansha Ltd.

For an 11-year-old, Yuzu has a lot on her plate. When her mom gets sick and has to be hospitalized, Yuzu goes to live with her uncle who runs the local veterinary clinic. Yuzu's always been scared of animals, but she tries to help out. Through all the tough moments in her life, Yuzu realizes that she can help make things all right with a little help from her animal pals, peers, and kind grown-ups.

Every new patient is a furry friend in the making!

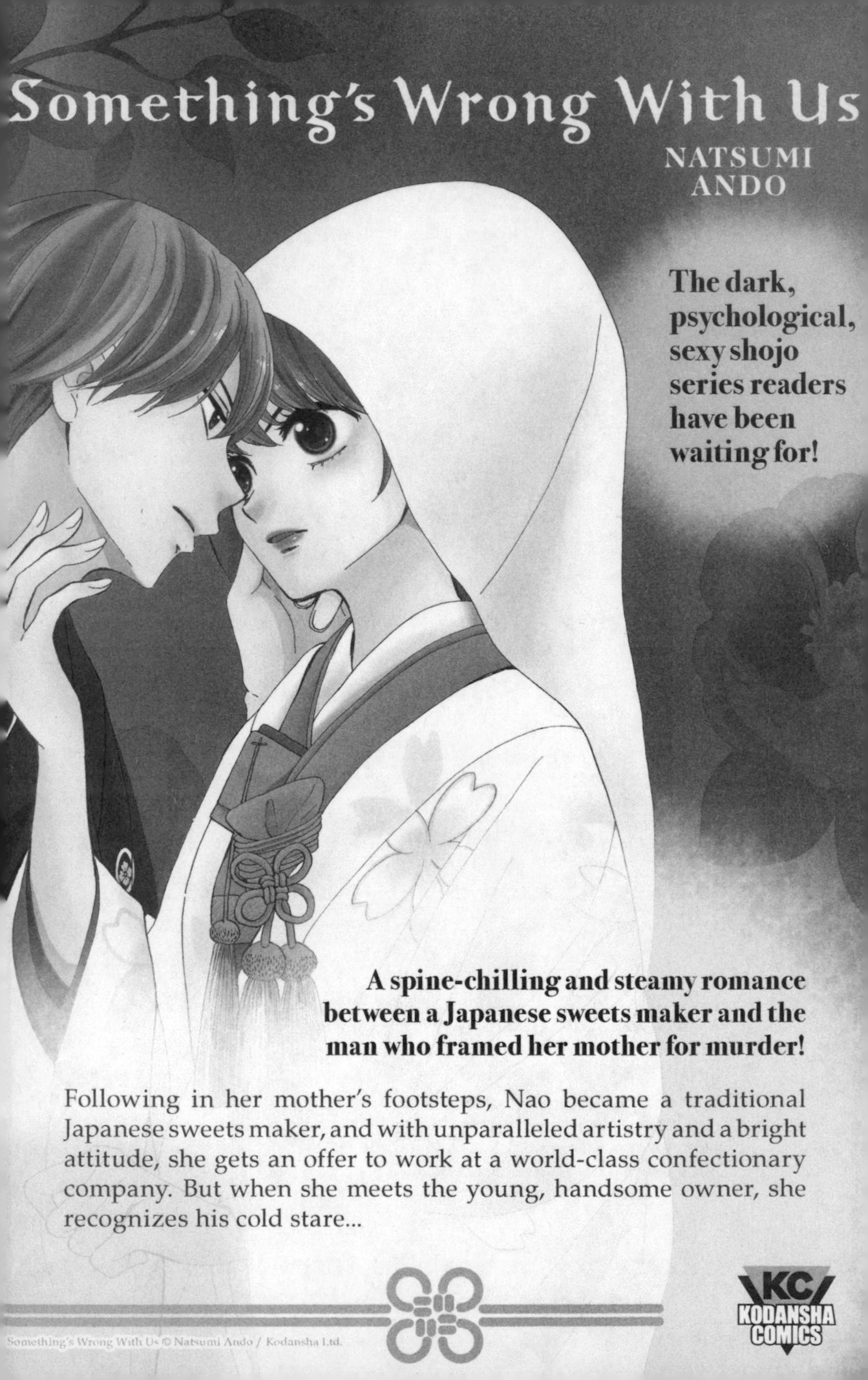
Something's Wrong With Us
NATSUMI ANDO
The dark, psychological, sexy shojo series readers have been waiting for!
A spine-chilling and steamy romance between a Japanese sweets maker and the man who framed her mother for murder!
Following in her mother's footsteps, Nao became a traditional Japanese sweets maker, and with unparalleled artistry and a bright attitude, she gets an offer to work at a world-class confectionary company. But when she meets the young, handsome owner, she recognizes his cold stare...
KC KODANSHA COMICS
Something's Wrong With Us © Natsumi Ando / Kodansha Ltd.

THE SWEET SCENT OF LOVE IS IN THE AIR! FOR FANS OF OFFBEAT ROMANCES LIKE *WOTAKOI*

Sweat and Soap © Kintetsu Yamada / Kodansha Ltd.

In an office romance, there's a fine line between sexy and awkward... and that line is where Asako — a woman who sweats copiously — meets Koutarou — a perfume developer who can't get enough of Asako's, er, scent. Don't miss a romcom manga like no other!

Knight of the Ice ©Yayoi Ogawa

Yayoi Ogawa

SKATING THRILLS AND ICY CHILLS WITH THIS NEW TINGLY ROMANCE SERIES!

A rom-com on ice, perfect for fans of *Princess Jellyfish* and *Wotakoi*. Kokoro is the talk of the figure-skating world, winning trophies and hearts. But little do they know... he's actually a huge nerd! From the beloved creator of *You're My Pet* (*Tramps Like Us*).

Chitose is a serious young woman, working for the health magazine *SASSO*. Or at least, she would be, if she wasn't constantly getting distracted by her childhood friend, international figure skating star Kokoro Kijinami! In the public eye and on the ice, Kokoro is a gallant, flawless knight, but behind his glittery costumes and breathtaking spins lies a secret: He's actually a hopelessly romantic otaku, who can only land his quad jumps when Chitose is on hand to recite a spell from his favorite magical girl anime!

KC
KODANSHA
COMICS

SAINT ☆ YOUNG MEN

A LONG AWAITED ARRIVAL IN PREMIUM 2-IN-1 HARDCOVER

After centuries of hard work, Jesus and Buddha take a break from their heavenly duties to relax among the people of Japan, and their adventures in this lighthearted buddy comedy are sure to bring mirth and merriment to all!

"Brilliant...the physical comedy and facial expressions will make you literally LOL."

—Sam Humphries (host of *DC Daily*; writer, *Green Lanterns, Legendary Star-Lord*)

- KAMOME -
SHIRAHAMA

Witch Hat Atelier

A magical manga
adventure for
fans of Disney
and Studio
Ghibli!

Witch Hat Atelier © Kamome Shirahama/Kodansha Ltd.

The magical adventure that took Japan by storm is finally here, from acclaimed DC and Marvel cover artist Kamome Shirahama!

In a world where everyone takes wonders like magic spells
and dragons for granted, Coco is a girl with a simple dream:
She wants to be a witch. But everybody knows magicians
are born, not made, and Coco was not born with a gift for
magic. Resigned to her un-magical life, Coco is about to
give up on her dream to become a witch…until the day
she meets Qifrey, a mysterious, traveling magician. After
secretly seeing Qifrey perform magic in a way she's never
seen before, Coco soon learns what everybody "knows"
might not be the truth, and discovers that her magical
dream may not be as far away as it may seem…

Magus of the Library

Mitsu Izumi

MITSU IZUMI'S STUNNING ARTWORK BRINGS A FANTASTICAL LITERARY ADVENTURE TO LUSH, THRILLING LIFE!

Young Theo adores books, but the prejudice and hatred of his village keeps them ever out of his reach. Then one day, he chances to meet Sedona, a traveling librarian who works for the great library of Aftzaak, City of Books, and his life changes forever...

Battle Angel Alita: Mars Chronicle volume 7 is a work of fiction. Names, characters, places, and incidents are the products of the author's imagination or are used fictitiously. Any resemblance to actual events, locales, or persons, living or dead, is entirely coincidental.

A Kodansha Comics Trade Paperback Original

Published in the United States by Kodansha Comics, an imprint of Kodansha USA Publishing, LLC, New York.

Publication rights for this English edition arranged through Kodansha Ltd., Tokyo.

First published in Japan in 2020 by Kodansha Ltd., Tokyo, as *Gunnm: Mars Chronicle*, volume 7.

ISBN 978-1-63236-784-6

Printed in the United States of America.

www.kodansha.us

9 8 7 6 5 4 3 2 1
Translation: Stephen Paul
Lettering: Evan Hayden
Editing: Vanessa Tenazas
Kodansha Comics edition cover design by Phil Balsman

Publisher: Kiichiro Sugawara

Director of publishing services: Ben Applegate
Associate director of operations: Stephen Pakula
Publishing services managing editors: Alanna Ruse, Madison Salters
Assistant production managers: Emi Lotto, Angela Zurlo